My Road
to the
SUNDANCE

...My Vision Continues

D1114008

MY JOURNEY

INTO

NATIVE SPIRITUALITY

My Road to the SUNDANCE
...My Vision Continues

Manny Twofeathers

Wo-Pila Publishing
Erie, PA

First Printing, August, 2002
Second Printing, August 2003

To protect the people in this book, we have only used first names in most cases, unless we had permission. Although the author tried to ensure the accuracy and completeness of the information contained in this book, we assume no responsibility for errors, inaccuracies, omissions or any inconsistency herein. Any slights of people or organizations are unintentional.

Library of Congress Catalog Card Number: 2001 135651

Twofeathers, Manny
      My Road to the Sundance. . . My Vision Continues

Originally published: My Road to the Sundance,
Phoenix, Az. Wo-Pila Pub., c1994
Second edition: The Road to the Sundance, New York, N.Y. Hyperion Pub., c1996

ISBN: 1-886340-18-8

Cover picture: Linda Goytia

This book is dedicated to all the Sundancers,
no matter where they dance . . .
All men, women, and children who have gone
to the Sacred Tree to pray.

I wrote this to honor them and in
respect for our Sundance.

This book is in
honor of my mother

HELEN T. RENDON

and in
memory of my father

MANUEL M. RENDON
(to whom I dedicated my Sundance in 1994)

Contents

Acknowledgements

I want to show my respect by honoring the Spirits of all the Sacred Directions. They brought me all I needed, to find my way to the Sundance.

I would like to thank all the people I have met in this new direction in my life, each and every one. You know who you are, so many of you are mentioned - I am deeply grateful.

A special thank you to Linda Goytia, who took the picture of me on the cover of this book - who promised she would send it and did. And many thanks to my agent, B.J. Robbins, whose belief in this book has taken it places I had only dreamed of.

Special thanks to Wendy Burgreen, for helping make this version happen again. To my nephew, Bruce Baltz for coming into my life and making it so much better, just by knowing you. To Dave Weinkauf for his support and prayers when we needed it most.

Thanks and much love to everyone in my family, especially Rockie, Stormy, Maria, Rebecca, Dorina, Oriona and Stone. You all had to endure so much while writing this book, I am so grateful for your support and love. A big thank you to my mother-in-law, Lynne Babuin for all her much-appreciated help, in more ways than space allows. Our dear friend, Sharon Passero, who was always there, offering encouragement - when I needed her. I am deeply grateful you are in our life.

Finally, I want to honor my wife, Melody (formerly Betty Hutton), for her excellent memory; for her expertise at the computer, editing and spending endless hours at it; and for her love, devotion, and patience with me. Without you this book would not have happened, Thank you.

The Seven Sacred Directions

The seven directions are a gift from the Great Spirit. They all form a perfect balance for us to live in comfort as humans. Without any one of the directions our Spirits would be just a few wisps of energy drifting without aim in the vast expanse of the universe.

The East Direction is where the sun rises every morning, bringing the whole world new life and us our daily blessings.

The South Direction is where the warm winds come from to bring an end to the coldness of winter and new life to all.

The West Direction is where the sun brings a balance to our days. The sun goes down to allow us to sleep and nourish our minds and bodies.

The North Direction is where the cold winds come from. They bring us relief from the hot summer and balance to the warmth.

The Above Direction is the home of the Creator and where the Eagle flies. From above comes our spiritual energy and above is where our prayers are answered.

The Below Direction is our Mother the Earth. It is the celestial body that is our home. The one that needs our love, respect, and protection; without her there is no life, for she gives us everything we need to live.

The Inner Direction is where our spiritual energy lives and learns. Our bodies should also have our love and respect, for it is a gift and a home for our spirits while they learn humbleness and to suffer.

Introduction

The Sundance is a way of sacrificing for the privilege of having a direct connection with the Creator. It is one of the seven special ceremonies brought to the Plains Tribes by the White Buffalo Calf Woman to allow a way to give thanks and show gratitude. It is a way to humble ourselves, pray for the healing of others, and ask for a better way of life for everyone.

It is a spiritual awakening for some, and a spiritual commitment for others. I had attended a few Sundances over several years, but never as a participant. Whenever I heard that one was taking place, I felt compelled to go and be around the energy, like a moth to a light. I never understood my attraction to it. I would stand for hours where I could see the dancers and wonder, "Why do they do this?" Whenever I left, I felt sad and empty although I never understood why.

The first Sundance I ever saw was being held in Fort Duchesne, Utah. I asked for and received permission to sell my crafts, but after the first day I realized my heart wasn't in selling. In the distance I could hear the singers, the drum, and the eagle whistles, and they seemed to be calling me to the Sundance Arbor.

The Ute people hold what is called a "Thirst" Sundance. They undergo four full days of hard dancing and praying without anything to drink or eat the entire time. It is extremely difficult just to complete the ceremony. The dancers blow constantly on an eagle-bone whistle, which dehydrates them very quickly, making the four days almost intolerable. But

Sundancers continue the ritual because they believe the Creator gave man the eagle whistle to call the eagle spirit. (An eagle flies the highest of all the birds, so that spirit is the one that carries prayers to the Creator.)

The eagle whistle is made from one of the wing bones, and tied to the front of the whistle is an eagle plume, which is an inside feather almost like the down of the eagle's breast. We use this feather because it comes from a place close to the eagle's heart and so carries with it the power of the eagle's heart and is very strong. When we blow on an eagle whistle, our breath moves the plume up and down, and this becomes part of our prayers. If you're open to spirituality, the sound made by the eagle-bone whistle will leave a permanent imprint on your heart and soul. The haunting cry stays with you, no matter where you go or what you do.

The Arbor is where the dancing takes place. It represents the Circle of Life and is divided into four sections symbolizing the four stages of life: infancy, adolescence, adulthood, and elderly. The Arbor also has four different gates to honor the four main directions. It is most of all the house of our prayers and where many different, but very important, ceremonies are performed. Of all the ceremonies, the Sundance is the main or final ceremony of the year, excluding the Sweat Lodge ceremony, which is performed all year—although not in the Arbor.

The Sacred Tree is a crucial part of the Sundance ceremony. It represents the Creator, but only after it has been cut and placed in the center of the Arbor. We attach our prayer ties (small pieces of cloth, tied with tobacco and prayers) to the tree, and it becomes our God in physical form during our Sundance.

A live tree is not used because the Plains people were always on the move; they had a different location every year when they held the ceremonies. Nowadays the Sundance Chief chooses a tree a year in advance. It is always a cottonwood, and he blesses it four times over the course of the year.

At that first Sundance in Utah, I stood for two days simply watching the dancers and praying, thinking how great it was for me, just being there. My spirit felt light; I wanted to fly. Then reality set in: I had to earn a living, so I left.

A few weeks later I found myself back in Fort Duchesne, long after the Sundance was over. Driving through the town, I had a strong urge to go to the Sundance Arbor, so I followed that impulse. With butterflies in my stomach I turned off the main highway. I didn't know why I was going there; I knew no one would be there. Maybe the Spirits wanted me to go by myself and feel the Sundance energy, to experience it alone. The closer I got to the Arbor, the more nervous I became. I kept questioning myself, wondering what I was doing there.

When I reached the road leading into the Sundance grounds, I was elated to see the tree was still there. All the offering flags were waving happily, and it stood proudly. I don't know why, but I had the distinct impression that the tree was happy to see me; that it was lonely and needed my company.

To respect its sacred space, I parked my van away from the tree, got out, and walked toward it. It was good to be alone with it and to have this moment of privacy. The closer I got, the stronger the tree's energy became. I started feeling the sorrow, the tears, and the pain from the Sundancers who had prayed here. I had to touch it.

As I touched the tree, I looked up and saw all the prayer flags and offerings, waving gently. When I did, I was overwhelmed. All the emotions and energies from the previous Sundancers, combined with the tree's healing energy, overcame me. I started to cry. Tears formed and spilled out of my eyes. It was as though the tree needed my emotions. I gave the tree what it wanted, willingly, without shame, as I prayed.

To this day, I don't know how long I was there, but when it was over I felt an enormous relief. I didn't realize that I had been kneeling, and as I stood up, I realized that I had also been under a lot of stress from my responsibilities. The Sacred Tree had paid me back for visiting it. It had given me relief from all the pressure and anxiety I had been experiencing. As I backed away, I felt humbled.

Getting closer to the van, I saw another car. It was a tribal policeman. He asked me what I was doing there, and I explained that I had just come to the tree to pray. I'm sure he could see the traces of emotion left on my face. Understanding, he quietly told me it was okay. He asked if I was a Sundancer, and I said no. He said he understood my wanting to pray, because he was a Sundancer and knew the power of the tree. We talked for a little while longer. He wished me well, and then I left.

Driving away, I was filled with happiness. I wanted to shout out my experience and let the world know my joy.

EAST — YELLOW

"New Beginnings"

R I S I N G

S U N

1985: SACRAMENTO, CALIFORNIA . . .

It all started at about 6:30 on a Sunday morning. It was pleasant and cool, and I felt great. For two days I had been displaying my silver and turquoise jewelry at a Native American conference in Sacramento, and at the end of the day, I was going home. A couple of my good friends in Sacramento had asked me to stay with them (a common native custom), and this gave me a chance to visit and to save some money.

I woke up early that Sunday morning, quietly took a

shower, got dressed, and eased myself out of the house. I figured I'd go to a nearby restaurant and have a great big breakfast. After that, I'd get my jewelry ready and set up early.

I had been away for several days and was beginning to miss my kids. I'm never cheerful that early in the morning, especially when I haven't had my coffee, but on this particular morning I was feeling extraordinarily happy. I felt a little strange and almost light-headed. A couple of times I tried to analyze my feelings, but I just felt too good to worry about them. Deep inside, I had a strange sensation that this was going to be a very special day somehow. I had a good feeling of anticipation, but didn't know what it was I was anticipating.

As you can imagine, on an early Sunday morning there wasn't much traffic anywhere. I had been moving down the freeway at a pretty good clip when my exit came up. I slowed quickly and eased my old van off the freeway. When I came to the first intersection, the light had just turned red, so I stopped and waited for the light to change back to green.

I waited and waited and must have looked at my watch three or four times in just as many seconds. As I sat there, I got a faint whiff of hot oil from the engine. I thought to myself, "I'd better watch how fast I drive this old van or I'll find myself walking."

When the oil smell disappeared, so did thoughts of the van's condition. My mind drifted; I wondered if sales were going to be better than the day before. Again I noticed that the engine sounded pretty good. It was idling really smooth and easy.

My mind returned to the present. Starting to get a little irritated, I thought, "When is this @#$%^&* light going to change?" I looked around, then glanced into my rear-view mirror, thinking, "If there are no cops around I'm going to cross." Then I thought, "The light must be stuck or something. It's probably broken." I was thinking very seriously of running it and started dreaming up excuses I could tell the cop if I got caught. A hundred thoughts raced through my mind as I sat there getting more and more irritated at the dumb light that wouldn't change.

I was hungry. I hadn't had my first cup of coffee yet, and that made my cigarettes taste terrible. Lights or whatever shouldn't keep a guy from the little things in life that mean so much! I'm sure you've heard about the old bear coming out of hibernation? Well, that is exactly how I was starting to feel.

We all act a bit childish when things don't go our way. I was approaching that state and didn't want my good mood ruined by anything—especially by a traffic light.

Then I thought, "Ha! Ha! I'll bet there's a cop somewhere pushing the buttons that make the lights change just waiting for me to screw up so he can bust me. No sir, you're not going to get me that easily. I'll wait you out."

About this time, through my irritated and aggravated state, I started to hear something. At first it was very, very soft, almost like a whisper at the back of my mind. Though I didn't know what it was, I thought I recognized it, and I started getting chills. It's very hard to write a sound, but I'll try. It started softly, a shrill whisper—"Sherii—Sherii—Sherii—Sherii." As it went on, it got louder and louder.

I knew I had heard that sound before and tried to figure out where and when. So familiar, yet its origin eluded me. It almost became painful trying to recall such a beautiful and haunting sound.

Since I had an older van, I thought, maybe it was developing a new crippling syndrome. God, I prayed it wasn't. The old van was already worth $30,000, just from repairs.

The "Sherii—Sherii—Sherii—Sherii" sound kept getting louder and kept going on and on.

I cocked my head, turning it slowly, trying to find where

the sound was coming from. It wasn't the engine. I thought it might be the radio, so I reached over and tried to turn it off, but it was already off. Perhaps something in the back was making the sound because of vibrations from the engine?

I turned completely around in the seat. Carefully I looked at everything back there. There was nothing. As I straightened out and sat back in the seat, the light was still red, and I sat, a little shaken, and listened to that musical, eerie sound.

As I listened, I felt goose bumps all over my body. I was having trouble swallowing, as if something had gripped me by the throat. My heart was having trouble deciding whether to stop beating or jump out of my chest. Although I was afraid, I knew deep inside my soul that a very special message was coming to me.

It was then that I finally recognized the sound. I felt covered by a warm, quiet mixture of sound and peaceful energy, and a great sigh escaped from my long-held breath. I knew without any doubt what I was hearing. It was not one but several eagle wing-bone whistles. Exactly like the ones I had heard at the Sundances.

I broke into a sweat as I fully realized what was happening to me.

In my mind I was swiftly transported to that sacred Sundance tree far away—to that lonely tree in Fort Duchesne where I had prayed and felt so much emotion. Again I was kneeling at its base with my hands on its rough bark. I could hear it talking to me.

I distinctly heard the words meant for me: "You have searched long enough. It is time that you look to us for your destiny and direction. There is much to do." I didn't think about where I was or what I was doing. My thoughts were of how soft the voice was, and I wondered what it meant. I couldn't quite understand what was happening to me.

Realizing I was back in my van at the traffic light, I felt my mind fill with questions. I sat there for a minute, confused and a little scared. Looking down at my hands, although I couldn't see anything, I swore I could still feel the tree's rough bark. Had I really been there or had my thoughts been so real I could feel reality with my mind?

I believe that all of us have experienced those little shivers of unexplainable feelings. That's what was happening to me that morning. The eagle whistle and thoughts of the Sundance were now freshly burned into my brain. The soft voice that had spoken to me, had left me badly shaken. For a moment I had been at the Sundance tree in person.

Coming out of this experience as if from a dream, I shook my head. Unknown to me, a car had pulled up behind me and softly honked its horn. I looked up. The light had changed to green. Putting the van in gear, I slowly crossed the street and continued to the restaurant.

I didn't understand what had happened in those few moments at the light. I did know that something very important had happened to me. Somehow I knew that it was going to change my life in a big way.

The different emotions I experienced in that moment are difficult to explain, yet very real to native people. Though many of us get away from our ancient beliefs, I suppose we never really lose them. They are deeply ingrained in our genes. And though many of us have become urbanized and walk through life going through the motions of living, eventually there comes a time when we realize that what we have spiritually is not ours.

What *is* ours is the deep spirituality passed on to us by the Spirits. When we realize that, most of us return to the Sweat Lodge and other ceremonies. We return to try to learn, and to once again belong to, something so natively ours. I have come to realize that this was my first vision, and it came to me because I was at a point in my life when I needed it. The Spirits were telling me it was time to return to my native spirituality. They were showing me the way, and it was my choice whether or not to follow.

After the show ended that Sunday evening, I drove back home to the Mi-wok Rancheria near Tuolumne, California. Driving through Oakdale was a breeze. I think I hit one red light and was through before I knew it. I headed east into the foothills of the Sierras. It was late when I reached the town of Sonora.

It had been raining a little in the foothills earlier. The road was still wet, and the tires sounded like they were singing as I drove along. I left Sonora behind me and realized that I was almost home. Where did the time go? My mind wandered, thinking about my vision. I hardly felt the trip. My mind was still full of the sounds of eagle whistles.

Arriving home, I found my wife, Vivian, waiting up for me. She had hot coffee ready. As she poured me a cup, she asked me how the weekend had gone. It didn't take me long to tell her that I'd had a good weekend, but I wanted to tell her about my experience. I tried to explain what had happened. I suppose she understood, but I could see that she didn't fully appreciate the importance of the occurrence. She took it very lightly.

I attempted to explain how I had felt receiving this spiritual visit, and tried to convey the confusion, fear, apprehension, and joy that I felt. Somehow I couldn't make myself understood.

After that, I became very inquisitive and aggressive, trying to find out about the Sundance, because at that point I knew absolutely nothing. In my anxiety to find out, I must have approached people the wrong way. I found myself unable to get answers from anyone.

It may be hard to believe, but some native people are

Christians through and through. They are brainwashed into believing that the Sundance is the work of the devil. How wrong they are.

There I was: a naive person just awakening to something new that felt so good. I stupidly thought that all native people believed this way. So when I asked the wrong people, they moved away from me as if I were a leper!

Oddly enough, though I had been to several Sundances, I never made any close friendships with anyone there. Perhaps this was because I was so out of touch with my own spirituality. I was lost and had left religion and spiritual life behind.

I was born and reared a Catholic, through no choice of mine and through no fault of my parents. They taught me what they thought was the best for me. By the time of their birth into this world, native spirituality had been suppressed by the Spanish Catholic religion for four hundred years and had been all but forgotten. Even today all my relations still practice Catholicism. I was the first to break from that mind prison.

Going into the church was always a little scary to me. I could never talk aloud; we felt that we had to talk in a whisper. The teachers who taught us made us feel important. They were getting us ready to do the church's bidding as we grew older. They were teachers during the week, and on weekends they would be partying and drinking.

My parents had a restaurant in Ajo, Arizona, for many years. The "after the bar closed" crowd would always go there to eat. I saw many of the same people—my teachers and other pillars of the community—drunk, fighting, staggering, and falling.

When I was ten years old, I decided to become an altar boy, helping the priest at Mass services. I did this for several months. I would get up early in the morning, ride my bike to town about three miles away, and sell newspapers to men on their way to work. I'd make two cents off each paper I sold for ten cents!

With that job finished, I would go to the church and get my black-and-white altar-boy gown on. Then I'd light candles and perform all my other tasks to get ready for the 7:30 a.m. Mass.

It always seemed majestic in the church. It was so quiet and peaceful, yet scary, in there. I never liked the smell of candles. It reminded me of funerals. I was always curious to see what the priest was doing behind the great big altar. That was where we got ready before Mass.

I watched as the priest performed his daily ritual. At the time it seemed like quite a ceremony to get his habit on. Wide-eyed, I would stand there watching, not wanting to move a muscle.

After Mass, I would head for school.

The altar boys met once a week. At one of the meetings, we got a new young priest. I was sick and couldn't make it to the meeting or even to church the following Sunday.

When the next week's meeting came around, I was there, but the new priest wasn't. I still hadn't met him by the next Sunday morning. After selling my papers, I went dutifully to church.

When I got there, I found the priest standing in front of the church. He appeared worried as he looked up and down the street, trying to control his irritation.

When I walked up, I said good morning. He answered kind of gruffly. I asked what was wrong. He replied that the altar boys had not shown up, and he needed to start Mass immediately. We took turns helping the priests, and that Sunday was not my turn, but naturally I offered to help him.

He turned angrily toward me and between clenched teeth said, "What the hell do you know about being an altar boy?"

He didn't even wait to hear my answer, just turned and walked back into the church. I stood there dumbfounded. All I could think was, this is the man who was above reproach? This is the man I'm supposed to respect and follow? Everything I had learned since childhood evaporated in a matter of seconds that morning in front of the church.

I stood there for a moment, torn between the truth just revealed to me and the fear of the punishment I was going to get if I didn't go to church. The truth won out. This single event made me wonder, even with my young mind, how much was truth and how much was not. I said a prayer to the Gods, or whoever was in charge, not to hold it against me and walked away from the Catholic church, returning only once for my father's funeral.

When I lost my dad recently, the funeral services were held at the same church I had attended in my childhood. The service started well enough, I suppose, with the priest discussing my father's good points—the usual litany about how much he would be missed. Then he turned my father's service into a recruiting exercise by telling us that it was too bad we had to come back to church under these circumstances. He went on to say that at least we were back in the church, and that we should continue to come to Mass. He carried on and on in the same recruiting mode for several minutes. He turned my father's funeral mass, which was a chance for me and my family to mourn and think of him, into an opportunity to guilt-trip us into coming back to the church! I was angry and disgusted by it all.

After leaving Catholicism, I looked into the Baptist Christian faith as a teenager. But I was only there to meet girls. It was fun for a few months, until I realized that I was still not satisfied spiritually. Disappointed in Christianity, I became a guy looking for thrills and good times. I made friends with a couple of guys, and we ended up in Seattle, Washington.

A few months after moving there, I was walking home from work when two people stopped to talk to me. They were both Japanese. One was an older man and the other a middle-aged woman. They smiled very politely, bowed, and greeted me.

I was a little apprehensive because in big cities when people smile at you they usually want something. So, with a bit of hesitation I said hello. They handed me a pamphlet and asked if I had ever been to a Buddhist meeting.

I said, "No, I don't even know what you mean."

It was a little hard to understand what they were trying to tell me, but I was ripe for the picking. Disenchanted by Christianity, I was open to anything else that might come along.

The Japanese couple realized I was interested, so they really poured it on and I attended some of their meetings. I found Buddhism very interesting and different, and tried to be serious and faithful to this new belief.

Through meditation you were supposed to get whatever you wanted by focusing on it while you chanted a very old chant, "Nam-yo-ho-ran-ge-kyo." The sound emitted when you said the chant made a vibration. This vibration enabled you to connect with the universe and receive anything you desired. I was always chanting for women, booze, and parties.

Boy, did it work! For a long time after leaving Seattle, I was burned out on booze and parties, though I never got tired of girls. I was also burned out on Buddhism. I realized that I had used it in a selfish way, perhaps because I didn't fully understand it. While I still respected Buddhist beliefs, I decided not to use any faith in that manner, so I stopped going to the meetings.

When the eagle whistles sounded for me that Sunday morning in Sacramento, I had been living on the Tuolumne Miwok Rancheria, a small reservation not far from Sonora, California. My wife and I had four children—Rockie, Stormy (Elena), and twin girls, Mary and Becky. Shortly after that, the lease on our rental house ran out, and we decided to move.

We ended up in Blackfoot, Idaho. There are many native people there who bead, and some of the best beadwork in the country still comes from that area. I had been making native crafts for several years but not in a very serious way, at least not to earn a living at it. When I married Vivian, we got more and more into making leather crafts. She was white and Blackfoot, and enjoyed making a living this way.

Our life in Blackfoot, Idaho, wasn't much different from anywhere else. We made crafts, cut beads, and I went on the road to sell them. Several years earlier, I had noticed that no one in the country made faceted hand-cut beads, so I decided to try to figure out how to do it. After many tries and fine-tuning I succeeded. We were the only people in the country who knew how to cut beads at the time, so we had a good market.

My little Dorina was born that June in Pocatello, Idaho. Her birth occurred just when I began my Sundance journey. It was an event that told me that I was on the right path.

That month I went to a Sundance at Fort Washakie, Wyoming, on the Wind River Reservation, where they were allowing crafts people to set up. We could sell in an area that was quite a distance from the Sundance Arbor. After deciding to go to Fort Washakie, I suddenly started feeling a funny little sensation in the pit of my stomach. I didn't know what was wrong with me, but I almost lost the desire to go there because of my fear and apprehension. It was as though I knew that by going there, my spiritual quest would become clear—a new path. Maybe I feared what I might find and didn't feel I was ready to do what was being asked of me.

I left Blackfoot early in the morning and stopped in Idaho Falls to buy groceries for my few days in Fort Washakie. Later I ate lunch in Jackson Hole, Wyoming, then passed by the Grand Tetons and the southern tip of Yellowstone Park. Between there and Dubois, Wyoming, is some of the most beautiful scenery in the world. Apparently, the Creator was either in a very good mood when He made that area or He had time on His hands and was feeling creative. He did a great job.

The afternoon that I drove in to the Arapaho Sundance, the weather was hot and sticky. When I stopped the van, it felt as if the heat consisted of tiny hammers, trying to beat me down.

I got out of the van. I stretched and felt the full force of the sun. Then I thought of the men and women who were going in to Sundance and how hot it was going to be. I felt sorry for them.

I went over to check on the setup. The guy in charge was not very friendly, and they wanted a large fee for a space. I decided to get a tribal permit instead for twenty dollars that was good for a year. Then I could set up anywhere on the reservation.

I set up at an intersection away from the Sundance. That's where I met Allen Enos. Allen was a young man in his mid-thirties, slender, about six-feet-one, with a light complexion and a soft voice. He always had a smile ready! He became my "Grandfather," the one who introduced me to the Sundance. (The term "Grandfather" is used as a form of respect by most traditional people. It is a word to refer to "God" or to someone we respect very much, or to a person who sponsors or introduces another person into the Sundance. Some use their tribal language words for its equivalent, and others use the word "Uncle" as the term of respect. That is why I refer to so many young men who came to Sundance as my "nephews.")

I had my cut beads laid out. There had always been just two places to get cut beads, in Czechoslovakia or Japan. So when my wife and I started cutting beads some people just couldn't believe that we knew how. We hadn't been cutting beads very long so we were very proud of them. When Allen walked up, he was surprised at how many I had.

He remarked, "Boy, the Japanese are sure cutting a lot of beads, and all sizes, too."

Japanese cuts are considered inferior to the Czech cuts. His tone of voice was almost sarcastic, and I was very offended by his insult.

"I beg your pardon," I said indignantly. "*We* cut these beads."

Allen looked a little surprised by my aggressive reply, but he did have the presence of mind to calm himself. He started to make another comment, but stopped. This took a great deal of self-control because he's a pretty tough character. I was happy he had calmed down because I know a warrior when I see one, and he was right in front of me. In my eyes, a warrior is someone who not only stands up for his or her rights with whatever it takes but is also a good provider who doesn't mind helping others, has compassion, and is very spiritual. And I didn't want to get into a fight with this warrior.

He said, "Sorry, I didn't mean to offend you!"

That set me back a little, and I apologized for the outburst. I explained how I'd heard that remark in the past, and it upset me quite a bit if someone compared our cuts to Japanese cuts.

Though we had started off on the wrong foot, I found out Allen was not a bad sort. We visited awhile, talking about mutual interests. I told him about my family, he told me about his, then he left.

The following afternoon, Allen came back to see me and I asked him if he knew where I could get eagle feathers. At the time I really didn't know why I was searching for them. I just wanted to have some in my possession because I had never had one.

He said that he had some and brought me a large paper sack from his car. As he handed it to me, I felt good receiving those feathers and asked him what I could give him in return, or what I owed him.

"Nothing at all. I don't sell eagle feathers," he replied.

During this period of my life, I knew nothing about traditions, and so I didn't realize the importance and significance of eagle feathers to our people. Here I was completely ignorant, offering to pay for something sacred. To traditional people, having an eagle feather means that that person has earned it. But a lot of others just have them because they are a native thing, without having earned them. Now I realize that the feathers of an eagle are sacred and are not to be hung on the rear-view mirror of a car or placed on a cowboy hat as a decoration. They are for us to use only in ceremonies.

Now it was my turn to apologize to him.

"It's okay," he said. "You didn't know, and it's a gift from me to you."

"So I can give you a gift if I want to?" I asked. Now I was being more careful about how I said things.

"I didn't do that so I could get something in return," he answered.

"Well, I want you to take these to your wife," I said, and gave him cut beads of each color that I had, which was quite a few. That exchange of gifts helped to start a friendship that has lasted for years.

Before Allen left, I asked him why he had decided to give me those feathers. He replied that he didn't know. He just had a feeling that I was going to need them pretty soon. Then I remembered my quest, or desire, to learn about the Sundance, so I asked him if he knew any Sundancers or anyone connected to the Sundance.

"Why do you ask?"

"I was told that I had to Sundance," I replied.

"By whom? Who told you, you had to Sundance?"

"Man, I really don't know," I said, and went on to tell him of my vision in California.

"You're right, it sounds like you were being told to do a Sundance," he replied after much thought. "So what are you going to do about it?"

"Well, I want to go into a Sundance, but everyone I ask refuses to talk to me about it."

"How serious are you about dancing?" Allen asked me.

"Well, I don't know. The Spirits said I had to do it. I guess if I can find someone to help me or teach me, I'll do it."

He said, "I'm a Sundancer, and if you're serious about this, be here by the last Sunday in July."

"What do I have to bring?"

"Nothing, just bring yourself. I'll call you the week before to see if you've changed your mind or if you still want to go."

It was getting late, and I started packing up my things. Allen helped me. We said our goodbyes, and I left Fort Washakie.

I was very excited because I had finally found someone to help me. The meeting reminded me of the old proverb,

"When the student is ready, the teacher will appear." Now I had found a Sundance and a Sundancer.

I returned to Blackfoot and continued working. There wasn't a day that went by that I didn't think about the upcoming ceremony. Most times while driving to and from powwows or a show, I would get so scared that I'd start praying. I still didn't know what I was getting into, only that I had made a very important commitment and was terrified that I would fail. I was too ignorant to be afraid of anything else.

I'm glad I didn't know about the thirst.

I'm glad I didn't know of the hunger and the long, hot hours spent under the blazing sun.

I'm also glad I didn't know that when you dance once, you commit yourself for four years! If I had known all these things, then I might not have had the courage, the will-power, and the strength to go through with it all.

At the time, I wanted to Sundance no matter what.

Good to his word, a week before the Sundance, Allen called. I told him we were leaving that day to come to Fort Washakie.

My family and I pulled in later that night and stayed at Rocky Acres campground, between Fort Washakie and Landers, Wyoming. The next day Allen came after us and led us to the Sundance grounds. It took us two days to set up camp. We had to go long distances to cut a certain type of bush used for walls and shade around the camp. This is a tradition for both the Shoshoni and the Arapaho, the two tribes that live on the Fort Washakie Reservation.

After making camp, we started gathering wood for the Sweat Lodge ceremony. Although people go into it to sweat, the main purpose of the Sweat Lodge is to purify.

Purification in the Sweat Lodge is a total body, mind, and spiritual cleansing in preparation for performing any of our sacred ceremonies, especially the Sundance. Once the ceremony starts, the people going through it must remain celibate. They can't even touch anyone who hasn't gone through the Sweat Lodge ceremony. Most lodges last about a half hour per round, each round lasting approximately twenty to thirty minutes.

At the beginning of each round more red-hot rocks were put into the lodge, keeping it good, hot, and interesting. The first three days of purification were spent praying: going into the lodge and concentrating on our reasons for Sundancing. We were getting ourselves mentally and physically prepared because of the difficulties we would face in the ceremony. We would have a four-round sweat at least once a day. They were good, hot sweats.

The Shoshoni people perform the Sweat Lodge ceremony differently from other tribes. We had four days of purification and prayer before the dancing began.

The lodge was right next to a cold, clear, fast-running river. It came in pretty handy because in the Shoshoni Sweat Lodge ceremony, the people could come out of the lodge between rounds and go into the river. Or they could just stand around, smoke, and visit.

During the dance many men can be driven to the brink of insanity. Some can't tolerate the thirst and hunger, even though it is part of the sacrifice to get your prayers answered. Some get so thirsty and hungry that their commitments cease to mean anything to them. They will go to any lengths to satisfy their desires, if allowed.

People ask me, "Why do you Sundance?" I always say, "So my prayers can be answered!" To some people it may seem quite an elaborate ceremony for just praying. Anyone can get down on their knees and say a little prayer. It takes a special person to willingly put themselves through this kind of sacrifice. Putting your ego and personal comfort aside for a few days takes someone strong in spirit. However, it is a lot more than that. To Sundance means something different to everyone.

Most of us pray only when we need it and only when we're in trouble. I'm as guilty as anyone in doing this. In the Sundance you learn the meaning of being selfless. It humbles you. The first obligation, or rule, if you will, is that you never pray for yourself. You let others pray for you.

When we dance, we are not just praying for now or for today, but for the whole year and the whole world. We are praying for all of humanity. We also pray for others in our family, for a sick relative or loved one. We are pleading for our brothers in the rain forests who are losing their land, as we once lost ours. We also pray for the starving people of the world, and for abused men, women, and children.

This is our way to humble ourselves to the Creator. We beg that He intervene on our behalf and help us strengthen our lives so that we may live better. We also give thanks for all the good things that Grandfather (God) has given us up to this point in our lives.

We are willing to sacrifice ourselves so that all goes well on our Mother Earth. Wasn't Jesus Christ also a Sundancer? He was willing to sacrifice himself so the world could evolve into a better place through spirituality and showing us the way. Not that I would compare myself and other Sundancers to Jesus Christ, but his sacrifice for others did help to change the world. In his time, he was a man with a prayer and a message—just like we are. Perhaps our sacrifice can help make a difference, too.

We spent four days relaxing, getting our eagle whistles ready—making sure they worked properly and were easy to get sound from. That's when I started needing the feathers that Allen had given me weeks before. As we were sitting there working on our traditional regalia, Allen smiled and looked up at me. "See Manny, I told you that you were going to need those feathers soon."

The regalia for each warrior dancer is a shawl, which is normally worn by women over their shoulders. Men wear it around their waists like a skirt and don't wear any shirts. Around our necks we wear our traditional ermine skin necklace and our eagle whistle.

In the bag Allen gave me I also found some good, long, fluffy plume feathers, which were perfect for my eagle whistle. I used what I needed. As other men came by, I gave the remaining feathers away, as needed.

Everybody was drinking large quantities of water. Some were drinking sports drinks. Finally I got curious enough to ask why everyone was drinking so much. They all turned and looked at me as if finally realizing that not everyone there knew all the rules. One guy said, "You'd better drink all you can. It'll be a long time before we drink again."

There was very little conversation all that afternoon. I could feel an uneasy or nervous energy radiating off everyone. This was a serious event, and they all knew how hard it was going to be. The days had been really hot. In the afternoon the ground was hot enough to burn our feet. I thought I was the only one there who was completely ignorant. I found out later, there were quite a few people going in for the first time. I was the oldest—in my forties—and pushing my years pretty hard.

Another thing we did that afternoon was eat a venison stew. Allen's wife, Zedora, fixed a large pot of it, and it was delicious. It had lots of vegetables in it, but not one grain of salt. They said that if we ate salt, it would cause us to dehydrate faster.

The first day of the Sundance finally arrived. This was the day that would change the rest of my life, though I didn't know it at the time. It was the day I had been excitedly expecting, yet dreading.

The night before, the sun finally dropped below the horizon. A frenzy of quiet activity started. Everyone was quietly making last-minute touches on themselves and their Sundance outfits. The smell of the dust in the air was suddenly very prominent. Dust stirred up by bare and moccasinned feet became part of the energy and part of the special moment.

The smell of the burning wood also invaded my nostrils and became part of my memories, as did the smell of the bubbling venison stew mingled with the different smells of wood smoke, dust, and sage. People all over were smudging themselves with the smoke of our medicine sage. The smell of humans was everywhere. Perspiration, nervousness, apprehension, and even joy have a distinct smell. They were all there. They were all creating a beautiful memory for my first Sundance.

Everybody was within themselves praying to Grandfather in their own way. The energy was charged up. There was electricity in the air surrounding us, the excitement was contagious. Everyone could feel the enormous energy. It was a wonderful feeling that I can still feel when I sit down and remember that evening.

When it was completely dark, Allen came up to me and said, "Well, Manny, here we are. How do you feel?"

Shaking my head, I replied, "Man, I can't explain it, but I feel like I'm floating!"

"That, my friend, is the Sundance energy," he smiled.

Suddenly from off in the distance where the Arbor was, we heard the drum. A beautiful sound mellowed by distance. Then one helper yelled, "Sundancers, let's go! Come on, it's time to line up!"

We walked from our camp to the Arbor, a bunch of

24

unidentified figures wrapped in colorful Pendleton blankets. As we walked, some of us were barefooted, and some of us were wearing moccasins.

The Sundance grounds we walked to that night were new. For years the Sundance was always held right in the middle of Fort Washakie. Then the government started building houses pretty close to the grounds. As the Sundance Chief once said, "One important thing about the Sundance is that every morning we must greet the sun as it rises. With all the houses, we can't see the sun as it comes up." Although that was the main reason for changing the location for the Sundance, there was another reason. In the center of Fort Washakie, there were also drunks who came around to taunt and yell obscenities at the Sundancers. They would call us devils and idiots for sacrificing the way we were. They called themselves "good Christians."

I felt good about the change because I was new and it was my first Sundance. This was a new place, and it was the first Sundance at this location.

Walking toward the Arbor, I stepped very gingerly. Not only were there many small, sharp rocks, there were cactus needles, which were tough on my bare feet.

After assembling behind the Arbor on the west side, everybody stood in two lines. I was sticking as close as I could to Allen.

I found out later that Allen always picked the spot in line that would place him in the Arbor on the north side. It's the hottest and hardest place to be in the Arbor for most of the day. Lots of Sundancers avoid that spot because whoever ends up there suffers the most. Allen and I were on that spot for three full days.

The Sundance sure makes you appreciate a lukewarm drink of water. It really makes you appreciate a small spot of shade or a little breeze on a hot summer day. When you get down to basics, it's surprising at how little it really takes to make you happy or at least satisfied.

We started walking, each line going around opposite sides of the Arbor. One line is led by the Sundance Chief, the other by one of his helpers. As we rounded the Arbor, we met the other line moving in the opposite direction. We were blowing our eagle whistles as we walked around and around. It was so dark there was no way of recognizing anyone.

It was an eerie feeling to be involved in something so strange to me. I felt that I had gone back one hundred years in time. I could see many people standing quietly, watching us prepare ourselves to enter the Arbor.

The smell of dust and sage was strong, yet comforting. It felt like a friend, something familiar. We continued our walk until we had circled four times. Then the Sundance Chief led us into the Arbor. We did not leave the Arbor from Friday night just after dark until Monday afternoon. In retrospect, it doesn't seem like a very long time. When you're in there, however, every hour seems like an eternity.

The Arbor, the resting place for the dancers, is not only to rest the physical bodies. It's also a place to meditate, to concentrate and pray for the things that you need, to think about the prayers you need answered. Some people who are new to the Sundance think the Arbor is a place where the Sundancers relax and have their cigarettes. This is wrong— there is nothing to drink, nothing to eat, and in many Sundances they even ask you to give up your cigarettes.

Eventually, I did find an escape from the suffering. It didn't happen for a couple of days, and when I did finally discover it, it was as if the tree, the Sacred Tree, had talked to me. It taught me to pray, pray, and pray hard. My prayers could be answered, and I could endure what I was going through. My prayers were my escape.

You know something? I had found what I was looking for, and felt such joy and peace with everything and everyone that I didn't have time to think of my suffering. I found out that things only bother you when you pay attention to them. So, if you ignore the suffering and focus on the beauty that you wish, it changes everything.

For three days, I went through many things, and I really don't know what to call the experiences. Can I call them better changes? Can I call them sufferings or spiritual awakenings? I do know one thing to be a fact: The Sundance changed my life like nothing else could have. I know, without any doubt, I'm a much better man. At least, I feel that I am and so does my family.

I was honored that the Shoshoni allowed me to participate in their most sacred ceremony with them. I can only return their respect and honor by not writing about what occurred during this Sundance ceremony. If it is ever to be told, I'll leave that to be told by a Shoshoni elder.

So we danced and danced.

And prayed and prayed.

I thought the first day was not very difficult. But everyone is different, and I could see other dancers were already suffering. As time went on, it was more noticeable. We danced late that first night.

The following morning we were up early. We greeted the sun, then had a little time to prepare ourselves for the day. Sometime in mid-morning we started dancing again. The sun got hot early. As the day progressed, it got hotter and hotter as we danced to and from the Sacred Tree.

When we danced back to our place, our feet would be burning. Sore feet from the heat or hot ground are one thing. But the bruises from the sharp rocks and cactus stickers impaling your feet make the suffering more intense. Add to that the number of times we danced back and forth.

Now I knew why Allen had asked me how serious I was about dancing. He later told me that many people say they want to Sundance, but when it gets right down to it, they find all kinds of excuses why they just can't make it "this time." It's very, very hard. The person who goes through the Sundance ceremony must have an important reason.

Personally I respect all Sundancers. Sundancers are a special breed of person. Every one of them has gone to suffer and pray willingly. I believe that no matter where the Sundance is or who is running it, they are all done for the right reason. They are all special. There is no easy Sundance. You go there to pray, and to suffer, and you should. You should sacrifice yourself so your prayers can be heard and answered.

As one Sundance Chief told me, "If you want to go on a picnic, take your whole family and go to the river. This is *your* Sundance. It's only for three days. Make the most of it. Pray and dance hard." He said this because late in the afternoon when it was the hottest, some Sundancers would sit out a few songs. There is no written rule that says a Sundancer has to dance every song. It is an individual choice.

By Sunday afternoon, everyone was getting very dry. I would try to spit, and my saliva was so dry it was like rubber strings. Some of us were having trouble talking. It was so hot. The constant blowing on our eagle whistles dried us out even faster. Swallowing was completely out of the question; by that time there is nothing to swallow anyway.

We always looked for a dancer who looked ready to collapse from heat exhaustion, hunger, and dehydration. We believe that this is when a Sundancer is truly close to the Creator and is very powerful spiritually. He is pulling the "Sun Power" down on himself and the whole Sundance. It is the ultimate in power and energy a person can receive during a Sundance, even if it's just for a few seconds. We strongly believe that when the body grows weaker, the spirit grows stronger.

This is what every Sundancer is striving for.

This is when a person receives his vision.

This is when we receive direction from the Creator.

The more people this happens to in the Sundance, the more power we all receive to get our wishes and prayers fulfilled. It is a great honor to have this happen to an individual. When a dancer is showing signs of exhaustion, he receives encouragement to keep on dancing. The drummers will pick up the beat and keep on singing and drumming. When that special dancer dances back to his spot, the other dancers push him back out.

It is a wonderful feeling and yet a pitiful sight to see. The person it's happening to receives respect from everyone. If the dancer falls, many dancers who are close, rush out to touch and share his energy and power. To show our respect for what he has just been through, we pick him up gently and carry him back to his spot. If he has a little shade, we lay him down so he can rest.

The Sundance goes on.

Sometimes we have two or three different groups who drum and sing for us. So we go on and on and on. The sun beats down on us for hours.

After two days of almost unbearable heat, the Sunday sun reached the end of its long, hot journey across the Wyoming sky. It finally decided to give us some rest from its fiery bright energy. Though dry, hungry, and tired, we felt our spirits rise with joy. We felt the ever-present evening breezes and the coolness provided by the evening shadows.

Late in the night, the dancers stopped and tiredly lay down on their sleeping rolls. The drummers also showed signs of fatigue. The songs got slower and further apart.

Finally, when there were only a few dancers left, the singers finished their last song. They got up, stretched, and by one's and two's left the Arbor.

The dance was over for the day. Here and there I saw dancers wrap themselves up in sheets and head for the outhouse. As I lay down, thinking and praying for my children, my parents, and everyone else, I looked at the beautiful stars lighting up the sky.

I thought, "Thank you, God, for all the blessings you've given me throughout my life. For my beautiful children, my brother and sisters, and my wonderful parents, who have always been there for me. Most of all, thank you for bringing me to this Sundance. I finally have a way to thank you for all you have given me." As I lay there giving thanks, I drifted off to sleep.

Morning arrived quietly. I heard someone cough and I awoke. Where I lay, I could see through the leaves of the Arbor wall. Although they were different constellations, the stars were still shining brightly. They had a cool, regal, almost aloof look to them. They looked different to me. I was not used to seeing this group of stars, and not used to waking up at this time of the morning.

I felt an urgency to get up. Mother Nature was calling. I had to answer the call of nature the first two days of the Sundance, but I figured that was normal. As I left my warm blankets and felt the cool air hit me, I had to move.

Getting up quickly, I went to the outhouse. It amazed me how much liquid I still had to get rid of. It had been three days since I had had anything to drink. Well, like one dancer said, "Just because you quit drinking, doesn't mean that your kidneys stop working!"

When I returned, everyone was in high spirits and putting on their finest regalia. I also pulled out my best shawl. It was bright red and had an eagle sewn on the front. I was very proud of it because Allen and his wife, Zedora, gave it to me. We wrapped them around ourselves like skirts.

The rumor started going around that we weren't going to get out until late that night. You can't believe how tough that is to hear after three days without food or water. Allen pulled me to the side and told me that the rumor always started for the discomfort of the first-time Sundancers. They do go late sometimes, but this doesn't happen too often.

We had to watch the flagpole in front of the camp of the Sundance Chief, who was away from the Arbor. If the flag was all the way to the top of the pole, we would be staying late. If it was at half-mast we would get out around twelve or one o'clock in the afternoon.

This was the last day.

As we danced and blew on our eagle whistles, I could hear dancers gagging because of the lack of moisture in their mouths. I was feeling pretty bad myself. Once, I started retching and couldn't stop. When I finally did, I was pretty weak and shaken, but continued dancing.

The reason we go without food or water and blow on our eagle whistles is to help us focus and to reach an open and accepting state of heart and mind. This brings us insight and helps us become open to receiving our visions. It says something about the way we live today that such drastic measures are needed.

Many spectators came into the Arbor for blessings. Some dancers brought in their families and others to be blessed. It was a little beyond my understanding, but Christian ministers were coming into the Sundance Arbor and asking the Sundance Chief to give them blessings. In turn, they asked if they could bless other people from their congregation in the Sundance Arbor. It was beautiful to see the mixing of beliefs the way it happened there. At least I'm glad that these people have the intelligence to recognize the Arbor as a sacred place, as sacred as any church anywhere.

The morning went slowly and seemed to stretch until the next weekend. The sun decided to take it easy on us poor Sundancers. Maybe it thought we had suffered enough. The morning couldn't have been better. It was the most pleasant of the whole time. It eased our suffering a little.

Suddenly, Allen grabbed my arm. When I looked at him, he pointed with his chin, directing me to look at the flag, now flying at half-mast.

"Thank you, Grandfather," I said to myself.

Suddenly the people were no longer coming into the Arbor. The blessings were over. The energy within the circle felt charged and exciting. Even the spectators could feel it. People were starting to smile and laugh. Some were holding their fists up to the dancers. A sign of victory, as if saying, "Good man, we are proud of you."

Then the Sundance Chief tied up his sheet.

Everybody started following his example. The sheets we had used to cover ourselves at times during the Sundance now concealed us from the spectators' eyes. At first I didn't understand why. Then it was explained to me. We were about to have our first drink of water in three days. This is sacred water, to be received with humbleness and respect. It was too personal to be seen by anyone else, other than your Sundance brothers and God.

They brought two large, old, metal milk cans, each filled with fresh spring water. After bringing the water in, the helpers placed it before the Sundance Chief. He prayed over the water, gave thanks for it, then with his blessing he poured it into buckets. His helpers brought it to us.

One by one, they let each dancer drink his fill. It was a quiet time, filled with reverence. It felt like his own personal ceremony was taking place, as each Sundancer took his first drink.

As the helpers stopped in front of me, one of them took a large dipper full of cool, sweet, well water out of the bucket. He raised it high enough to clear the edge of the bucket. Water splashed and dripped off the sides of it. It looked fantastically delicious. The helper was not moving fast enough. The whole process seemed to be in slow motion.

I was sitting on the ground watching as all this was happening. My throat felt stretched tight as my head tilted back. I tried to swallow as I looked at that beautiful water, but all I could do was croak. The feeling was so intense that I couldn't have talked even if I had wanted to. He slowly lowered the dipper to me. By then I wanted the water so bad that I was ready to stand up and reach for it, yet I held myself down on the ground waiting for the water to come to me. I felt I had earned the right for the water to come to where I was sitting.

At long last the dipper was in my hands. Wanting to just guzzle it down and get some more, I stopped myself and thought of the last three days. Then I thought of the flag. What if it had been all the way to the top? I still wouldn't be drinking. I thought of the Spirits that had helped me so much.

I raised the dipper in gratitude and respect, and to honor Grandfather and the Spirits. Slowly I tipped the dipper, letting a small amount of water drip out and splash on Mother Earth to honor her. Now I felt that it was my turn. With shaking hands, I raised the dipper to my mouth. That first sip was like nothing I had ever experienced. It was heaven. I could feel that wonderful, wet trickle, slowly working its way down my dry throat. It was like putting water on a sponge. I continued to take small sips.

After the first taste that didn't do much, I was finally

starting to make a little saliva in my mouth. Each time I took a sip, my lips trembled. Little drops escaped my lips. They would race down my chin, then drop off, landing in my lap. At long last I was feeling halfway human again. Reluctantly I surrendered the dipper. It passed on and on to the other Sundancers until the helpers reached the end of the line. Everyone had water, and we started taking our sheets down.

Earlier that morning we had given our sleeping rolls and anything else we didn't need to relatives, so we didn't have much to carry out. Finally, we lined up and the Sundance Chief held his hand up for us to follow him.

It was finally over.

As we filed out of the Arbor, the spectators lined up on each side of the entrance. As we walked between them, the people reached out to touch us. They thanked us for our prayers. Everyone was smiling, laughing, and shaking our hands. It was a wonderful feeling. I got very emotional and shed a few tears of thanks and gratefulness.

The people who had prayed and stood by us until the last drumbeat had suffered almost as much as we had. I found out later that many people had fasted with us. They went without water for three days and in a way it's harder than what we had done. They had water, food, and other cold drinks right in front of them and still went without drinking. It's harder to resist if what you want is right there in front of you. You have no one to stop you except yourself.

Lots of people wanted our sun energy, the energy that for three days we had pulled down onto ourselves. That energy is powerful, it's clean, it heals and cures.

As I was walking, I felt exhilarated, I felt so good it was like walking on feathered ground. Now I didn't feel the small, sharp rocks that had made my life so interesting for the last three days. I was no longer worried about the small cactus stickers that had attacked my feet at every opportunity.

Now that the time for eating was close, I didn't feel any hunger. At the end of the line, I could see a large crowd ahead of me. Sundancers wrapped in white sheets dispersed and headed in different directions to wherever their camps were. I could see them all clutching something in their arms.

Suddenly it was my turn. A Sundance Chief's helper stood on the ground right behind a pickup truck. He was handing each Sundancer an unexpected surprise: a large, striped watermelon. I thought I didn't have any liquids left in my body, but the sight of the big, beautiful watermelon made saliva slowly moisten the whole inside of my mouth.

Again, I had received another surprise. It's amazing how little things have so much meaning. When a person has suffered and has had to do without the basic things in life, little things mean a lot. A chair to sit on, a drink of water, a small meal, becomes all that is important in life. Even a small piece of bread becomes something to think and dream about when you are in that state.

My wife and family were all there waiting for me. My children looked like they had also been in the Sundance—tired and drained—especially my twin girls. I believe that in their innocence, and because of their love for me, they tried to take the pain, hunger, and thirst from me. Since then I have found out that in their own way they are very powerful individuals, especially Becky, who has always been the runt of the family. Her energy is so strong, only my influence as her father can keep her on the right track. I realize that someday I'm going to let her go, to do the things she needs to do for the Creator. She has strong leadership qualities and has had this energy since childhood.

When I saw them and felt their anxiety for me, my emotions welled up. My heart felt as though it was convulsing. "My God," I thought, "these babies have been suffering for me as much as I have."

The enormous swelling I felt in my chest rose into my throat and brought tears to my eyes. Right then, I felt so much love for them and the whole world that I knew this was the reason I Sundanced.

We walked back to camp. It was a quiet and slow process. I set the slow pace and everyone stayed next to me. The children wanted to touch and hug me as we all walked along, which made the progress even slower. Despite my intense joy at seeing my children, the main reason I was dragging my feet was that I felt an unexplainable sense of loss. I felt an emptiness inside as if I were leaving a part of myself behind.

The only comparison I can come up with for this feeling is when a woman gives birth. After giving birth, she goes through a feeling of loss or emptiness. The Sundance is a trial and test of your spirit. It's exhilarating, yet incredibly difficult, like childbirth. Although I will never go through childbirth, I did share and witness the birth of my youngest daughter, and I have my wife's testimonial to what she felt.

What I saw and experienced at that first Sundance is as close to going to the other side without making the permanent transition. During this experience, I gained strength, appreciation for the basics in life, and respect for all humanity.

I learned how to cope with pain, hunger, and all other things that make life unpleasant. I learned that we must consider others before we act. If we hurt others, even unintentionally, we hurt ourselves.

As native people, we don't always have specific words for everything. We do believe that if we do wrong to someone else, it comes back to us. Some people call this Karma.

Our connection with nature, our Mother Earth, and

with the heavens, allows us to know and feel things that others overlook. It's not because of any other reason except that we have developed a sensitivity to the earth. The elements and human connections have never been lost.

I believe that every living thing on this earth is born with that special sensitivity, but, through no fault of our own, we learn to overlook many laws of nature. For our convenience and progress, our environment suffers. Believe this, when nature decides, she's going to put things back where she wants them. We are not going to change nature. We have to respect nature and try to live with her, which is something we forget. Native people have learned that trying to force nature—or as we call her, Grandmother (the earth)—to bend our way, is to look for disaster.

What I mean to say is that instead of trying to be so logical, we should use a little of the common sense God gave us. Have we become so intellectual that we can't believe in the simple things? It's almost as if we follow down a road of destruction because we learn to believe only what we can see . . . and see only what we want.

When the Creator formed the earth, He had us in mind and made everything perfect and balanced. When all was running smoothly, He created humans and set up the food chain for the vegetables and animal world. *So why did He create us?*

The answer is hard to find, but very simple in content. We native people believe that when the earth was brought to life, the Creator had to think of everything.

Even before He created the animals to walk the earth, He knew that He was going to create humans, and spirituality would be needed. So He had to supply a means for them to protect themselves spiritually as they were learning.

The best thing He brought us was the "mother plant." This very first plant He created was called "sage," or "*Pejuta Wakan*," as the Lakota people call it. It is sacred to all traditional native people. We believe that the Creator gave it to native people to use in whatever way we need. It was not to be sold in every store and by everyone. What many people don't understand is that this medicine sage is not the same thing that grows in Europe, and it's not cooking sage. It's a special sage that has always grown in this hemisphere and has always been used by spiritual people for spiritual reasons. For our peoples, raping the land of sage for profit is equal to prostituting your sister or mother.

The Creator knew that we would need the smoke from the sage to cleanse our bodies and our spirits. Therefore He made different sage plants so the sage could survive at different altitudes and in different areas. He wanted His children to have sage available to them everywhere.

After Grandfather made sure we had what we needed for our spirituality, He created humans. He made each of us different. He knew that we had to be different because He was going to give us distinguishing features from the other animals.

We have free will, creativity, intelligence, courage, integrity, resourcefulness, pride, and, best of all, the ability to love. However, the Creator also gave us the ability to overemphasize our own worth in the form of the ego. We must all learn to have respect for each other and all other living things on this earth. We also need to learn to stop being judgmental of others. No matter how we feel, we all share this earth mother together. Whether we like it or not, we are all brothers and sisters.

When we learn these simple things, we have taken the first step to becoming a useful part of this earth, instead of a detriment.

When we finally arrived back at camp, the women had laid out a feast on a long table. I was only the third Sundancer to arrive back. The others were standing around just waiting. My reserves and control started collapsing when I saw all that beautiful food! They had prepared steaks, stew, fry bread, cold chokecherry juice, chokecherry pudding, coolers full of cold soda pop, cold watermelon, and boiling-hot coffee. There were so many wonderful things to eat. I looked around and realized everyone was as hungry as I.

We waited for one of the Sundancers to do a blessing and give thanks for a good Sundance. With that done, everybody started digging in. I didn't know what to eat first, so I had a small piece of meat wrapped in a tortilla, burrito style. Then I had a piece of watermelon. Then I asked for a cup of coffee. I never realized how good food tasted. The food mixed with the smell of burning wood made me realize how much there is to appreciate in this short life of ours.

I found out later that I had lost twenty-five pounds in those three days. Unfortunately, it doesn't stay off. Dehydration causes the weight loss, so once you replace the fluids in your body, you are right back where you began.

After everyone had relaxed and eaten, and the sun started to go down, one by one, each Sundancer began relating what had happened to him—what he had felt, seen, or experienced. It was beautiful to sit, listen, and wonder where all this energy had come from, and listen to stories and the crackling of the burning wood in the campfires. The small children scooted off to bed, and the older people just kept on talking and visiting. It felt good to not be dancing on those sharp little stones. I was glad to be smoking a cigarette, having a cup of coffee, and just relaxing.

If you have ever sat around a campfire as the earth quiets down after a long day, you'll know that it's a unique experience to feel our Mother Earth relax after watching over her children all day long.

As it got later, the adults started drifting to wherever

they were staying for the night. Not everyone was camping with us. As they left, they bid us farewell because some were pulling out early. Lots of dancers and people who helped us had to get back to work. Some had traveled long distances and had gone to great expense to attend or help at the Sundance.

As I've said, nobody is told they have to come to or be at the Sundance. Dancers, helpers, and everyone else are there because they want to be—which impressed me. Invariably the last thing everyone says is, "See you next year!" And even though you're still in a semi-shocked state, you are already looking forward to the next time.

That night, I lay there under the stars trying to go to sleep, but I couldn't. I kept reliving the Sundance. I was still high from what I had received—that huge spiritual uplifting and happiness at having found the Sundance. Most importantly, I was struck with wonder at the new world that was open to me now, and I knew I would never be the same.

I lay there so at peace with myself and my newfound world that I felt as if I never closed my eyes. Before I knew it, the sun was coming up.

In the distance I heard a couple of cars start and quietly drive away. The drivers seemed reluctant to leave and break the peaceful spell of that sacred place. The departure of those first two cars was like a signal. From all around the Sundance grounds, I could hear people starting to talk. Car doors slammed, babies cried, and more cars left the camp. Someone in our camp put kindling on the hot coals left over from the night before.

After everyone had gotten up and eaten, we started to break camp. It took several hours to accomplish. With all that done, our footprints and tire tracks in the dirt were all the marks that remained. Even the holes where our shade poles had been were refilled. There wasn't one tiny piece of trash, paper, or anything, anywhere. Everyone left their camps clean.

Not long after that first Sundance I went to Oklahoma on a selling trip. The native people of that state are the finest you can meet anywhere. They made me feel so welcome, and I fell in love with the countryside around Tulsa. I set up at a large native arts and crafts show in Tahlequah and met quite a few wonderful Cherokee people. Tahlequah is considered the capital of the Cherokee nation. It is where all the people searching for their Cherokee roots go to find out about their heritage.

I was so taken by the people and area that when I returned to Idaho, I talked Vivian into moving there.

The year went by so quickly, that before I knew it, it was time to return to Wyoming for another Sundance.

SOUTH — WHITE

"Warm Winds"

RAIN

We left Oklahoma about two weeks before the Sundance was to begin because I wanted to arrive at Fort Washakie with plenty of time to help with the camp and Arbor.

We got our camp set up early, but I was not allowed to help with the Arbor. It's never set up by the dancers; it's always done by the helpers. In fact, I have never had the occasion to see it being put up, since I was always dancing.

The erecting of the Arbor can be complicated and difficult. It takes many men a long time to put it up, and sometimes it feels as though it's not going to be done in time for the dance.

At one Sundance, I really got worried because it was late afternoon, and there wasn't anyone around the Arbor. I mentioned it to Allen. He just shrugged a shoulder and told me not to worry. The next time I thought about it, I looked again. Like magic, the Arbor was complete.

This day there was still no one around that I could see, but I stopped worrying about it. That was someone else's job. Our job was to pray and to dance.

We had plenty of time to cut brush for our camp and dig the holes for the frame. The frame consists of whatever materials are available, usually two-by-fours, four-by-fours, tepee poles, or whatever is on hand. Since it's not a permanent structure, we don't feel that what we use to make it is important—only that it serves the purpose. You know what they say, as long as the shell covers the nut . . .

As the days went on, more Sundancers arrived. Some would come by and stop at our camp. We were happy to re-establish old acquaintances from the year before. A Sundancer, Benny, grinned when he saw me and asked, "Hey, Manny, come back for seconds?" This being my second time made me an old-timer. I felt welcome and proud of myself.

Some guys only come to the Sundance once and never return because of the suffering they experience. Others will do anything to get there.

We heard of one guy who was riding his motorcycle to the Sundance from western Montana. Because he thought he was going to be late, he was speeding and got stopped. Fortunately, there was a Native American police officer at the station where they took the man, so when the Sundancer explained why he was speeding, the officer understood and spoke on the Sundancer's behalf. They released him so he could get to the Sundance. He was lucky that he had found someone who respected the Sundance and the people who take part in it.

I guess that even if it's not supposed to be a macho thing, people still reserve judgment on how a man can act under extreme conditions. Those people, the Shoshoni, and I guess all native people, place a great deal of importance on bravery. Bravery has always been and continues to be a large and very important part of our warrior societies and our way of life.

In the Shoshoni Sundance, women don't enter the Arbor. If they want to Sundance they must have a male member of their family inside the Arbor, and then they are only allowed to remain outside the brush wall of the Arbor next to their relatives. They are on their own about whether they drink or eat during the Sundance; no one watches them or forces them not to.

In the old days, the people judged you on how you endured hardships. People wanted to know if you would and could persevere in times of trouble. Could you be dependable and trustworthy? Many people believe that the Sundance is a test of these characteristics, so this time several Sundancers were a little bit nicer greeting me than they had been my first year.

Now that I knew what was happening, things were a little easier. However, there were some things they had forgotten to tell me: for example, when you dance once, you have made a commitment to Sundance for four years, and once you're in the Arbor, you can't leave for *any* reason.

The reason it becomes impossible to leave is that once all the Sundancers have come together, we become one entity. We become a solid force, and, as one, our power is tremendous. All our prayers will be answered. If even one person leaves the circle of a Sundance, it can cause a weakness in the rest of us. It weakens us not only as individuals, but it also harms our ability to function as one. It's like when a person loses an arm, a leg, or another part of the body. The body is still alive, but its abilities become limited. This is the reason you should know what you're getting into from the very beginning—before you start—because once you're in, there is no going back. If necessary, you would be kept there by force to keep from breaking the Sacred Circle.

My second Sundance happened much like the first. I was feeling pretty confident. I thought that my first one had been fairly easy. In a year you forget many things: the aches, pains, thirst, and hunger.

One elder I told about my feelings looked at me for a long time. Then he said, "Don't be so cocky about it, and show more respect. The Spirits are there to help you, but if you take it lightly, they have ways of humbling you and making you show respect. They can make the Sundance very hard on you."

He was absolutely right.

We had gone in on a Friday just like before, and the first night was quickly over. The drum started early the next morning and then they started singing. The songs were beautiful, and the energy was good. Everyone was happy and excited, and dancing strong and hard.

We would rush at the tree and, after touching it for power and energy, dance back to our spots. We were blowing furiously on our eagle whistles the entire time. I danced without regard for my physical condition. I danced without regard for the future of my next three days. Most dancers would pace themselves so they could last the entire dance. They advised me to do the same, but I didn't. My energy was so high that I just couldn't help myself.

I wanted to dance. I wanted that Sun Power on me. I wanted to feel the total glory of the Sundance. I had fallen in love with the Sundance and its beliefs. I knew that I had found the very best for myself. I didn't understand it all, and I knew I never would. Some Sundancers dance all their lives and learn more every time they dance. It's very much like an ongoing lesson in life.

I heard that some people, for whatever reasons, will call down the Sun Power on other dancers. The object is to elevate those dancers with so much power and energy that their dancing creates a pull of energy, causing them to have a vision right there in the Sundance. I also heard some dancers do the same thing with malice in their hearts—calling down the Sun Power on one dancer, causing him to dance until he drops from exhaustion. Once a dancer has reached that point of dehydration, he suffers immensely through the remainder of the Sundance. Though it's a very hard thing to do, that's what every Sundancer is there to experience, a vision and connection with the Creator.

I don't know if that's what happened to me, but I was badly dehydrated by Saturday evening. This was only the first day, and I was starting to have hallucinations as it grew later. The evening saved me.

I don't believe anyone knew what I was going through. The only one who could have known how I felt was Allen, and he only made a slight, passing remark about how tired I looked.

Sunday morning, after greeting the sun, everyone got ready to start dancing. Although there was only room for one drum at a time, when one group of singers tired, another group took its place. There must have been five or six groups of singers, and they were eager to be singing. They started singing all those beautiful Sundance songs, one after another. Such beautiful songs, every one of them. (They stay in your mind, and long after a Sundance, you find yourself singing them over and over in your head for months.) They didn't give us much time to rest.

This new day was the same as the previous morning, it got hot very early. There wasn't even the slightest breeze stirring, and I was incredibly thirsty.

By the middle of the afternoon I started retching because my mouth was so dry from dehydration. There wasn't saliva in my mouth, instead there was a gummy substance that made me sick to my stomach. I was starting to feel the effects of the previous day. After another night without water, it became hard to pray as my thirst took over my concentration.

In the next few hours I suffered like I never had in all my life. I had gone without water for long periods before, but never like this. I can't tell you how I looked, but I can tell you how I felt.

By now hunger had ceased being a big problem. The thirst and deep, dry feeling now dominated my thoughts. It started behind my eyes, reached into my mouth, down my throat, and engulfed my entire body. Although the thirst centered in my mouth and throat, my arms and legs felt detached from the rest of me. It felt as if my head were floating high above me.

The feeling was almost beyond words. Mostly it was a beautiful, glorious feeling because I knew why it was all happening to me. Yet, a small part of my brain questioned my sanity: Why am I doing this to myself? Is it worth it?

Then thoughts of my children invaded my brain, and my friends who needed prayers all reminded me of why I had made my commitment. I realized that in spite of the fatigue and fuzziness, it was worth everything I was going through.

We are all guilty of getting ourselves into situations in which we question our actions and priorities. And we also have a tendency to be selfish. We ask ourselves, "What am I getting out of this?" But why must we always think of ourselves first? The Sundance is about thinking of others before yourself. When you sacrifice yourself, you are showing God and the whole world that you are willing to give of yourself so that others may live better.

The drumming and singing continued. The hot sun was blazing down on us as if trying to give us as much of its heat and energy as we could take.

By now, many of us were really suffering and some dancers were staggering, which automatically makes the drummers sing faster and harder. It also makes the songs longer. They are trying to see if any of us are on the verge of collapsing, and, if we are, they will keep on singing until someone does fall. It is a great honor to fall with exhaustion during the dance. It brings great honor to the Sundance, the Chief, and all the dancers. The more dancers who go into this state, the greater the honor.

As I rushed at the tree I was praying hard for my father and my mother. Each time I danced back from the tree I blew hard on my eagle whistle. I was asking God to please answer my prayers. I had so many people to pray for, each time I danced back and forth I focused on another person.

When I first made the commitment to Sundance, I was afraid to face the unknown because of my lack of knowledge. In one of my prayers before the Sundance, I asked the Creator to help me. I asked Him to give me the courage to go through the Sundance and the strength to complete it. If He did, I would let my hair grow long in His honor. I also promised Him that I would let it grow until my commitment was over. Long hair has always been a possession of pride for the native warrior as well as a challenge to a warrior's enemy. Traditionally, by wearing your hair long you are taunting your enemy and asking if he is man enough to take it.

After I completed my first Sundance I started to grow

my hair and told my parents about my choice. "Well," my Victorian father said, "no man with long hair can come into my house." I felt rejected and hurt by my father's reactions to my choices, but I didn't blame him for acting the way he did. My parents brought us up to be humble, keep a steady job, and wear our hair short. That's what the Christian society demanded of us, so in a way I understood. My dad just didn't know any other way. I tried to tell him why I had to let it grow, but he would not listen to reason. So I explained to my mother about the Sundance and the significance of growing my hair. Although she understood, she had to stick by my dad, right or wrong. Because of my commitment, I didn't see my parents for five years.

Although I was hurt by their rejection, I also understand why my parents never claimed their native heritage. In the 1940s, the prejudice against "Indians" was rampant. It was better to be a Mexican than an Indian. In the summer there was a community pool in Ajo, and swimming privileges were segregated by race. Fridays through Sundays were for the white kids only. On Mondays and Tuesdays the Mexican kids got to swim. On Wednesdays they let the black and Indian, or Indio, kids swim. And on Thursdays the pool was disinfected and refilled with clean water.

I grew up as a Mexican, although my ancestry was mixed with native blood, and so I didn't understand the discrimination. The irony behind all this is that many young Mexicans today are claiming their "Indian" heritage and searching spiritually for their roots—like I did. Today, there is a new sense of pride in being Native American, and things aren't as bad as when I grew up.

Over the next several years, I kept praying at every Sundance that my father would accept me the way I was. I was praying hard for him this time when I backed away from the tree, staggered, and fell down hard. I felt my breath leave me. My head was reeling, and I went into an almost hypnotic state. I could see everything going on around me, and I could hear those beautiful Sundance songs, but I couldn't control my arms and legs. My legs were twitching, trying to cramp. I wanted to get up and dance some more, but I couldn't will my legs to move. It was a frightening feeling. I had my bedding rolled up in my spot just behind me. As I tried to get up, my legs just stretched out in front of me.

Allen had gone out to the Sacred Tree, and as he danced back I saw him stagger. When he was back all the way, he stopped and looked at me with a question on his face. He didn't say anything. He just looked and understood that now I was going through a very personal experience.

I didn't know it myself, but I was going through a very real vision. The hunger, the thirst, and the heat were combining their energies to put me in contact with the Great Spirit. Now I knew He was giving me his undivided attention. In essence, He was letting me know that moment was mine. He had listened to my prayers. Since I was willing to sacrifice, He was now willing to answer my prayers, and He was also going to let me know about my future through a vision that would later be interpreted by an elder. This was the moment when I was going to receive direction for my life.

My world, my eyesight, everything as I knew it went blank. Just as suddenly, everything came into focus, but seemed so unreal. I could see the green leaves of the Arbor brush—so bright, so green, they almost glowed. The sky was an intense blue. Everything I looked at was vibrant and in clear, sharp detail.

The sun was extremely bright, but it no longer felt hot. It didn't bother me in any way. It felt so pleasant, I just wanted to sleep. I was the only one in the Arbor. All the other dancers seemed to disappear. There was no more drumming or singing. It was absolutely still. I was lying just north of the Sacred Tree with my feet pointing toward it. My eyes were closed, yet I could see all those things.

Suddenly, I heard a loud, flapping noise. I opened my eyes and there between the poles in the roof of the Arbor, I saw a huge spotted eagle descending into the Arbor. He was so big I knew he couldn't possibly fly between the rafters. But they were invisible to the eagle. He flew right through them as though they didn't exist, soared to where I was lying, and landed lightly on my chest.

I couldn't move. My body was rigid with fright. I felt the pressure of his weight on my chest. I could smell his feathers, hot from the sun. I could feel the warmth of his body.

As the eagle stood on my chest, in slow motion he looked into my eyes. I could see very clearly the golden flakes in the iris of his eyes. I tried to read a message or figure out what he wanted me to do. I couldn't, but I got the distinct feeling that I didn't have to be afraid.

I felt myself relax, and as I did, each of his talons slowly gripped my chest. Slowly, one by one, the talons pierced my skin and dug into my flesh. I flinched, expecting pain, but, surprisingly, felt only the popping sensation as each talon broke through my skin. As I lay there, the eagle continued to look right into my eyes.

His look said, "I told you that if you overcame your fear, it would not hurt."

So I lay there, held my breath, and waited to see what was going to happen.

The eagle slowly spread its magnificent wings, and ever so slowly, started flapping them. I could smell and taste the dust disturbed by its wings. In two or three huge flaps, we were off the Arbor floor. As we lifted off, the eagle seemed slow because of my weight.

About this time I felt my soul separate from my vision. It was as though I were leaving my vision to become an observer. The eagle had told me that he was going to take me up to show me where I could help others.

The eagle spirit and I soared high above the ground, so high I could see the curvature of our Mother Earth. He was showing me that I would be helping people in all directions, and that I would be ready when the time was right. A medicine man would tell me and show me the way to help people.

I could see my vision below me—the eagle with my body, flapping between the ground and the rafters. I realized that I had split into three separate entities of myself: my physical body on the ground, my spirit being pulled by the eagle's talons, and my soul watching the entire scene from above.

As we soared higher, I felt fear, but only because I had nothing to hold on to. My spirit seemed suspended next to the eagle spirit as he spoke to me in thoughts. Suddenly, I was back in my vision. Again I could feel the wind stirred up by the eagle's wings. We moved past the rafters, and the realization hit me: I was being taken from the Sundance! My thoughts screamed, "I don't want to leave this Arbor. I'm not done with my Sundance!"

Boldly, I grabbed for the rafters and yelled at the eagle to let me down, that I didn't want to break the circle. I reached out with both arms. When I grabbed the rafter, I felt the pain in my chest where the eagle's talons had pierced my flesh. The spotted eagle kept flapping his wings hard, then harder and stronger. It was as if he were trying to break my grip from the rafter. Desperately, I hung on. His huge wings were so powerful for a moment I felt like letting go. Then I felt the power of our Sundance and the importance of not breaking the Sacred Circle, so I hung on.

Suddenly, one then another of his talons started ripping out of my chest.

I felt the pain then. It was a good pain because I knew that I was not to leave the Sundance. I was not going to break the Sacred Circle.

As the last talon ripped out of my flesh, my grip on the rafter finally broke. I landed softly on the floor of the Arbor.

As I woke from my vision, I was still next to my bedroll. I opened my eyes and looked around. Everything was the same as before. The drummers were still singing; the Sundancers were still dancing and going to the Sacred Tree.

Had it only been a dream?

Had it only been thoughts going through my mind? Or hallucinations?

I really wasn't sure what had happened. All I knew was that it seemed real, very real. So real that I still felt pain on both sides of my chest above my breast. I felt as if the eagle's talons had virtually torn out my flesh. It felt so real, I looked down and touched my chest to see if I was bleeding.

I staggered. I had to get on my knees and stand up. I stood swaying and wondering if I would fall. I felt confused as I stood there looking around. Everything was back to normal. Nobody seemed to have noticed a thing that had happened to me.

It had been so real for me that I just knew everyone else must have seen and felt what I did. It took me a few minutes standing there to clear my mind and come back to reality.

As I stood there shaking my head, I looked at the tree. I could feel an intense energy coming to me from it. It was almost like magic. The tree was helping me and giving me strength to continue.

There were also two small trees, freshly cut and placed between each dancer. I got up and felt a coolness come to me from those trees with their bark removed. They were moist and damp.

By now we were all dry, so we accepted gratefully the feel of moisture from those beautiful trees. It was so wonderful to feel dampness on our parched skin.

The singers were still drumming and singing.

I put my eagle whistle in my mouth and rushed at the tree. When I got to it, I embraced it and asked Grandfather to give me strength and direction. I thanked Him for what He had given me and for what He had chosen to let me see. I still didn't realize that it was a vision.

I danced back to my spot and blew furiously on my eagle whistle. I couldn't believe it. I felt like I was getting drops of moisture back into my mouth from my eagle whistle. It was wetting the inside of my mouth at first, then I felt my throat moisten. I was getting help from the Creator and the strength and courage needed to survive this very hard Sundance.

The elder had warned me to be careful, that some dances were more difficult than others, and this one was proving to be just that. It was overwhelming, almost more than I could take, but I feel it was also a test by the Creator. As though He were telling me, "You had an easy one. Now try a hard one."

Suddenly, I felt so good with that little bit of moisture in my mouth and my throat. I felt happy. I started looking around at my brother Sundancers and thinking, "I'm going to make it. This is it. I have had the sign that tells me I am going to finish the Sundance."

I looked at everyone and noticed they were going through difficulties. They were dehydrated and suffering. I started praying for them, saying, "Grandfather, help my brothers," and the answer I got for my prayers was almost like electricity. Slowly the whole Sundance seemed to start picking up and getting more life into it. Even the singers and the drummers perked up. The energy had changed. It was so beautiful that everyone felt happy. The dancers looked better, and it was getting toward evening and was becoming cooler.

The dance continued, and I had no problems after that. Late that evening, as everything finished, the drummers went back to camp. We were finished for the day.

Tired from the long, hot day, the Sundancers lay down and rested. This was Sunday night. We knew that the hardest, longest part of the Sundance was over. We knew the next day would be the last. Everything was right.

I lay there thinking, thanking the Creator for helping me as he did in that one special moment. I got up from my bedroll and walked to where the Sundance Chief was sitting on the west side of the Arbor. As is tradition when seeking counsel, I brought him some tobacco.

I shook his hand, sat down, and said, "I want to share something with you. I need some guidance from you."

He asked, "What do you need?"

He didn't even know my name because so many Sundancers come and go every year that he can't keep track of everyone.

I told him what had happened to me that day, how I had suffered. I told him how, in a way, I wish it had happened in the middle of the Arbor so everybody would have known about it.

He said, "That's okay, it was only supposed to happen to you. It's your vision. My interpretation is that there are other Sundances. The Lakota people pierce their chest. I think the spirits were telling you that you have to do that some day. Also that you are to help heal others, no matter who they are. But not yet, not until you are ready."

I asked, "Why do they bring the vision to me here?"

He explained, "Because that was one time that your mind, body, and spirit were ready and open to receive this message. So it came to you in a very sacred place. Then you would know that it was real and not just your imagination. It wasn't just a dream or just a thought. This did happen to you. This is how we get our visions."

He answered my questions, and it scared me to death. Just the thought of piercing made me ache all over. I thought, "My God, I can't do that." However, that was his answer.

I asked him one final thing, "When do I have to do this?"

He said, "When you are at the Sundance the first time, you make a four-year commitment. The reason the Spirits demand this is so that they can see that you are sincere in following the Sundance spirituality and traditions. You must go to the Lakota Sundance and pierce as your vision told you, but first you must finish your four years with the Shoshoni people."

After receiving the interpretation of my vision, I returned to my bedroll and lay down. Everybody was starting to get into their blankets because the air was starting to get a little chilly.

I lay quiet for a while, just listening to the sounds. By the center of the Arbor the guards started their fire and kept it going all night. As I drifted off to sleep, my mind was full of wonder at what had happened. I couldn't believe my mouth had saliva. It was no longer dry like it had been for two days. The last thing I recall was looking through the branches of the Arbor leaves, at the stars.

I woke about one or two o'clock in the morning. It was cold, and the wind was blowing very hard. We got hit by a big storm that night. It was almost like an answer to all of our prayers. We couldn't touch or allow any water to touch our lips or go into our mouths, but we could feel the humidity in the air. When you're parched the way we were, moisture can be absorbed through the skin.

At the Sundance, many people said not to let water touch you in any way—even on the arms, the hands, or the face—when it rains. It just makes your body cry out for more moisture, and when it doesn't get it, the suffering is twice as hard as it was before.

It was cold, windy, and stormy all night. We had quite a bit of rain, but by morning it was clear. It was Monday, so we all got up and put on the best shawl skirt that we had. We put on our finery because we wanted to look good. We wanted to show that, although it was hard on us, we were proud of what we had done and of the suffering we had endured. Proud to be allowed the privilege to pray for other people.

The Creator had seen fit to let us survive, to live and talk about what we had experienced. We knew we had done our small part. Everybody got ready and greeted the sun. We always get up before the sun rises, to greet it and allow its warmth into our hearts.

The dancing went on for the remainder of the morning. Finally we concluded the Sundance that Monday afternoon at about one o'clock. Leaving the Arbor was the same as before: we got our watermelon, and people thanked and greeted us. It was such a joyous occasion. It felt as if every breath we took, every second of thirst we suffered, was all worthwhile simply because of the gratitude shown by the people who waited for us to leave the Arbor.

In preparing the Arbor, some people endure much hardship and strenuous work. They keep us going with their support. They cook for and feed the drummers and singers. There is so much to do, it's almost easier to be inside the Arbor dancing than to be outside.

It is toughest on the Sundance Chief. Four days before the Sundance, during the purification days, the Sundance Chief has one full week of fasting. He allows himself only a very small amount of liquids, such as coffee or tea, but never water in its pure state. For a full week, the Sundance Chief already suffers. Then he suffers, fasts, and is without water with us for three and four days during the Sundance. Finally, for four days after the Sundance, he prays and gives thanks for all we received.

Tuesday morning I got up and went outside. I saw the Chief's lonely figure standing there in the middle of the desert. He raised his pipe and arms to the Great Spirit, the east, and the rising sun.

When a man is chosen by the Spirits to be a spiritual leader, he must be willing to lead by example. He can't ask others to do things he hasn't done himself. That's the reason he starts his ceremonies and suffering long before the dancers have arrived.

It is such a beautiful ceremony, but it is not for the weakhearted nor the timid. It takes great courage to be a Sundance Chief, to commit yourself to that sacrifice. It's not easy. Anybody who sacrifices for another should be respected and helped in any way possible.

My family and I returned to Oklahoma and continued our daily quest for our livelihood.

Early the next summer, we left Oklahoma so that we could attend powwows before the Sundance. The powwows we go to are gatherings of people where natives from many different tribes dance for competition, and where local people get the opportunity to buy arts and crafts from the people who make them. We attended a couple of small powwows in Colorado and then went to Taos to see some acquaintances.

We had been there a few days when Carpio, a friend we were staying with, asked me to drive his car down to Santa Fe. They were having auditions for extras for the miniseries *Gambler III*, with Kenny Rogers. To make a long story short, although reluctant at first, my whole family ended up as extras on the set. I played a Sioux chief.

Before the shooting of the film started, I asked Kenny Rogers' brother Leland if they wanted to have a Sweat Lodge with us. After agreeing to it, we built it right on the movie grounds. There were several of us, including Kenny Rogers; his brother Leland; the producer, Ken Kragen; and the director, Dick Lowry. It was a good sweat. Kenny was surprised at how long we were in the lodge.

It was fun being with people who were new to the Sweat Lodge ceremony; they were great. It was here I met Larry Sellers, a Sundancer from Rosebud, South Dakota. Immediately after they filmed my segment, we left for the Sundance.

We went through the usual ritual, preparing our eagle whistles and getting our ceremonial outfits ready. Of course, it was always good to see the people at the Sundance. They became very important friends to us.

The Sundancers greeted me more enthusiastically than they had my first and second years. They made me feel like I was one of them now. The days passed as the Sundance came and went. It wasn't quite as hard as my second one, but it was still tough. Everyone suffered quite a bit. Thirst was again a major factor in my suffering.

I always prayed for my family, my wife, and my children. I especially prayed for my father and mother, that their health would last and they would be well. Also that my father would come to accept me with my long hair.

On Sunday I saw something that almost caused me to have a nervous breakdown.

It all began when the drummers were taking their noon break, and we had only one group singing for us. Most of us were just resting. Some guys were asleep. I was lying on my bedroll. The man next to me was one whom I had looked up to and respected since I had met him. Though he was younger than I, he had been around the Sundance all his life, so in my book, that made him pretty special. At the time, he hadn't been married long, but he and his Cheyenne wife had a small baby.

Right outside the Arbor, she was sitting with the baby. In the guise of showing him the baby underneath the baby's blanket, I saw the woman hand him the baby's bottle full of water. And I saw him put the nipple of the bottle in his mouth and start sucking on it.

I was shocked. I turned and looked at my wife, sitting in her chair just beyond me. She also had a surprised look on her face. I asked her, "Did you just see what I saw?" She nodded her head. She couldn't say anything. I then asked him, "What in the world are you doing, man?" Although I tried, I couldn't quite keep the anger out of my voice.

He tried to be casual about it and said, "Oh, it's okay, I'm just rinsing my mouth out."

Angrily I retorted, "If it's all right, why don't they let all of us do that?"

"It's okay, it's okay, Manny," he said, trying to calm me. He didn't want anyone else to know what I had seen.

It devastated me. All I could think of was, once again I'm being let down hard. Maybe I just demand too much from others. Maybe I expect too much. I'm not very tolerant when a word is given. I'm not one to forgive going back on a man's word.

He immediately returned the bottle to his wife. My wife was livid, as she also took the Sundance very seriously. She told his wife to take the baby back to camp and not bring water to the Arbor ever again. His wife got up and almost ran from the Arbor. She knew they had done something profoundly wrong. They also knew that it wasn't a secret any longer. Someone had seen what they had done. I turned my back to him and didn't even want to see his face. I was deeply hurt by what he had done.

Now thinking back, I wonder if I had judged him too harshly. Did I have the right to judge him at all? He didn't hurt me, he only hurt himself. Then again, everything that occurs within the Sundance circle does affect everyone in it. Did he in fact weaken our spiritual strength? Were all of our prayers answered? Or were some left unanswered because of his actions?

I think most of my anger was because he used an innocent child to cheat. The breakdown didn't happen until the next day, when I had had all night to think about it. After the sun-greeting ceremony, I called Allen aside and told him what I had seen. He couldn't believe it either.

During the telling, a combination of hunger, thirst, fatigue, and emotion surged through me. The result was devastating. I was distraught and heavily disappointed. I even tried to give away my pipe. It's hard to write what I felt, how hopeless everything looked because of one man's actions. I was crying in front of my brother Allen and couldn't seem to control myself.

This is when I believe I had my spiritual breakdown. He understood and waited patiently until my grief had expended itself. For days afterwards, I felt empty and cheated.

In retrospect I believe it was indeed a spiritual breakdown. Since then, I've given the experience a tremendous amount of thought and have realized that I learned two important lessons. First, the experience showed me that no matter how deeply embedded in spirituality anyone is, the fact remains that we are still scared, lonely, and weak human beings. Second, I learned that no man should be put up on a pedestal; no one human being is above reproach. If you put someone up on a pedestal, they will surely fall some day. This has been demonstrated repeatedly with religious and spiritual leaders. Perhaps the Creator is showing us to rely on ourselves and Him only.

At the end of the Sundance, something else dramatic happened to me. As I was coming out, we were all happy, tired, and hungry. We were very thirsty, and the people were standing outside, greeting us and shaking our hands. While walking up, I looked to my right. Just beyond the people sitting in front was an older woman. Our eyes made contact. I just smiled, nodded my head, and went on. When I got to the end of the line, they handed me a watermelon. I turned left, and a young man came and touched my right shoulder. He said, "Excuse me, sir. Would you pray for my mom?"

I couldn't hear him too well because he had mumbled the request and there was so much noise. People were talking to each other and laughing and congratulating the Sundancers. I wasn't feeling normal yet. I frowned and looked at him. I said, "I am sorry, what did you say? My throat is very dry." I could hardly speak.

Again, he repeated, "My mom wants to know if you will pray for her."

It took a second for me to comprehend this. I asked, "Why me?"

"She wants you to pray for her. No one else."

"I'm just a Sundancer, I'm not a medicine man," I said lightly.

"That's okay," he went on. "She wants you, no one else, to pray for her."

"I would be honored, if she thinks I'm the right person."

"Yes, you are the one she wants."

I turned around, handed my wife the watermelon, and said, "I will be right back."

I went with him to his mother, who was sitting down. She had the most beautiful face, a wise-looking face. She had long gray hair, and was so regal, so elegant, you would have sworn she came from the ancient courts of Europe.

To be so honored in this way, to pray for one of our elders, is an honor beyond description. I was close to tears. I knelt down before her and looked in her eyes. I asked quietly, "Grandmother, am I the one you called for? I'm not a medicine man. I'm just a Sundancer."

"Yes, I want you to pray for me, son. I feel that you can do something to help me."

"Please tell me how can I help you?"

She explained, "I have arthritis throughout my body so bad I can hardly walk. I can't walk without a cane or someone helping me. If you could just bring me a little relief from the pain I would be grateful."

So, I put my hand on her right knee, grabbed hold of both her hands with my left hand, and started praying. I don't recall what I said, but I know that I was praying so hard that tears came to my eyes. I tried with all my energies within me. I don't know what to call it, it could have been a personal contact with God, maybe. She might have thought that I was able to do more than just a prayer.

I guess I prayed for two or three minutes. As I stood up, I said, "Grandmother, I feel very inadequate in doing what you ask of me. I have done the best I can. I know it wasn't very long, but I'm tired and very thirsty."

With relief on her face, she said, "That is all I wanted, for you to touch me and say a little prayer."

"Before I leave," I told her, "I want you to understand one thing. Although this prayer was short, I am not through praying for you. For the next four days no matter where

I am, I will be praying for you. I will pray that you receive help."

"That's all I want," she said gratefully. "Thank you."

As I turned to leave, I touched her shoulder and walked to where my family was waiting. While walking away, I turned to look back at the woman and her son, but they had vanished. On our way back to camp, my wife asked me, "What did she want?"

I said, "Just a prayer. That's all she wanted was a prayer and a little relief from her pain."

I felt very humbled by the experience. She had chosen me out of seventy-five other Sundancers. To me that was a great honor. Had this been a reward for my faith? Was what I had seen the other Sundancer do a test of my beliefs, a test of my faith in the Spirits and the Sundance? Had the Spirits seen in me a man who believes in them so much that they granted me the ability to help others with prayer?

That night I went out by myself away from all the other people camped there and prayed for her.

I never knew her name, that beautiful lady. I've never forgotten her or her energy. I wish now I had asked her name, or to know her children, her grandchildren. I went and prayed, and for some reason it was so intense that I cried for her again.

Now I stop and look back at that experience and realize it was a test for me. Perhaps she was sent to help me learn a lesson. We believe that sometimes the Creator sends a helper to teach us. If she was a helper, I think her mission was to show me I was now ready to help people. In helping her, it gave me confidence in my ability to help others. I believe that through her, Grandfather was showing me how close I was to my vision coming true.

Though I was tired, thirsty, and wanting to eat the watermelon in my hand, would I give that pleasure up to help someone unknown to me? If it was a test, I suppose I passed it.

The following morning we left and traveled toward South Dakota. I'm not sure why we headed in that direction, we were just going. I kept listening to the radio for information about tornadoes: where they were going, and how far away from us they were. One crossed in front of us, and one crossed behind. We came to a little town called Valentine, Nebraska, and camped at a trailer park. That night, I went out.

While I was praying for her, a big thunderstorm came. For some reason, when I prayed for her I became emotional again, maybe because I was still fresh from the Sundance. There was thunder, lightning, and hail, so I had to cut the prayer short, but that didn't take away any of its power.

We left there the next morning and passed through Mission, South Dakota, and the Rosebud Reservation. At the time, I never knew what my connection might be to that area, or what pulled me there. We drove through the village of Parmalee, South Dakota, and stopped at a small store, way out of the way. I don't know why I asked the owner, "Are there any Sundances going on around here?"

He said, "Yes, there is one going on." Then he gave me directions.

However, my wife said she wasn't ready for another Sundance so soon after the last one, so I let her talk me out of it. I'm not going to put the blame on her. I was also tired, and the Sundance had worn me out. That summer before we left for the Sundance, we had looked around and found a house in southwestern Colorado. We put a down payment on it and told them we'd return after the Sundance, so we headed back in that direction.

Not long after that, I made a sales trip up around

Jackson Hole, Wyoming, and up through Fort Washakie, where the Sundance took place. I made a swing back toward Denver, Colorado, but before getting to Denver, I got very sick. I was out of energy and had trouble holding my head up.

I got to the convention center, where they were having a native arts and crafts show. While there I got a booth and set up my arts and crafts to do some retailing, but during the show, I almost fell down twice. I didn't know what was going on. At first I thought maybe I was just hungry, but I had eaten plenty, so I knew it couldn't be that.

The second time it happened, I almost fell out of the chair. Some concerned friends took me to a male nurse on the grounds. The nurse asked, "What's the problem?"

I said, "I think I've had a heart attack."

The guy went haywire. He was in worse shape than I was. He started to shake and say, "Ah, ah, ah, ah . . . I better call 911 . . . uh . . . the ambulance." He looked around frantically. He couldn't find the phone, and all the time it was sitting right next to him.

As sick as I felt, it was still comical watching his reaction to the situation. He finally got an ambulance for me. When they got me in it, they checked me out, put me on an IV, and sped me to the hospital. They were still checking me out as the ambulance raced through the traffic. At the hospital, they put me on a cardiovascular receiver and discovered that I'd had two minor strokes within an hour. I didn't even know what was going on. I thought it was just bad dizzy spells. Then they told me that when I got back home I should check with my doctor to see what was wrong.

At the time, I didn't even have a family doctor, so I just found one in Durango, Colorado, who told me my biggest problem was that I had serious high blood pressure. Apparently, it affects some people more at high altitudes. And we had just bought a house two or three months before that sits over eight thousand feet high! There I was staggering around. I couldn't do anything. I was almost totally unable to function at home.

I told my wife and kids I couldn't handle it. I had to move to a lower altitude, so we moved back to Oklahoma.

We returned to the town of Inola and found a house to rent. The following summer I got sick, and my blood pressure was up again, so I couldn't make it to the Sundance. Allen called me and said they had moved the Sundance grounds from up on the mesa, where I had been Sundancing for three years, back to downtown Fort Washakie. He continued, "I'm not going to the Sundance this year. I don't like that place. Too many drunks come around yelling obscenities at us and stuff. It's not a good place for a Sundance. So I won't be going."

Throughout the sickness, with everything I had gone through, I felt empty—as though a big piece of my life had been cut out by not going to the Sundance. Yet I knew that healthwise I wasn't ready, and the location wasn't good for me. So, I thought, this is the way it's supposed to be.

That year would have been my fourth year.

In my mind I couldn't picture myself going back to the Sundance if I had to sit and listen to drunks and other people who didn't believe our way. By now I figured that I wasn't going back to the Shoshoni Sundance. I asked Larry, the Sundancer from Rosebud, if I could finish my fourth Sundance there.

He said, "Of course you can, Manny. You're more than welcome to come with us. We'll help you any way that we can."

Three weeks before the Shoshoni Sundance the phone rang, and it was Allen.

"What's going on?" I asked.

He said, "The Sundance is back on, Bud. It's back on the mesa where you danced your first three years." He was very enthusiastic and happy. "You're going to love it. It's really going to be a good one this year."

I groaned, "Oh my God, I already committed this summer to the Rosebud Sundance with Larry." I explained everything to Allen. He seemed crestfallen, but told me to do what I had to do.

Now I was sick to my stomach. I really didn't know what to do. The Shoshoni people honored me by allowing me to dance with them. I couldn't let them down. So I told Allen, "I'll be there."

He said, "Okay."

When I told my wife that it was back on in Wyoming, she said, "What are you going to do about South Dakota?"

I said, "Well, we'll go to the Shoshoni, and I'll dance there. Then we'll go to South Dakota and tell Larry that I've already finished my four years."

So, that year we went. We prepared just like the other three years.

Incidentally, when you make a commitment for four years, nothing says you have to do them consecutively. The agreement with the Creator is to dance four years. If it takes you six years to finish four years, that's fine, just as long as you finish them.

We went there, we prepared, I Sundanced, and it was a very hard one. I want to point out that I hardly ever mention hunger because hunger is not a factor. When you get so dry, you forget everything else. What really becomes prominent is your thirst. The hunger you can live with. You can go several days without eating. Although the first twenty-four hours without food can be hard, after that it gets easier. So, we went through the Sundance. Other than its difficulty, and losing another twenty-five pounds from lack of moisture, it was a good Sundance, and a beautiful one.

There's nothing common about any Sundance, they are all difficult and have special things that happen when you're there. Although it would be hard to top my second and third Sundances, because of my vision and somebody asking me to pray for them, it was still special.

We finished with the Sundance and said our farewells to all our friends. Before the Sundance was over, I had brought my gifts for the giveaway and honored the drum by giving gifts to the drummers. It is our way of thanking the spirit of the drum. It doesn't matter that it was not the same drum I had been dancing with the previous years. I was giving thanks. That was my giveaway; I had to have a giveaway because it was my fourth Sundance and I was finishing my commitment.

I honored many of my friends whom I had danced with for four years, who had encouraged me and had given me strength or energy to get through rough spots. I honored Allen, Benny, Edgar—the Sundance Chief—and most of all I thanked and honored the Creator. I asked Him to look after my family, I was deeply grateful to Him for helping me these four years.

After it was over, we drove north to Rapid City. When we were looking for Larry, we visited another Sundance because we heard he might be there. When we stopped, we saw men dancing and piercing, which frightened my wife. She wouldn't even get out of the van. Although she wouldn't admit it, she was deathly afraid of the piercing ceremony, even just seeing it through the bushes that lined the camp. This was also the first time I had seen it from the outside, and I realized I was glad I'd finished my four years. Frankly, the whole scene scared me, too.

We ended up in Mission, South Dakota. We got a few groceries there and tried to find Larry. I already had directions. We went to where his stepmother lived and found him.

Grinning, he said, "You're sure here early. The Sundance isn't until this coming weekend."

I explained cautiously, "Larry, we just came by to tell you that I can't do the Sundance. I have already finished my four years. They called me and told me that the Shoshoni Sundance was on again. That's where we are coming from."

"That's okay, Manny. I appreciate you coming by and letting me know, instead of just not showing up. No, you've got no obligation except to yourself. If that satisfies you, it should be good enough for everybody else."

I didn't know what he meant at the time, although I would find out later.

WEST — BLACK

"Setting Sun"

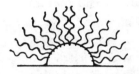

D A Y ' S   E N D

After we left Larry's house, there was an eerie silence in the van. When I told Larry that I wasn't going to be dancing with them, I felt an emptiness inside that I couldn't explain. Then I got to thinking about what he had said to me about my being satisfied with fulfilling my commitment.

What he didn't say was that I had made that commitment not only to myself but to the Creator as well. I realized that my commitment had been made for me by my vision. I kept remembering my vision and thinking about what it meant for me. It had been so vivid, I couldn't just forget it.

We headed back to Oklahoma, and when we arrived home Sunday evening, I knew it was when the Rosebud Sundancers were going through the purification ceremony. The actual Sundance wouldn't start until the following Thursday.

Monday I worked in our shop all day. But no matter how hard I worked, I couldn't tear the thought from my mind that I was abandoning the Creator by not completing my commitment. Although my promise was made under unusual circumstances, that is what Larry had meant. I said I'd be there, and the Creator wasn't going to let me forget it easily. He was going to make me uncomfortable.

Tuesday morning I got up and worked again all day, making crafts—lances, war clubs, and war shields—trying to get the thought of the Sundance out of my mind. Most of my time at the shop was spent alone. My kids were in school and my wife was at home.

By Wednesday morning I couldn't handle it anymore. I was watching CNN to see what had happened during the night while I was asleep, when my wife walked in and said good morning.

I said, "I'm going to the Sundance."

"I knew it, I could feel it," she said. "I'm surprised you waited until Wednesday, I thought you were leaving Monday morning. I've got your suitcase all packed. I fixed you some sandwiches after you went to bed, so you are all ready to go."

"I am really sorry I am spending this time and money going."

She said, "You know you have to go."

She knew about my commitment, she just didn't want any part of it because, unlike the Shoshoni Sundance, the Lakota Sundance involves the piercing and ripping of flesh. I can't blame her for fearing it either, because it is something alien to many people. They find it hard to accept seeing other human beings suffer, but that's all part of our prayers.

I drove all day and all night. When I arrived the next morning, they were already in the Sundance. Heartbroken because I had tried so hard to make it, I found Larry. Everyone greeted me and made me feel welcome. My friend Steve's sister, Chrys, and I walked to the Arbor. I saw Larry and Steve, and they were happy to see me.

Larry said, "You came back, did you?"

"I had to, Larry."

With a knowing smile on his face, he nodded his head. As though he knew that I would be there, but also that I had to find out myself.

He said, "Look Manny, get yourself together, get some rest today because it isn't easy. It's really hard. You can come in tomorrow morning."

"I could use some rest," I said gratefully.

When I got back to camp, the women there to support Sundancers told me what I needed: a head crown of sage wrapped in cloth, ankle and wrist bands in the same material, and a skirt. They got some long stems of sage for me and helped me put everything together.

The next morning I lay there for the longest time, wide awake, anxious to get going into this new Sundance the Creator was showing me. I felt excited and nervous. I don't know how much I slept that night, but it couldn't have been long.

When it was time to get up my stomach lurched. This was it. I jumped up and went over to Steve's tent and called him. He got up, and we put our towels around us and walked barefoot to the sweat lodges. It is an exhilarating feeling to be up that early for such a special occasion.

But this Sundance was a lot different from the others. They had four sweat lodges behind the Arbor, and the fire pit was burning. The flames were high. Several people started to gather.

The morning air was cool. As we walked up to the sweat lodges, I had a little tingling sensation at the pit of my stomach. I felt apprehensive, somewhat nervous, and a little scared, and so many things were going through my mind. I kept thinking of the vision that I had had two or three years before.

The first thing I felt was the heat from the big fire. It was warm and friendly and seemed to wash my apprehension from me. Not only did the fire have a calming, soothing effect on me, it also seemed to relax everyone else. There is something very special about the fires that are heating up the Stone People (we show the stones respect because they are so important in that ceremony) for the sweat lodges, getting them ready to bring us their breath. We would have our bodies, minds, spirits, and energies purified by them.

As we walked away from the sweat lodges, we heard someone call. The faint and muffled voice from the sweat lodge said, "Come on in, we've got room for two more." Made of slim branches, the sweat lodges are small enclosures built low to the ground and covered with blankets to help keep in the steam. So we got down on our hands and knees, and crawled into the sweat lodge.

When entering any Lakota sweat lodge, a person always says the words *"Mitakuye Oyasin,"* which mean "all my relations." A very loose interpretation is that you're asking the spirits to cover all the people of the world in your prayers. We believe we are all related, which is why the Sundance colors are red, yellow, white, and black: the four races. We are all one people.

When we got in the sweat lodge, the leader called out, "All right, bring me seven rocks, seven Grandfather rocks." By that, he meant he wanted some rocks about the size of a head. The fire keeper walked over to the fire pit with a pitch-fork and got the first rock. As he brought it into the lodge, the leader guided it into a special spot and placed it in the small hole in the center of the lodge. They repeated the process six more times.

As each rock was brought in, one Sundancer sprinkled a few pieces of cedar on top of the hot rocks. Right away they started popping and sending out a beautiful, rich scent of cedar into the sweat lodge. All of us were sitting there, waiting solemnly.

The Sweat Lodge is a very important ceremony in our culture. Anyone who has been in one knows how close you are to the other people. Almost immediately after the first stone was set in the hole, the sweat started beading up on my forehead. It trickled down my neck and back. It was so pleasant after coming in from the cool air outside.

When the seventh stone was in place, they brought a bucket of water. We asked a blessing for it from the Grandfather rocks, then closed the door flap, plunging our-selves into total darkness.

Once we leave the sweat lodge, there is never a discus-sion about what we heard or talked about while inside. If someone discusses anything heard in the sweat lodge when they go outside, we believe the problem returns to the per-son talking about it. The whole purpose of the Sweat Lodge ceremony is to leave all your problems inside, and to ask for blessings on all of our relatives. We also give thanks that we are all at the Sundance, and we ask for strength and the courage to go through it.

All I could think of was the sensation I had had during my vision, and my chest, after three years, began to itch again. I admit that I felt a little bit of dread and hoped that I wouldn't fail.

It was a quick, one-round sweat, which is traditional in

the Lakota Sundance, because we purify each morning before entering the Sacred Arbor and every night after leaving. Sometimes the lodges can get pretty hot. Most of the time the Sundance leaders are the ones that run the *Inipi*, or Sweat Lodge ceremony. They are pretty considerate of the dancers and don't want to dehydrate them or cause us to have a harder time within the Sundance.

We came out of the Sweat Lodge and shook hands with the others, people I had never met in my life. Coming out of the Sweat Lodge is like being born again. Going in there and leaving behind all our aches, pains, and troubles feels like starting life all over, without any human or spiritual problems.

In essence, we are all coming from our Mother Earth's womb, the Sweat Lodge. Some believe that because we sweat together, we become brothers and sisters—even though there is a separate Sweat Lodge for the women. This time there were many female Sundancers. As givers of life, the women brought a very powerful, beautiful, and special energy into the Sundance.

The leaders allowed us each to take one blanket and put it under the Arbor. Between songs we could rest and pray. I was very nervous and scared, especially since I had seen others get their chests pierced. I prayed. I asked Grandfather to please help me, to give me the courage to do it well, like a warrior, like a man. Like a person who believes, truly believes, in our spirituality. Many others were also praying. I know now there were quite a few new people, just like myself, going in for their first time, although I was one of the older ones.

We started lining up on the west side of the Arbor. It was nice and cool. I thought, "I should have kept my blanket with me." But we couldn't, so we stood there, waiting. I had goosebumps all over my body. There was a beautiful, quiet hush. I could hear the murmur of the people who were still around the fire pit and other Sundancers' voices as they talked quietly.

From way over on the other side of the Arbor we heard one man hit the drum. It seemed to startle everyone, though we had been waiting for it. It took my breath away. Everything stopped, even the murmurs. Now we were all waiting for the first eagle whistle to be blown. The drum sounded again.

That Sacred Drum. The heartbeat of our people sounded to call all the Sundancers, to let them know it was time to come and get into line. It was time to see the sun, greet it, and welcome it into our Sundance, time to sacrifice ourselves for others.

The Sundance Chief blew his eagle whistle loudly, three or four times, and started moving forward. When they saw him move, the drummers started drumming. The slow and measured beat of the drum escorted us into the Sundance Arbor.

Then the song started. Oh, what a beautiful song it was. I had never heard this song in my life until then. It gave me goose bumps all up and down my body. I was choked with pride. These songs have been handed down to younger singers for hundreds of years, and every tribe that has the Sundance ceremony has its own songs in its own language. I was humbled by the knowledge that I was listening to the same songs that Crazy Horse, Sitting Bull, and all the other Sundancers before me had heard.

I felt grateful and honored to be in the lineup with the Lakota warriors and warriors from other tribes. We started blowing on our eagle whistles, first one, then another, and we kept blowing on them. I felt the lurch in my stomach again. The time was drawing near. I was starting my first Lakota Sundance. Overwhelmed, I started blowing my eagle whistle to keep my emotions in check.

People from all the different camps had come out to watch us. They came to see their loved ones, brothers, cousins, and uncles, going into the Sundance. To pray and to support them.

I prayed, "Grandfather, give me strength and courage to do this with honor."

They were drumming and singing the "Going In" song. We believe that good Spirits live in each of the four main directions—east, south, west, and north—so we stopped to honor the four directions, four times, then we entered the Arbor. When I walked in, I became emotional, yet happy. I was finally at the Sundance that I had had a vision about so many years before. Tears filled my eyes. It may not be manly to do this, but I didn't feel bad because I was in the presence of the Creator.

I didn't go to the Sundance for my ego. I went there, humbled, and I wanted my prayers answered. I wanted my family taken care of. As we went in, we made a complete circle inside the Arbor. They went into another song, and the beat picked up, lifting everyone's spirits. It was so good to be alive and in the Arbor.

As the sun rose higher and the sky got brighter, I was overwhelmed at the sight of so many dancers. Men and women, all beautifully dressed, all there together to pray. There were about a hundred of us in there. All the colors the Sundancers wore were bright and beautiful. The traditional Sundance colors—red, yellow, white, black, for the four directions—were visible, as were blue for the sky above, green for the earth below, and purple for the inner spirit.

We danced and danced. I was finally getting over being cold; dancing was warming up my body. I was carrying my own sacred, ceremonial pipe on my left arm, and my eagle-wing fan in my right hand. The bowls of the Sacred Pipes are made from pipestone. There's only one good place that stone is found, in Pipestone, Minnesota. It's believed that the reason it's red is that the stone was colored by the blood that native peoples have shed from war and from suffering. As custom dictates, my pipe was given to me by a friend. A person must never buy his own pipe. We believe that when you need it, it will come to you. As we danced around the Arbor, I felt great and very proud. I had come so far, and I was finally here.

As the day progressed, we went through all the ceremonies. We greeted the sun, and each placed his pipe, or *Chanupa*, down on the altar. We had been dancing about an hour and a half by the time we finished the "Pipe" song, so we took a rest under the Arbor. Right away I saw other people getting marks on their chests and backs, then walking out to the tree to release their ropes. This is part of the preparation for the piercing ceremony. Knowing I would be one of them soon, I felt my stomach lurch as I watched them. My time for being pierced was entirely up to me. It would be done when I asked for it.

That was another thing that made my stomach reel. How long would it take me to decide? Would I have the courage to walk up to a Sundance leader and say, "I am ready to pierce"? Just the thought made me dizzy and swallow hard. As the realization hit me, that I was here to go through with it, I felt alone. My family was not with me. Steve and the others were only acquaintances so far. I had come alone, and I had to stand alone.

There were a couple of Sundancers inside the Arbor who had been pierced the day before. We rested a few minutes, got our blankets situated, and introduced ourselves. I found out that these Sundancers were to stay pierced three or four days. As is customary, they wouldn't break loose until the last day. It impressed me, their tolerance of suffering, their ability to cope with the pain and to withstand all that tugging and pulling on their flesh for four days. It also humbled me.

Suddenly a Sundance leader stood up and said, "*Ho-ka-hey*, come on, let's go, it's time to dance."

Everybody got up, and being the new one, I followed what everybody else did. I was fortunate to have a few friends to explain things to me before they happened. We formed the circle, and the singers started another song. At the time, I didn't know it was a piercing song. We danced and danced, and I noticed a Sundance leader dancing toward another Sundancer, his feet in perfect rhythm with the beat of the drum. The rhythm of his body movements as he danced and moved around portrayed his confidence and pride. His hair, long and flowing, gave him a regal, almost saintly look.

When the Sundance leader reached the man who was being pierced, it was clear that the man was waiting for him. The Sundance leader grabbed his wrist bracelet, and they moved out of the circle, dancing around the Arbor, then to the Sacred Tree.

You can't believe or understand how I felt inside. The dread that was in me was immense. I thought, "What am I doing here? Why did I make this commitment?" With my next breath, I assured myself, "It's okay, this is your vision. You must be here."

So I started praying, "Grandfather, when I go to pierce, please give me the energy and the courage to finish. To do it like a man, a warrior, a spiritual person. Please don't allow me to do anything to dishonor my people and the other Sundancers."

I kept on and danced hard. Maybe I was being a little selfish; some of my prayers were for myself to have the courage to do it right. It's a very hard decision to make, to go there willingly and get pierced. You do it without any anesthetic or any of the modern conveniences to take away the pain. Just to let somebody else cut your flesh takes trust and faith in the Creator. I couldn't believe I was even considering it, but I was.

I spoke to other Sundancers about it, and they told me, "It's a commitment between you and Grandfather. You don't have to do it."

As is human nature, I welcomed a way out, or a way to justify not going through with it. For a few minutes, I thought about not going through with the piercing, but then I realized I didn't come all this way from Oklahoma just to back down. Fear is a small thing to overcome when the rewards are so huge. Making that contact with the Creator, having your prayers answered, means so much more than just a little bit of fear or pain. I realized when the other Sundancers told me I didn't have to pierce, the Spirits had been testing my sincerity and my decision to be there.

We had more pipe songs; during them no one was pierced. Then we had more piercing songs; during these, sometimes as many as six or eight men were pierced.

Many women were dancing and a few were also getting pierced. They would pierce on their arms or wrists. I'm sure it was just as painful as it was for the men.

We then had a piercing song, during which several men were being pierced on their backs. They were tied to several buffalo skulls—each weighing between twenty and thirty pounds—bound together in a row. Depending on the dancer, they would tie three or more skulls together for him to drag.

By dragging the skulls, we honor the buffalo by giving back all that he has given to us. He gave us his blood, flesh, pain, and life, so we could have nourishment to survive. He gave us abundance in all ways. This was our way to show respect and gratitude for *Tatanka*, our buffalo brother, and the sacred tradition. Also, we respect the buffalo because we believe that he is the bearer of courage and strength both physical and spiritual.

We danced for three hours. It was really hot. I was still tired from the Sundance in Wyoming just two weeks before because I hadn't had enough time to recuperate.

As has happened on occasion, sometimes we are short on drummers. Often there will be powwows going on in the immediate area, and many drummers would rather go to the powwows instead of the Sundances. At the Sundances it's all voluntary. Unlike at powwows, no money changes hands. The drummers are fed and given all they want to drink. They are drumming for a spiritual ceremony. So sometimes we are unable to get enough drums, and we have only one or two drum groups to sing. This makes it harder on them, so they have to rest quite a bit. Since all liquids and foods are forbidden around the Arbor, they have to go to our camp or somebody else's camp to eat. Without drummers and singers we can't dance, so we must rest until they come back.

However, this time we had it pretty good. We had three different drum groups, and they kept us busy dancing. We danced and finished out the day.

They allowed us to return to camp on an honor system. Nobody holds an axe over your head and says you can't do this or that. You made the commitment with the Creator. Nobody watches you. If anyone does anything wrong, he or she must answer to the Creator.

This is one of the things I learned. In the Sundance, don't try to be judgmental of everything and everyone. Let people do their own thing, as you do yours. Each of us has a mind of our own, and what is right for one person may be wrong for another. That doesn't mean that it is wrong for both. It only means that we think differently, and we should try to honor and respect other people's ways of thinking.

As my first day ended, I felt energized and knew that

the Spirits had been with me and that my guides had led me to the right place. The other things I had gone through were almost like stepping stones to get me to where I was now. If I felt that I had fallen in love with my first Sundance with the Shoshoni people, I felt even more so that way with the Lakota people. I felt I was home.

I woke up early the next morning because of my anticipation of the day ahead. I've never been one to need an alarm clock. At 3:45 a.m., I was awake. By 4:30 they started calling us.

Steve was already up, and as we headed for the sweat lodges, I knew something was different about my energy. I felt light-headed. I believe I was also feeling the Sundance energy. It's a very tangible thing when you're willing to receive it. For the first time, since taking the Sundance path, I felt strangely at peace with myself and completely unafraid. It wasn't resignation, it was a calm acceptance of whatever the Creator was bringing me. I felt so light on my feet, as if I were gliding instead of walking to the sweat lodges. For a moment I thought maybe my blood pressure was high, but everything was wonderful.

Since developing high blood pressure, I sometimes find it difficult to breathe in the sweat lodge and my blood pressure will rise. I'm not even supposed to go into sweat lodges, according to my doctor, but I do it anyway. I walked up to the fire pit area where they had the fires going to keep the rocks hot. I saw this other man there, who was a Sundance leader.

He looked at me and said, "Come on." He waved at me with his hand. "Join me in the sweat."

I followed right behind him. The sweat lodge filled quickly until there were about thirteen men inside. They brought the rocks in. We sprinkled them with cedar and thanked the Creator for the past two days.

We thanked Him for allowing us to Sundance on this third day, and the Sundance leader started singing the "Four Directions" song in Lakota. I offer the words in English.

To the West the Sacred Stone Nation
To the North the Sacred Stone Nation
To the East the Sacred Stone Nation
To the South the Sacred Stone Nation
To the Heavens, Great Spirit, take pity on me
The People to the Heavens
Grandfather, take pity on me the family.

I had never been able to sing in the sweat lodge before because the heat was so intense that I was unable to catch my breath. But this time, I found myself clearheaded, and my throat was so clear that I felt a big bubble of joy just burst inside me. I started singing, and sang the whole song with the leader.

I said to myself, "Today I pierce. I pierce first round, first song."

Once I made that commitment, I felt elated. I couldn't believe that I was making a commitment to let someone cut into my chest so my prayers would be heard. I felt very, very humble, as if I were finally *there*.

Each time you learn something more about the Sundance and experience something new, you feel as if you've reached a higher plateau of spiritual understanding. As if you arrived at another place. It's like adding pebbles to the entire pile that is you. You add those small stones one at a time and each of them brings a bit more knowledge.

No matter who we are or how knowledgeable we are, we never stop learning. We never know it all. The Creator is so infinite that He is always feeding little tidbits of information and knowledge so we can become better persons. I cherish every piece of information, every little stone that I can add to that pile. I'm grateful that with all this, the Creator also gives us choices and free will.

Coming out of the sweat lodge, I headed back to camp and never said anything to anybody. I went through the motions of getting ready as if I were in a dream. Everything was close by me. I dressed and was ready in three minutes. When I got to the Arbor, the first person I saw was the Sundance leader who had brought me into the sweat lodge.

"Brother," I said and shook his right hand with both of my hands, "thank you, thank you very much for a wonderful sweat this morning."

He gave me a puzzled look, so I explained about my trouble breathing in the sweat lodge.

"It was the first time I have been able to sing this song all the way through. I feel that it was you who inspired me to sing the way I did."

"I am happy that you sang it with us. Manny, thank you for showing gratitude and respect like this. Not too many people think about it anymore. Though we are spiritual, we forget to give credit where it's due. Thank you for that."

Then I told him, "When we go in, I'm piercing first round."

"*Ho!* I'm glad to hear that," he said smiling.

He knew I was a new man. He knew I had only danced yesterday, but my spiritual energy was so high that he also knew it was time for me to pierce. He asked, "When did you decide? When did you know?"

"When we were singing the 'Four Directions' song, I knew it was time for me to go."

He said, "Okay, it'll be done just the way you want it." Then I realized that the "Four Directions" song had taken me back to my vision—to when the spotted eagle and I had soared high in the heavens, when he had shown me where I was to help people, in the four directions.

Now, mentally and emotionally I was ready. Physically, I hoped I was, too. I didn't know what my tolerance for pain was. I'd smashed my fingers and stubbed my toes a few times. I'd even cut myself accidentally in my life. I'd had toothaches and headaches, but could I cope with this? Did I have strength and courage to go through with this ceremony? After thanking the Sundance leader, I went and sat by myself in the Arbor on my blanket.

I felt so alone. I guess that's the way life is when a person faces a challenge. He might have support from friends or relatives, but ultimately we must face pain, heartbreak, and personal trials alone.

I prayed for guidance. I prayed for direction.

All the spirits were coming to me and saying, "This is the time. You are at the right place. It is your turn to offer your flesh, blood, pain, and suffering for the people you want healed. Don't worry. You are ready."

It was a fresh morning in South Dakota. The fire pit, the sweat lodge, Grandfather's breath, the steam coming off the stones, all made memories for me. It stayed burned in my mind, the memory of my first piercing Sundance, my first Lakota Sundance.

Now being a bit wiser, I was committing myself to another four years. I did it without any remorse or hesitation, and without expectations except to ask for blessings from the Creator.

We lined up again. The Sundance Chief started blowing his eagle whistle, so we moved forward. I waited for the dread and fear to start in the pit of my stomach, but my wait was in vain. They never arrived. As we entered the Arbor from the east side, I felt myself calmed by the sound of the drums.

We greeted the sun, prayed, and danced for over an hour and a half. It was a beautiful first song. We placed our pipes, *Chanupas*, at the altar and went to our blankets to rest.

The Sundance leader walked up to me and asked, "Is this it?"

I looked at him, eye to eye, and replied "This is it, Brother."

"Okay, where do you want to be pierced?"

I pointed to the places on my chest.

He asked, "Once or twice?"

"Let's go for both sides. I came from too far away to get pierced on only one side."

He took the time to explain to me, "Manny, this is your first time, are you sure you want both sides? Most new guys and first-timers will only pierce once to make sure they can endure the pain."

"I'm sure. I want both sides done. I can do it. The Spirits came to me this morning and told me that I was ready."

He says, "That's fine. It's all up to you." So he marked both sides of my chest. When my friends saw that my chest was marked, they came and shook my hand. They told me to be strong, to have courage.

One Sundance leader, Lessert, said, "Manny, it's painful, but you're a warrior. Don't worry."

"Lessert, I want you and Norbert to do the piercing for me. Will you?"

Laughingly, he replied, "You bet we will. How many you want?"

I asked Steve if I could use his rope, so we left the Arbor, untied the rope, and laid it out. By now I had time to think again. My stomach and brain were turning. I was getting very nervous. My heart was beating faster and faster. I kept telling myself this was my decision. This is where I should be. This is where the Creator wanted me to be.

The next song started, and Lessert yelled, "*Ho-ka-hey*." We all got in line in our appropriate places and danced out. Every time we danced, we ended up in the same spot. I felt good.

From then on it was almost like a whirlwind of action. Henry, an art professor at the University of Maryland, who would become a very dear friend of mine, knew I was going to pierce because of the marks on my chest. He grabbed my wrist and gently pushed me forward out of my spot. This way the Sundance leaders knew I was piercing.

The Sundance leader danced up to me. He grabbed my sage wrist bracelet and took me around the Arbor, always going clockwise until we got to the west side.

He took me to the tree and said, "Brother, you are going to experience something very, very sacred. You are going to be very close to God, to the Creator. Make the most of this time because you will be one on one with Him right now."

He continued, "This tree is a sacred tree. It'll give you confidence and courage. It represents God. Ask it for whatever you want. Give it your prayers, respect, honor, and it will do as you wish. This is the place where many good men, good warriors, come to pray."

Then he left me, and I stood there for a few minutes. I prayed. I felt reluctant to leave the tree when another Sundance leader came and asked, "Are you ready?"

It seemed everything started to move in slow motion, perhaps because I was anticipating the event, but it didn't seem to be happening quickly enough.

With a nervous smile, I nodded *yes*.

They laid me down on a buffalo robe.

I handed them my scalpel.

They took the crown off my head.

They said to put it in my mouth.

They told me to bite down on my crown, because the piercing is very painful.

Lessert said, "If you will pray, and pray hard to the Creator it won't hurt because He'll be answering your prayers."

I lay there on the ground, looking up into the sky. Then I handed Lessert my piercing bones. He got down on his knees next to me, and his father knelt by my left side.

I felt both of them grab my chest and rub it with some dirt, because I was sweaty and slippery. This way their thumbs and fingers wouldn't slip.

They pinched up my skin, and I felt as the knife went into my flesh.

I felt a sharp, intense pain in my chest, as if somebody had put a red-hot iron on my flesh.

I lost all sense of time.

I couldn't hear any sounds.

I didn't feel the heat of the sun.

I tried to grit my teeth, but I couldn't—my crown was in my mouth.

I prayed to the Creator to give me strength, to give me courage. I was doing it for my children. I begged that the Creator look after my children, their health and happiness. That all their needs be taken care of.

Then I felt them do something else.

They were putting my piercing bone through the wound.

As Lessert was tying it up, I felt something on the left side of my chest. I was concentrating so much on my prayers that to me it felt like somebody tugging on my arm. I barely noticed. When Les got through tying my rope around my piercing bone, he and his father grabbed my arms. Les said, "Come on, get up. You're done."

I said, "Wait a minute, Lessert. I want both sides pierced."

He said, "They are."

I looked down, and you know what?—I was pierced on the left side, too. Yet I had felt absolutely nothing. I felt nothing because my prayers to the Creator gave me courage and strength to endure.

When I stood up, I did feel pain. I felt pain, but I also felt that closeness with the Creator. I felt like crying for all the people who needed my prayers. I prayed they could get enough to eat. I prayed for all the people who are sick in the world. It brought tears to my eyes. It shamed me to have tears appear, because I thought if the other dancers saw them, they might think I was crying because of the pain. But the pain did not compare to what I was receiving from this sacred experience. The rope at my end was tied to the two piercing bones in my chest. The other end was tied to the Sacred Tree about twenty feet from the bottom. I was tied to the tree with that rope as securely as a child is tied to its mother by the umbilical cord. The only way off that cord was by ripping myself off.

Lessert told me to go ahead and get into place, wherever I wanted to dance. I pulled my rope and danced out. I was dancing because they were still drumming and singing. It was still going on. I will never forget those songs. They are so beautiful, so calming. I went out as far as my rope would reach. I leaned back and the flesh on my chest pulled out tight. As I was praying to the tree, I could feel the pain in my chest. All my friends had come around to stand behind me and give me support, to receive that energy from me. All that energy I was going to pull down from the sun to help us, to help answer our prayers.

Running through my mind were thoughts of disbelief that I was actually doing this. Every time I leaned back on my rope, I felt intense pain in my chest. It became a raw ache that reached all the way down to my toes. Every time I looked at my piercing bones, I saw the faces of my children. I knew this was for their protection and my way of giving my pain for them. This was why Grandfather had brought me here.

It felt glorious and explosive. The energy was high and brilliant. I danced and then Lessert waved at me with his fan. He said, *"Ho-ka!"* as he pointed at the tree. "Go to the tree and pray."

I got to the tree, knelt beside it, and put my arms around it. I thought of my mother and father. I asked *Tunkashila*, Grandfather, to watch over them, then danced back to my spot and pulled back on the rope again.

One dancer next to me whispered, "Pull back, pull it tight. Stretch your flesh. It will break easier when you're ready to break loose."

Looking into my eyes, Steve danced in front of me with his eagle fan; he started tapping and hitting on my rope in a downward motion. He was trying to help me stretch the flesh.

I smiled at him and said, *"Wo-Pila*. Thank you, Steve."

Again, Les waved his eagle fan and yelled, *"Ho-ka-hey."*

Then I went back to the tree and prayed the second time. Embracing the tree, I could smell the warm cloth wrapped around it. The tree felt soft because there was so much cloth from the many people who had tied on their prayer ties. They wanted their prayers answered. I danced back to my spot.

Les yelled, *"Ho-ka,"* a third time.

I went to the tree and prayed. I prayed for everyone that I could think of. I prayed for people I didn't know, I prayed for all those I might meet during the coming year. There is so much to pray about. So many people that need prayers. It boggles the mind to remember people by name, or try to remember those who need your prayers to heal them.

Finally he said, "*Ho-ka,*" for the fourth and final time.

I danced back to the Sacred Tree. Again, I embraced it. I knew that when I left here I would be breaking free from it. It would be like separating myself from my mother, like breaking the umbilical cord. I would be free. I prayed for the courage to break loose on my first attempt.

Lessert walked up to me and said, "When you go this time, go fast, go hard. You have to break loose. The only way you can get off this rope is to break away and tear the flesh out. So run backwards fast. Don't worry, those guys will catch you."

I prayed to Grandfather: "This is it. You brought me this far, please don't fail me now. Give me the courage to finish this piercing ceremony like a man, like a warrior."

As I finished my prayer, I started running.

I went back, back. I looked at the tree and said silently, "Grandfather, please give me strength."

I ran faster and faster and faster.

I hit the end of the line.

I heard my flesh tear, rip, and pop.

I saw the rope bouncing way up into the tree.

It dangled there for a second, then dropped.

While this was going on, I fell backwards.

I had broken loose.

It was surprising how strong the flesh was. It didn't tear easily. It took all my strength and weight to break loose. Steve and a couple of the other Sundancers caught me when I fell.

I was so happy, I let out a big yell. I jumped up and down. I had finally done what I had envisioned at that Shoshoni Sundance, so long ago. I was at the top of my spiritual being then. My energy was flashing. The energy around me was sparking many people. They gained a lot, I feel, because my energy was so hot. I brought that Sun Power down on myself and all the people who came to support me.

Steve grabbed my arm bracelet and took me around the Arbor to the spot where I had started. As I ran by the other Sundancers, they were all patting me on the shoulder. Most of them were men who had been pierced in the past, who knew about the pain, the happiness, the jubilation. All or most would be pierced before the weekend was over.

I felt high, like I had reached that ultimate plateau of human spirituality. But eventually I found out that I was wrong. There was more to follow.

After several more Sundances, I realized that this was not the ultimate. There are other plateaus to experience. New heights of awareness to achieve in the Sundance circle, and other circles as well. This was just the beginning of my journey.

We finished that Saturday evening. After leaving, I walked around visiting other people and other camps, wearing my scars like badges of honor. Although it isn't seen as showing off, it is viewed as an honorable thing we have done. The piercing of the body, the giving of our pain, blood, and flesh so others may live well.

Saturday evening, I thanked Norbert Running, the Sundance Chief, and told him that I'd like to stay, but I had to get back to Oklahoma. I had left my family unattended and without money, and it would take me all of Sunday to get back.

He said, "You came, you danced, you pierced, you have to go. Everybody understands, including the Creator. The commitment you made was to Him and not to me."

On Sunday evening, when I arrived home, my wife was a little upset because I had pierced. I knew it bothered her, but she didn't make it a big issue, and I was grateful. She knew that I had done something that was important to me and that I had done it to try to help others. I had so many people who needed prayers—my parents, my sisters, and brother. It appeared the Creator had chosen me, from my family, to be the Sundancer. I felt honored. This is why I felt that I had to be there, and my wife seemed to understand.

NORTH — RED

"Cold Winds"

S N O W

In January I left Oklahoma to do a show in Santa Monica, California. I met some Sundancers and ended up spending a lot of time there selling crafts because we needed the money. And during the winter, California was the only good place to sell my native crafts.

My wife was making crafts at home, while I made them in California. With the crafts she sent me, I was doing well and always sending money home. By mid-May, my wife decided she had had enough of that kind of life.

Once I was talking to her, chatting about what was

going on. Our conversation was a little tense, but nothing special, I thought. She wanted us to invest in a trailer, and I said no. So she said, "I guess that's all I have to say. I'll talk to you later. I love you."

I didn't answer her. I just hung up.

The next morning, I received an overnight letter from my wife. She told me not to bother coming back; she didn't want to hurt me anymore. She wrote: "This life is over. I am tired of being a telephone wife."

I went into a state of shock. I couldn't believe what I was reading. After fifteen years of marriage, I never expected to hear this. Other than our talk the day before, everything seemed fine.

What hurt the most was the thought of being left out of my children's lives.

I couldn't blame her, though. After being away from her and the kids for so long, I had gotten to a point where I didn't miss them as much as before. That frightened me. It was almost as if they ceased to mean anything to me.

I started praying to Grandfather. I said, "Grandfather, what's happening to me? I'd hoped for a better life. This is why I Sundanced."

The realization of what was happening hit me hard. I blamed myself, then I became consumed with anger toward my wife. Then I blamed myself some more. My mental state began to deteriorate. Filled with grief, remorse, even bitterness, I felt abandoned.

In my attempts to pray, I felt even Grandfather had left me behind. When you're beating yourself up, you don't think you're worthy of Grandfather's help. Then I rationalized in my head for a while that this may be a good thing. Maybe I was supposed to be free again. When this happened, I started drinking. I drank to dull the pain.

When I ran out of booze, I would feel the pain over the loss of my children. Deeply hurt, I drank for about a month. I felt a rage against this woman who had done this to me. I had trusted her completely and had never questioned anything she did. Yet, suddenly, she told me not to come home.

All this time, I was wandering aimlessly from place to place, from powwow to powwow. Once at a powwow in Cupertino, California, I was dancing in a competition in the arena, but my mind wasn't on dancing, because of my emotional state. The song was a "Sneak Up," a special dance for hunters or warriors.

I didn't realize I was dancing the wrong way for that song until one dancer casually danced near and informed me it was a "Sneak Up." Embarrassed, I just turned and walked out of the arena.

Tom, the emcee, and my friend, made an excuse for me. He said, "Sometimes us old-timers go to so many powwows that we forget one song from the other." He knew what I was going through. Everyone did, and they tried to help me through it.

I went outside and looked off into the distance. I didn't know that someone was taking a picture of me. (It's the one on the cover of this book.) The woman who took it wanted to try to capture the moment. She told me about it later and asked my permission. At the time, I was angry that she had invaded my privacy. When I look at it now, and the expression on my face, the picture seems to say everything. Right then, my mind was on my loss. The Creator had decided to take away all that I held dear to me: my family.

The feelings of grief and devastation were hard to take, and I realized then that all I had now was the Sundance. The Creator was teaching me to depend on my spirituality for strength. The pain would pass in time, but the Sundance, my spiritual foundation, would be forever.

After that, I was still wondering, what had I done? Why did this happen? I blamed myself during the entire month while I was drinking.

Then suddenly, one morning, I woke up. I was in Monterey at a campground. I rolled over, sat up in bed, grabbed a bottle of beer, and took a drink. I stopped and looked at the bottle and at the mess I called a bed. I looked at the overflowing bag of dirty clothes. I looked at myself and what I had become in just one month. I didn't like what I saw.

Then I asked myself, "What in the world are you doing? You are having a beer for breakfast. This is absurd. You've never had a drink this early in your life. Why now?"

I checked my pockets and found only three dollars. Then I checked the crafts box. It was empty. Well, there I was, almost flat broke, no food, no crafts, and no prospects. Again I thought to myself, my God, what am I doing to myself?

I got up, took a shower, and shaved. I felt better than I had in weeks. I headed out and stopped at a big hardware and crafts store.

The only way I could get a fresh start was to steal materials I couldn't afford. I walked around, debating whether to do it. It bothered me to consider stealing what I needed to make some money. Ironically, the items I needed were to make one of our spiritual symbols, the Medicine Wheel.

I took a deep breath, and decided that above all I had to survive. This was the only way that I knew how. I asked forgiveness. Then I went and found the largest chamois cloth they had. It was smooth, soft, pliable leather. I walked around the store for a long time until, finally, I slipped it into

my shirt. I paid for the other items that were under a dollar, and I walked out.

I don't do this kind of thing. I got scared, scared that I might be stopped, that I could be caught and thrown in jail for that little piece of chamois cloth. But I needed that leather to make the Medicine Wheels. I needed something to sell, to make, to buy myself some food and some gas, at least to get myself going again.

I was at rock bottom.

I didn't know what I was going to do. I didn't even have enough money left to pay for another night at the campground. I stopped my van in a parking lot. It wasn't too far from where I had taken, or should I say stolen, that piece of chamois cloth.

I cut up the leather into strips and wrapped the wooden hoops I used to make Medicine Wheels. The spirits were with me. The Creator was also close to me in my time of need.

Everything went so smoothly, so fast, and the wheels turned out beautifully. I finished them in record time. I knew of a store, in Pacific Grove, so I went there and showed the owner what I had. The woman said, "Oh my God, you've got Medicine Wheels? I have had more calls for these in the last couple of weeks. I'll take all six of them. I'll need more. How many can you make me?"

I said, "As many as you want."

She said, "Make me another thirty, then I'll have thirty-six. Then I'll have three dozen, and that'll hold me for a good part of the summer."

I asked, "Would it be possible to get a little advance on the order? I need to buy leather and stuff to make them with."

She said, "Sure, I'll give you half the cost of my order. Okay?"

I figured the money for the six Medicine Wheels plus the deposit on the other thirty put me in good shape. Good, I was happy. Now things were starting to look much better.

I ate a good breakfast, then returned to the same store where I had stolen the leather. I was afraid to go to the manager and admit what I had done because I felt terrible and so guilty. I also thought that maybe they could still throw me in jail.

Instead of confessing, I walked in and bought all the supplies I needed. I wanted to compensate them or apologize in some way for what I'd done, so I bought more than enough to make the other Medicine Wheels. I felt a little better, but to this day I still feel bad, and I've never forgotten about it. I have been into that store on two other occasions since then, and I've always bought more than I needed. In the end, that piece of chamois has cost me quite a bit because of my guilty feelings.

The Creator must have forgiven me because my life has returned to normal. I never blamed anyone for my actions or for the situation I found myself in.

I finished the order, and that gave me plenty of money. I filled up the gas tank in my van, bought more supplies (leather, beads, feathers) and returned to the campground. I made shields, Medicine Wheels, and leather necklaces. Within a couple of weeks I was back on my feet. I was forgetting the pain too, or at least it had diminished. I was feeling a lot better about myself. I could take the heartache a little bit better.

So I headed south toward Los Angeles. I drove on to Torrance to see my native brother, Wolfhawk, and while we were eating dinner, the subject turned to the recent changes in my life.

I said, "Wolfhawk, I don't know what I did wrong. I don't know where I messed up, where I screwed up."

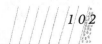

He said, "Manny, let me tell you something. I've seen you work and work many hours, putting the welfare of your family first above your own comforts. I've watched you send money, and more money, home."

He continued, "You didn't screw up, she did. It's not your fault, man. I wondered how long it would take you to realize it. Apparently you haven't let yourself see it, yet. So it's my job to tell you, to let you know, that it was not you who screwed up. It was her."

He said, "Let it go. Send money to the kids. Tell them that you love them every chance you get. Write to them on their birthdays, on Christmas, on Easter. Send them a card, send them twenty dollars, thirty dollars, a hundred dollars when you can. Remember always to tell them that you love them so they won't forget you."

I took his advice.

I learned how to make an old/new article called a "Dream Catcher." (By "old/new" I mean that it's an old belief or tradition that, after many years of being forgotten, is once more becoming very popular.) Many people are familiar with how Dream Catchers help people overcome nightmares and bad dreams.

Long ago, they were only made by the medicine man in the tribe. He would be called on if someone was having difficulty sleeping, or having nightmares. The medicine man would consult the spirits, then make a Dream Catcher for that individual. He went through many prayers and a sacred ceremony while making each Dream Catcher, and it was considered bad medicine for anyone else to create one for any other reason or by any other method.

It all started when I decided to teach myself how to make them. When I made the first one, several of my friends saw it and laughed. They said, "That one is for nightmares, not for dreams."

I thought it was pretty good, but I wasn't quite getting the stitch right. I racked my brain trying to figure it out.

When I was at a powwow in Fresno, California, I ran into a good friend of mine from Bakersfield. A wonderful little lady, her name is *Wia Chanupa*, meaning "Pipe Woman." She took one look at my Dream Catcher and said, "God, Manny, that looks awful. I wouldn't show that to anybody!"

Wia showed me that I was missing just one little step and after she showed me how to fix it, I got busy making more Dream Catchers.

I never did fix that first one I made, but apparently it didn't matter. I was at a powwow when a woman from across the arena saw it and came running. She said, "I'll take that Dream Catcher."

"Well, it's sixty dollars."

"It's okay, I'll take it."

After paying me, she said, "If it was a hundred fifty dollars, I would still have bought it."

"Well you know, I want you to be happy," I grinned.

"Oh, no, that's okay. Sixty is fine."

At times, I would sit in my van, right on the beach for a week, and make Dream Catchers. It was very hard to sit there alone hour after hour, working. It gave me time to think. Sometimes I felt like my chest was going to burst; I missed my kids so much.

When the thinking became too painful, I would get out of the van and ride my bike up and down the Strand at Redondo Beach—just to be around other people—until I was too tired to think any more.

It wasn't long after that I saw four friends of mine, Jesse, Sonny, Lonnie, and Marty, up in San Juan Bautista. They were going to their first Sundance.

I told them, "Look, guys, it's pretty tough there, and I'm an old hand at it now. I've been to one Lakota Sundance, and I have four under my belt at the other place, so I'm an old-timer to the Sundance circle. I'll be there the day before to support you when you go in the Arbor, and Wednesday night to help you and give you any advice that I can."

They thanked me unanimously, and said they hoped I could make it.

I headed to South Dakota and arrived the day they were going into the Lakota Sundance. I pulled in at about seven o'clock in the evening. The boys were sitting in the tepee, and they were very happy to see me. They were as anxious and as frightened as I had been my first time.

I sat and talked with them until long past midnight. Finally, it was time to go to sleep, so I left them alone and went to bed.

In the morning when they went in, I was encouraging and wished them luck. It was important to me to be there when they went in because I had been alone for my first piercing Sundance. I was glad they had each other for company. I felt that I had done my job by keeping my word that I would be there, and I was proud of all of them. They all danced, and three of them pierced that first day.

Marty did not pierce because he had not made that commitment to Grandfather. Personally, I think if he never pierces it might be better. He is a Vietnam veteran (173rd Airborne) and was badly wounded in action. I feel he has given enough pain, flesh, and blood for all of us. He is a good warrior and "nephew."

Shortly after the piercing ceremony, I said goodbye and left.

I had another Sundance brother, Lionel, who was going into his first Sundance over in Porcupine, South

Dakota, on the Pineridge Reservation. I had told him I would help him prepare for his *Hanblecheya* vision quest and his Sundance.

When I arrived, the weather was hot and muggy. Lionel and I shook hands and hugged. He motioned for me to sit and asked if I wanted something to drink. He had his tent pitched right under a nice, shady tree and had been there a few days already, getting the Arbor prepared for the Sundance.

I stood for a second to stretch my legs and look around. I caught my breath as I looked east. The land and high, white sandstone cliffs were magnificent. The cliffs were outlined with the green of the grass. Mingled with the glorious, deep, green grass were soft, dusty, grayish blue stalks of medicine sage. The colors made the place seem mystical and beautiful.

The Sundance Arbor was in a nice secluded area that was mowed and raked every year so that it would be a decent campground for people who come to the Sundance. With no electricity or running water, the only conveniences were those you brought with you.

I noticed that Lionel was a bit nervous and apprehensive. This was his first time to dance, so he was happy to see me. I was a familiar, friendly face from home.

We spent the afternoon visiting, drinking coffee, and talking about mutual friends. I told him about Sonny, Jesse, Lonnie, and Marty. They were also friends of his. It comforted him to know some of his friends had just gone through their first piercing ceremony.

After eating, I helped him put together his crown and his ankle and wrist bracelets. We also made some tobacco ties to put on the Sacred Tree. I helped him prepare his flags and the altar for his Chanupa, his pipe.

We had coffee late that night. By this time most of our

visiting was done. We sat there for long moments in silence, feeding small sticks into the campfire. From time to time, others would stop and visit, then leave. It was so pleasant to sit and relax after so much driving.

Following tradition, I went to look for David, the Sundance Chief, to give him some tobacco. I found him sitting behind Lionel's tent drinking a cup of coffee and talking with Al and Bernice, two of the elders who were also husband and wife. When he knew that what I had to discuss was important to me, he stood up, and we started walking away from the others. I told him what had happened to me with my family, how I was hurting and missing my kids.

He gave me a great deal of advice. What he said made me realize there may be a good reason it happened, though I won't go into the details. I respected what he told me, and I accepted it.

Then he said, "The only thing you can do now is pray for your children. Pray that maybe someday they will return to you. When they grow up, they will want their dad. They'll want to know where you are. They'll want to be with you. Meanwhile, pray for them, and pray hard. The biggest thing is to pray for forgiveness for your wife."

He continued, "I don't believe it was her fault. Circumstances pushed you two apart, and maybe through prayer she'll reconsider."

"No," I replied, "I have too much pride. It is over."

There was a long pause. We had both stopped walking. He stood for a long, quiet moment. I stood waiting. Finally, as if he had received confirmation from the Spirits, he nodded his head.

As we started walking back to camp, he said, "Well, if it is over, just be strong, and take the best road open to you, the Sundance. Did you come to dance?"

"I came to visit and help support Lionel."

"*Washtelo*, good," he answered. "Please make yourself at home. You're always welcome here."

His energy was quiet and unassuming, yet so powerful. I quickly came to respect this man, and he's the one I now follow in the Sundance. He has got the energy that others are seeking. He comes by his spirituality quite naturally, from a people whose very existence depends on their deep, spiritual beliefs.

After our talk, we returned to camp for more coffee and met with three other young men who impressed me: Bo, Marvin, and Tony. Bo was one of David Swallow's Sundance leaders. He was also the son of Pansy, the women's Sundance leader. Marvin and Tony were married to Al and Bernice's two daughters. They were Sundancers, drummers, and singers, and respectful young men.

I spent seven wonderful days there. I volunteered to go to Rapid City, and returned with the things we needed, and some things we didn't. The time passed, sometimes slow, sometimes fast, but always hot. Every evening was a blessed relief, because it always cooled off.

David took Lionel up to the mountain on his vision quest— one way to seek guidance for your spiritual life. This was four days before the Sundance began.

Before he left, I said, "Brother, if you need anything spiritually, please let me know. I'll be in tune with your energy. Send a message if you need help, and I'll be with you."

About two o'clock in the morning I felt something hit the side of my van. It startled me, and I woke up instantly. Then there was another, louder thump, farther away from me, toward the front. And then there were three small bangs on the front bumper. The sound worked its way around to

the driver's side, and when it got even with me, it stopped. I jumped up and looked around.

I thought maybe someone I just met was trying to scare me or pull a joke on me. I looked and no one was there. It was dark, but I could see well enough in the moonlight, and I couldn't spot anybody.

It got me thinking, "What is this?" Then I swallowed hard and realized, "My God, my brother Lionel is in trouble. He's asking for my help."

So I found my smudging shell and grabbed a big piece of medicine sage. After finding my lighter, I lit the sage, got out of my van and started praying. "Grandfather, please help those three."

There had been three who went up the mountain, so I asked help for all three of them in case it was one of the others asking for help. I forget exactly what I said, but I know I prayed hard for them to have the courage and strength to do their "*Hanblecheya,*" which is the Lakota word for vision quest.

"Help those warriors make it through the night. Help them find their direction and advice," I asked Grandfather. I knew that one of them was in trouble, and was worried it was my brother Lionel.

Suddenly, off in the east, I heard David start drumming and singing. Apparently he also knew that someone needed help. His voice and the drum were hauntingly beautiful. Muted by distance, the sound seemed to come from somewhere out of the past.

Two days later, when they came down from their vision quest, we learned who it was.

I had just finished eating, and I was enjoying a cup of coffee. David was leaving to get the three men from their vision quest. They had been up there for two days and two nights. Besides Lionel, there were two others that went up; one was a white man, Thomas, from Nebraska, the other was Lakota from Pineridge. He was the one who had the problems. He got scared and began hallucinating. He thought everybody had forgotten about him, and so he walked back down.

He asked me where everybody was, and I told him that David had gone up the mountain to get him. Embarrassed, he was nervously trying to explain why he had come down. I didn't realize it at the time, but even I wasn't supposed to acknowledge his presence because doing so breaks the spiritual energy from the *Hanblecheya*.

The experience humbled me. *Hanblecheya* is a hard thing to do, and still many people would judge him harshly. I think it made me realize how serious all this is. It's very sacred: the *Hanblecheya*, the *Inipi*, the Sundance. Everything is important to us, and no part of it should ever be taken lightly by anyone.

If a person walks away from the *Hanblecheya* sight by himself, he has committed a terrible sacrilege. When one who is seeking a vision leaves without the spiritual people who took him up there, it is considered bad medicine for him and his family. It is disrespectful of the Great Spirit and of the ceremony. Not only that, it is very embarrassing for the relatives or anyone associated with the person.

No one should insult or show disrespect toward anything related to the Sundance or native spirituality. Amazingly enough, there are so many people who go to one *Hanblecheya* and suddenly feel they are experts. They see one Sundance, and they are experts at the Sundance. By invitation, they see and participate in a Sweat Lodge, and the next week they are at home, calling themselves shamans and building a sweat lodge, usually improperly.

Most people don't even know the meaning of the word "shaman." According to the 1994 Grolier Encyclopedia, the word comes from tribal groups in Siberia, where a shaman-

istic religion dominates the tribe. It has nothing to do with, and should not be used in connection with, Native American culture or spirituality.

These people who call themselves shamans are running their own Sweat Lodges and charging money for it. This is wrong and only brings bad medicine to those who participate. Our spirituality is not for sale to anyone at any price. That people would even consider profiting from our ceremonies makes us angry, and some of our people who find out about it will attempt to put a stop to these practices.

I don't want to pass judgment; the Creator will take care of that. Often people act out of ignorance, or their intentions are good. This we realize. However, it's time people were made aware of what they are doing to our spirituality.

People should understand that when they do a vision quest, or a Sweat Lodge, they are opening themselves up to the spirit world. We also believe strongly that there are good spirits and bad spirits. We might call them spirits or call them medicine. There are bad energies out there, and people have to understand that they leave themselves wide open to this. They shouldn't be interfering with things they don't understand. Besides that, it is sacrilegious to prostitute another man's spiritual beliefs. We don't appreciate it, yet so many people are doing it for sheer profit.

After meddling in this way, some people call me to help them out of whatever they have brought on themselves. Some say that they feel snakes in their heads. Others say that they can't sleep because spirits are hitting them and keeping them awake for days at a time. One person told me someone's spirit guide took her spirit guide to another planet! When we try to give these people advice, they either don't want to hear it or never believe it.

Experiences with such people made me realize that I

had stepped into a spiritual world that is there to benefit and help to the fullest. There is no limit. I can be helped, I just have to believe, show respect, and pray. The rest will come naturally. As the old saying goes, *"Action is the fruit of thought."* So when you think of something, it will come true if you pray for it. A prayer is no more than a thought going from you to the universe or to the Creator.

The problem of the young man coming off the hill was straightened out when David returned. He counseled the young man. He didn't condemn him or hold against him what he had done. He just told him he shouldn't have done it.

I always say the Creator is not there to hurt us. He's only here to hold us to our word and serve as a spiritual foundation for us.

Wednesday afternoon we went to get the Sacred Tree for the Sundance. When David told everyone that we were leaving for the tree, people pulled up their cars to get in line for the procession. As we pulled out, there were a dozen cars lined up. We drove an hour to the turnoff, then five miles off the highway along a rough, dirt road to where the cottonwood tree was that would become the Sacred Tree.

After cutting it down, we carried it on our shoulders to the flatbed trailer and tied it down. People were sitting all over and around the tree, holding on to it. Protecting it from any harm. It was so beautiful.

A mile and a half from where we had cut the tree down, we saw a friend of ours. His name is American Eagle. He and another gentleman were walking ahead of us. Suddenly a great, big bull stood in front of them. It was a Hereford bull, and he stood looking at the procession of cars and the pickup with the tree, then pawing the ground and looking at us.

I could almost read his thoughts, "What in the world are they doing on my turf?"

American Eagle and the other man walked toward the bull. American Eagle was carrying his medicine staff. He shook it at the bull. The bull was irritated and started pawing the ground faster as though preparing to charge. Luckily we were close enough to the two men so that David could yell at him, "Hey, American Eagle! You better leave that bull alone. He doesn't know you're carrying your medicine stick with you. You'd better get back in the pickup before he hurts you!"

It was fortunate that we got there when we did. The two men got in the pickup. The bull—intimidated by all the cars, the tree, the truck, and the noise—trotted off. He certainly hadn't been afraid of two old-timers getting closer and closer to him, almost threatening him. We all had a good laugh, but it wouldn't have been funny if something had happened.

The drive back was beautiful, because as we drove down the highway with the tree on the trailer, people would pull off to the side of the road. They stopped their cars to allow the tree to go through because it was a sacred tree. This didn't happen just once. We passed many pickups, cars, and vans. Everybody slowed and stopped on the side of the highway.

We got the tree within a couple hundred yards from the Arbor and stopped the trailer. Everyone gathered around the tree. As one, we picked it up and put it on our shoulders. The tree measured about fourteen inches in diameter at the base. It was green and very heavy. Slowly we started moving. The walk was dignified. Although many of us were struggling, we were all quiet. As we carried the tree, we had to make the traditional four stops before we got it into the Arbor.

After moving the tree into the Arbor, we finally were able to lay it down. The ground inside the Arbor is sacred. It is the only place the tree can touch the ground. Anywhere else, and the tree loses its purity and cannot be used for the Sundance. Long ago, if the Sacred Tree touched the ground, the Sundance would be cancelled.

While the tree was lying there in the Arbor, many prayers were offered to it. We thanked it for giving its life so that we might have our Sundance, and we let it know it was going to become a sacred symbol for us.

Everybody who was going to dance and pierce had to tie on their ropes. They stretched their ropes out to different areas of the Sundance Arbor. When everything was ready, we started pulling the tree up with all the ropes. Once we hoisted it up, we formed a circle around the tree to keep it standing straight. A hole had been dug in the center of the Arbor. It was deep enough to support the tree. A crew of men started burying the base of the tree. They tamped the dirt down so that even a strong wind couldn't blow it over.

When it was finally standing proudly, it was late in the evening. It had all sorts of flags and colors, including offering flags made by many different people. Everybody had their ties up and ropes on the tree. They were ready for the next day.

The tree ceremony was over.

It looked like everybody was happy and ready. You could sense an intangible feeling of joy in the air. It was dark when we were through, and slowly everybody started disbursing back to their own camps. Everyone knew that morning would come very, very early.

I returned to the camp with Lionel. David, Bernice, and Al were sitting around drinking coffee and having supper, and we joined them. After everyone was through eating, we

sat around the campfire, visiting. Tired and ready to hit the sack by this time, I decided to go to bed.

The next morning, as I put my clothes and shoes on, I heard somebody yelling, "Ho! Sundancers, let's go. It's 4:30, its time to get up. The sun is almost up."

Even though the sun was still two hours off, the Sundancers have to get up that early so they can go and do a Sweat Lodge purification, then come back to camp and get dressed.

I still got up even though I wasn't going to Sundance with them. I had my own Sundance to go to and was just there to help Lionel, which I had done. I didn't want to sweat that morning because I had to leave soon and wasn't sure if it would be that day or the following day.

I went over to the Sweat Lodge area to see if anything was needed, found out nothing was, so I returned to camp. I still hadn't had my first cup of coffee, and they had a fresh pot on, so I followed my nose to it.

After my coffee, I returned to the sweat lodges again, to see if I could help. They had already designated men to pass the hot stones into the sweat lodges. I felt sort of lost and left out. It was strange not to be in the Sundance. I kept asking if anyone needed my help. One guy asked me to help him with his eagle whistle, so I helped him get it going again. Another guy asked me to help him finish his ankle and wrist bracelets. I was glad to be of assistance. It is an honor and privilege to be accepted by everyone because I am an elder, and I'm there to help a brother.

Everybody was happy to be there, in such a friendly atmosphere. Everybody was feeling energetic, although a little cold since it was so early in the morning. On the first day of the Sundance even the smells were invigorating. The smell of burning wood, sage, and cedar filled the air. It was burning in the sweat lodges. You could even get faint whiffs of the hot steam coming out of the sweat lodges.

As things progressed, I saw the men leave the sweat lodges and return to their camps to get ready. Everyone was ready with their beautiful colored regalia on and skirts made out of shawls. I watched in awe and thought, "Next week I've got to go through this at my Sundance."

Slowly, they got in line. They looked for friends they wanted to be next to during their four days of suffering. By being together they gained support and magnified the energy that comes to every Sundancer.

Finally, I heard the Sundance Chief. *Sheriiii-Sheriiii* . . . He blew on his eagle-bone whistle and told everybody, "Get ready, men. Get ready. We are going in to pray." The line started moving forward as the drums started, slowly at first. Gradually, the beat picked up and they played the "Going In" song. You could hear it playing across the Arbor over on the south side.

As they moved around the Arbor, they made the traditional four stops to honor the four directions. A couple of Sundancers held cans that had hot coals burning inside. They kept putting cedar boughs in the cans. The leaves smoldered and smoked. It was a purification smoke, and it smelled wonderful.

They followed each other around to the left, dancing. Everybody who was dancing was supported by brothers, cousins, aunts, and uncles. Many campers gathered around the Arbor to see the procession of dancers and people who had made the commitment.

After everyone was in place, the "Going In" song turned into the "*Chanupa*" song. The dancers all walked back under the Arbor, single file, as the song finished. Ten to fifteen minutes later the drummers and singers started singing again. A

Sundance leader stood up and said, *"Ho-ka-hey* . . . let's go. One more round, let's go."

They started the second song. I sat in the background under the Arbor. I was there to offer my support. I kept looking at all my brothers and sisters who were out there, suffering. They were going through a lot, and I was thinking, "At least I'm standing on the outside. I can keep my shoes and shirt on."

As the day grew older, the sun started getting hotter and hotter. I thought to myself, "My God, how could they be taking it out there?" I looked at one after another to see how they were holding up. No one was complaining or saying it was too hot. Humbled by the experience, everybody seemed to be honored for the opportunity to dance and pray for others. It was such an incredible feeling, standing there, watching them suffer without thinking of themselves. My chest swelled with pride to be a witness to this sacrifice and to know I was one of them. This Sundance belonged to everyone there.

The day passed slowly. I could see the dancers starting to tire a little bit at a time as the heat reached its peak. Then the sun slowly started sliding downhill to the other end of the horizon.

David Swallow Jr., being a good leader, had seen the condition of the dancers and let everyone know that it was their last song.

Before they could come out of the Arbor, they had to do one more thing. The "Pipe" song. They picked up their pipes, then danced out of the Arbor. The pipes were placed in a sacred lodge, where all the pipes are kept during the night. There was always a guard placed in front of the door so no one could enter the lodge and disturb the pipes.

From their first Sundance until the fourth, almost all

Sundancers have pipes, but they have not yet earned the right to perform the ceremonies with them. The pipes are theirs, but they are only in their care until they have finished their first commitments. After four years, they become pipe carriers. Only at that time are they believed to be responsible and knowledgeable enough to heal and to offer blessings, all in the name of the Creator.

It was about six o'clock when they came in from the last round. Everybody started going into one of the three sweat lodges. As they got ready, they dropped to their knees and quickly crawled in.

Everyone was happy as the day ended. Everybody had danced and prayed, and now it was time to relax for the night.

At the time, David didn't have any tepees set up, which would have given the people who wanted to remain in the area around the Arbor a place to sleep. So he allowed everybody to return to their camps.

My camp was simply my van. I parked right next to Lionel's tent, so I was close to everyone else. When I got there, they already had coffee and a pot of stew cooking. Getting some of both, I savored the first bite, rolling it around in my mouth. After going all day without food, I was hungry. I took my time.

Al and Bernice were about my age and had been dancing all day. Tired, sitting quietly, they talked and sipped their coffee. Elders are allowed to return to camp at night to eat and drink a little for health reasons. I sat close to them after helping myself to another cup of coffee. There were quite a few people there—their daughters, sons, Richard, Lionel, and other people I didn't know.

Bernice said softly, "Manny, you would honor us if you would dance with us tomorrow, just for one day."

I didn't know what to say. Then I replied, "Bernice, I

have my own Sundance to go to. I am honored you are asking me to dance, but I have another commitment already."

"We know, we just want you to honor us and dance with us one day. I've got to tell you something, Manny. This afternoon tired me out. The sun was really hot. But every time I looked and saw you dancing, it didn't matter that it was hot." She stopped, took a sip of coffee, and continued, "Just the way you were dancing—your motions, your sincerity—helped me. The look on your face really inspired me and kept me going when I felt the most tired."

Al looked up and nodded his head quietly. He says, "Me too, Manny. We would like you to dance with us."

Their son Richard added, "Yeah, Bro', come on, man, dance with us one day. Dance and suffer with us for one day."

When people offer you that much respect, you can hardly refuse such a humble request. At some point you have to consider their feelings above your own. I had no choice, really, but to say I would.

So, once again I forgot tradition. I forgot it in the spirit of the moment. When you make a commitment to Sundance, it's never for just one. It's a four-year commitment. When they talked me into it, they talked me into dancing with them for four years.

That wasn't their intention, I'm sure. It really doesn't matter because I'm committed to the Sundance for the rest of my life, as long as my health holds out. If I'm financially able, and it won't jeopardize my family, I'll Sundance from now on. It isn't as though I got talked into it with my eyes closed; my eyes have been wide open every time I have made a commitment.

I felt wonderful that they should honor me in such a way. After agreeing to dance with them, I saw Bernice get up and walk away. A few minutes later she returned.

She said, "Manny, since you agreed to dance with us, I want to honor you with one of our shawls. This will be your skirt. Honor us by wearing our family colors. Everyone who sees you in the Sundance will know that you are dancing with us and for us . . . for the Tail family."

It was such an honor, I got all choked up and thanked her. I told her, "You don't have to do this. I've got my own shawl."

She said, "Take it, it's okay. You are going to honor us by wearing it."

Bowing my head respectfully, I accepted the shawl. There was a chorus of glad voices. Everybody was saying, "All right, Manny, all right." Everybody was happy, laughing, and smiling, shaking my hand and slapping my back.

"I have to get a crown and ankle and wrist bracelets made," I said.

Everybody jumped in to help, and in five minutes they had them ready for me. They tied a couple of small eagle feathers on my crown. Suddenly, there I was, all ready to go into another Sundance that I had never thought of doing.

All I had come to do was help my brother Lionel through his *Hanblecheya*, his vision quest, and the Sundance. This was his first Sundance, and I wanted to see him off on the right foot. Now these beautiful people honored me.

I went to my van after everybody left and headed for their own blankets. I slept well, considering I was a little nervous about the next day. Only I knew what I had to do in this Sundance, too.

Next morning I was up early and did my traditional morning sweat. Afterwards, I headed back to my van and got all dressed up.

I was back at the Arbor when David arrived. He knew from the night before that I was going in, and was glad to see me join the circle. We talked and waited for the other guys.

One at a time, everyone arrived from their camps ready to dance. We started lining up. Everyone was in the same order they had been in the previous day. I got to fudge between two other guys who had been in the day before. Usually when you come in late, you always go to the end of the line, but it was a small Sundance.

I could feel the little pins and needles from the mown-down bushes. The ground was cool under the soles of my feet. It was such a good feeling to be there. The Sundance Chief started to blow his eagle whistle, letting everyone know it was time to dance and pray.

Somebody yelled, *"Hoka-hoka-hey,* time to go."

The drums started, and again I relive that incredible feeling of entering the Arbor, into that all-healing Sacred Circle.

We went through the first dance and greeted the sun, prayed at the tree and put our pipes on the altar so they faced the east. Then we rested.

While we were resting, I went to the Sundance Chief and said, "David, I want to pierce first round."

An incredulous look came over his face. He said, "Manny, you don't have to pierce."

Al heard me and also said, "No, no, Manny, you don't have to pierce."

Turning to face both of them, I said, "Al, David . . . you honored me by asking me to dance with you. Where I come from there are no free rides."

Al looked down at the ground almost as if he were sorry for what he had asked me to do. They never thought for a moment that I might pierce for them.

I grabbed Al's hand, and I shook it. "Don't feel sad. It is my honor to do this for you. I am happy that I can pierce for you and your family. Look at me and smile with me, brother. Laugh with me because this is what it is all about. It is about praying for each other, helping each other and knowing that you have somebody who is willing to suffer for you."

Al looked in my eyes and smiled. He shook my hand and said, "*Ho . . . Washtelo . . . Wo-Pila.*"

David, sitting in his chair, stood up and shook my hand. The man told me that if this is what I wished, it was a commitment between me and the Creator. "We will do as you ask."

They hadn't even prepared the paint to mark the chests with yet. It's not typical paint. It's a mixture of red dirt, clay, and water. A Sundance leader came over, and they told him to wet the paint. "Manny's going to pierce on this first round."

When they painted my chest, the look on Bernice's face was filled with emotion. She said, "Manny, you don't have to do this." She hadn't heard the previous conversation.

"Bernice, I have to."

She looked at me and said, "You are my brother, and I have to honor and respect what you want to do."

When the next song began, right away they started singing the *"Chanupa"* song. David went over and said something to them. They changed it from the "Pipe" song into the "Piercing" song. As we were going out, I stood right at the entrance of the Arbor where we do the dancing and praying.

It was as though a signal went out. When the "Piercing" song could be heard throughout the camp, people started coming to see who was getting pierced. The shade around the Arbor started filling up. Everybody went by, shook my hand, and thanked me. I was thanking them, though not as individuals. In my heart I was thanking them for this day.

When they were finally all in, Richard, a Sundance leader, came and took me right to the tree. After praying for a couple of minutes at the tree, I walked around and handed David one of my throwaway scalpels.

I looked at David and said, *"Ho-Wana,"* meaning "I'm ready."

I called Lionel to come in and be with me while I was pierced. I lay down, and they pierced me on both sides. I remember looking at Lionel's face. He had a look of pain and anguish. The people around me went through so many strange feelings and sensations. When I looked at them, I saw that they were praying for me, and hurting for me. They cared about my pain, about my blood and my flesh that I was giving up. I saw it in their faces, I saw it in their eyes.

After being pierced, I stood up and I moved back away from the tree. I started dancing. Almost everyone standing under the shade was now behind me, supporting me on that first dance. I danced and danced. Four times I went to the tree. On the fourth time after going to the tree, I prayed and I asked for strength and courage. I wanted to do this right for my new Lakota brothers and sisters.

I gathered up my rope as if I were going to lasso something in front of me. As I started moving backwards, I let go one coil of rope at a time, I was going back faster and faster. Finally, as I dropped the last coil, it never made it to the ground. I hit the end of the rope. For that one split second of time, I felt like something had reached from the heavens and touched my chest, my face, my head, and my heart.

The next second, I jumped up and yelled. I was happy to have honored these people. I was happy that I had done it with bravery, that I had succeeded.

That was the turning point of the day. The day ended as beautiful rays lit the Sundance Arbor from over the mountain tops. Everybody was happy and jubilant. After the sweat, everyone shook my hand and thanked me for the dance. We spent the rest of the evening just visiting.

I told them, "Tomorrow I have to leave, but I'll be here in spirit with you. I will be dancing with you every day."

Lionel smiled, "Will we see you next year?"

Smiling back, I replied, "You bet!"

I got up early the next morning to watch them go in to the Arbor. After they were inside, I said my goodbyes and left, heading south and east toward the Rosebud Reservation.

A mile before I got to the mass grave at Wounded Knee, I could feel the restless spirits from that horrible time, asking me for my prayers. Just as I do every time I pass the spot, I stopped and paid tribute to all the men, women, and children who had their lives taken so suddenly, and so tragically. I stopped, prayed, burned sage, and cried for their pain and the injustice of it all.

While I was driving, my mind wandered. I felt lost because I had left Lionel behind. We were very close spiritually, and I considered him a true brother. I was feeling lonesome because I had no one to talk to or share my thoughts with. Maybe this was why I kept going from place to place: to have a cup of coffee and someone to share conversation with.

My thoughts traveled from one friend to another. Where could I go next? Who could I visit after the Sundance? I was always careful I didn't overstay my welcome, even if I was lonely. I feared rejection if I stayed too long.

The loss of my family had subconsciously taken its toll on me. My self-confidence had been dealt a terrible blow. I began thinking of my children again. To see them and talk to them would be the answer to all my prayers. One thought that occupied my mind was, "When am I going to see them again?" I ached for the arms of my children around my neck.

When I got to Rosebud, I went straight to the grocery store in the town of Mission. I replaced bread and canned goods that I had used at the Sundance and purchased anything else I might need for the next four or five days. I bought ice for my cooler and a couple of gallons of water.

Then I headed over to Rosebud Village. As I drove through town, I started seeing people I knew, people I had Sundanced with.

Our Sundance was on top of a hill and was appropriately called Ironwood Hilltop Sundance. Already, people were starting to set up the camps where they had stayed for years.

I drove around and saw two native men, Emmanuel and Thomas, from California. This was their first Sundance, and I was their "Grandfather." I knew they would make me proud.

There was one area, sticking out from the hill, south of the Arbor. We called it "California Ridge" because so many people from California came and camped there at the Sundance. I went there first. Setting up camp for me was just a matter of stopping my van, and I was home.

I spent Wednesday morning getting myself ready and putting the final touches on my regalia.

In the afternoon, we headed out to get the Sacred Tree. This was a much larger Sundance than the previous one. There must have been twenty or thirty cars following the truck with the trailer to go get the tree.

Traditionally, while everyone is cutting down the tree, the Sundance Chief selects another one for the following year. He takes tobacco to it, prays to it, and lets it know that it will be our Sacred Tree soon. There is more said to the tree, but only a Sundance Chief knows what is said.

When we went to cut down our tree, we realized that it was right in the middle of a poison-oak patch. There must have been more than one hundred people, and every one of us trampled through it. We had to push the poison oak out of the way with our feet and hands to get to the tree.

Two children who are pure of heart, spirit, soul, and body are supposed to strike the first blows. So we had a little girl take the first axe strike to the tree, and then a little boy. Then they let the older guys, like myself, take a few swings. It was quite an honor to be selected.

After the old warriors took their swings, they let the young warriors chop it down really quickly. When the tree was close to coming down, they pushed it, and all the young warriors got under it. Slowly, slowly they took one whack at a time, until it was resting firmly where it couldn't fall and touch the ground because it was supported by all the men. When it was cut loose, we trampled back out.

Even with all that poison oak, to the best of my knowledge not one person involved in the ceremony got a rash or anything from it. Now that's unheard of. You can imagine two or three or maybe ten people being immune, but for everyone to be like that? This is powerful medicine.

We were there for a sacred purpose. We were there to get that Sacred Tree, the tree of life that meant so much to us.

We carried it up and put it on the trailer. Again as we traveled down the highway, people pulled over and stopped. Those who lived in the area knew the sacredness of the tree. They would stop as a sign of respect.

We must have traveled about ten miles, then we took it off the trailer. This time it was a larger tree, but there were more people to carry it, so it wasn't quite as difficult.

We made our four stops before we got to the Arbor, then inside the Arbor near the center, laid down the tree. This time I was there in time to tie my own rope on it.

When I was in Porcupine, I went to David with a problem and asked him what to do. I told him that the Spirits had entered my mind in a dream I had during the summer while sleeping in my van in California. The Spirits gave me a message: I had to pierce every day of my Sundance. It would be for my children. I should pierce once on each side, every day for the full four days. The dream scared me to death.

When David consulted with the Spirits and asked them if they truly wanted me to do this, the Spirits answered yes. That's what I must do so my children would be protected. The only way to guarantee that they would never be abused or mistreated was to pierce every day during the Sundance.

After settling down, I looked for a Sundance leader. I told him what had happened. We went into the Sweat Lodge together. He asked the spirits to bring him some kind of sign or word about what to do. Again the Spirits came and said, yes, that is the way they wanted me to go if I wanted my children protected.

Normally, the Sundance Chiefs don't allow people to do more than one set of piercing. If someone wants to do two, it should be two in front and two on their back, while dragging buffalo skulls. If they feel they must drag buffalo skulls, or if they have made that commitment, then it's okay. Doing more than that in one Sundance is frowned on, or it isn't allowed at all.

The leader told me, "You know, the Spirits are telling you to do this. We should still go and talk to Norbert and make sure that it's okay with him. He runs this Sundance."

The Sundance Chiefs are trying to keep glory-hunting people out of there. If someone is looking for glory, we let them know this is not the place to build their ego. So we went to Norbert, and we told him what had happened, word for word.

Norbert said, "Well if you made that commitment, and they told you that, that's the only way to do it. You've got my blessing."

He went on, "I know that this will be a hard and painful

Sundance for you. Not only are you going to feel the pain of those piercing wounds, but you are also going to feel the heat of the sun, thirst, and hunger. Another pain that you are going to feel is the pain of your limbs. Your arms are going to hurt, and your legs will ache. You will pay a heavy price for what you're asking. But you have the strength and the courage to do it."

So with that done, I started praying heavily. I prayed for the courage and the strength to accomplish what I had to do. Since I had already completed one piercing, I told them that was the first one of my four days.

When we went in Thursday, I didn't pierce. I danced. And then Friday morning I was the first one to pierce. I can't begin to relay to you how hard it is to go through that much hunger, pain, and thirst. Even though I had Sundanced many times, each time was just as difficult as if it were the first time. It took all the energy I could muster to keep myself on my feet.

The tiny veins on the tops of my feet started bursting. The tops of my feet turned black and blue, like a big bruised club at the end of each leg. All those vessels bursting, along with all of the hours dancing in the hot sun, increased my suffering. Pierced and pulling back on the tree, I smiled at Harold, a new Sundance brother I had met, who was from Pennsylvania. He was fast becoming a close friend. I had met him and his wife, Carlotta, the year before, when we both pierced simultaneously.

I pierced Friday, Saturday, and again Sunday. By Sunday, my entire chest was inflamed, one whole mass of pain. Piercing ripped my flesh open every day. It was gratifying for me because I knew that every time I ripped my flesh out of my chest, my children were being protected.

No single piercing was for any particular child; each piercing was for all of my children. I prayed that my children would come back to me someday and be kept from harm. I prayed hard for this.

I finished that Sundance, my third Lakota Sundance and my seventh Sundance overall. What a wonderful relief to complete it, and what a beautiful feeling. I know I've said it before, but I had found something that I really felt strongly about and truly loved.

The Sundance will always sustain you. All you are expected to offer is belief, respect, and prayers.

A B O V E — B L U E

"Star Path"

O R I O N ' S
L I G H T S

While I was at the Lakota Sundance, I knew something dramatic was going on in my life, but I couldn't quite put my finger on it. I was soon to learn that my wife was, at that very time, processing divorce papers.

When I left South Dakota, I returned to California only to find a letter from the courts of Oklahoma informing me that on July 31, there was going to be a divorce hearing. If I didn't appear in court, they would take it as an indication that I wouldn't contest any of the court rules or terms they laid out. They would go ahead and grant her a divorce under those conditions. I am almost positive that she knew I wouldn't be there to receive the letter. She knew I'd be at the Sundance.

Of course, when I received the letter, it was a month-and-a-half old, so there was no way I could have made it on time or contested it. Now it was final. It was hard to believe, it had all happened so fast. I didn't fight for my children, because the very best I could ever be was a poor mother. I figured I would send them money and learn to live with the situation. My ex-wife was a good mother to them.

Soon after, friends from Oklahoma kept giving me reports that she was not treating our kids well. Their welfare concerned me, and that was why I was praying so hard that Grandfather would take care of them and that no abuse would befall any of them. I was willing to give my blood, my flesh, and my pain to have my prayers answered.

It really hurt when I found out the divorce was final. Not that it hurt to be divorced. What hurt was to lose my children. I didn't know what I was going to do without them. So much of my life focused around them, and suddenly they were gone from my life. I wondered what they were thinking of all this, and of me. I wondered what their mother had told them and if they blamed me. I certainly couldn't go to Oklahoma. Not yet. I didn't know what I would do when I saw her and felt it was better to stay away. I was still angry.

After that Sundance, I traveled up into northern California. Life was treating me really well. Everything I made I sold. It started to get late in the fall, and I began to feel human again. I was sending the kids some money every week—always money orders in their names, so they would know their dad was trying to take care of them and was thinking of them. Much later, my son told me, "Mom said you sent us money in our names because you thought she couldn't cash it. She cashed every one of them and would give us five dollars of it, then use the rest for herself or the house."

No matter what she did, she was a good mother and a good wife to me for fifteen years. I hold nothing against her.

I headed to Quartzsite, Arizona, and sat in the desert for two weeks making Dream Catchers. At the time there weren't too many people making them. Those of us who were had found it hard keeping enough made for the people who wanted them. After the two weeks, I walked into one store, and they didn't even ask me the price.

The owner said, "Manny, you've got Dream Catchers?"

"Yes, I've got a bunch."

"We'll take them all," he said.

It didn't surprise me. They were very, very popular. Naturally, I was happy and grateful that the Creator had given me such a great way to make money. It was especially good for me because of my high blood pressure; the work was quite relaxing and not too stressful.

Heading back to California, I parked my van at the house of a friend, Wolfhawk, who lived in Torrance. I put myself on a minimum of at least ten Dream Catchers a day. It didn't matter what size or what color. I made them all sizes—from five-inch wooden rings to eighteen-inch rings. At the end of every week, I had seventy Dream Catchers made. Not bad for a guy living in his van without too much overhead. Things were going well for me.

Winter came and went in Torrance. I told my friends I wanted to head back to Tucson, Arizona, because in February, there would be a big gem and mineral show—the largest in the world. Every hotel and motel room in town would be full. Many motel rooms would be turned into retail and wholesale stores for the exhibitors, who would fly in from all over the world. It was a great place for me to whole-sale my crafts.

My only concern was sending money home occasional-ly and trying to make sure my kids lived well. Of course, I didn't want to send too much because from what I had heard, not all the money was spent on them. Apparently some of it was going to support my ex-wife's new drinking habit.

I headed down to Julian, California, to see my buddy Emmanuel. I had brought Emmanuel into the Sundance. He was a good friend. When I got there, he was happy to see me and asked how I was doing.

"I'm doing great. I'm just kicking back, making Dream Catchers."

"Well, look," he said, "I just moved into another house. This cabin is just sitting here empty." He continued, "If you want, you are welcome to stay there. The rent is paid for another month. There's a bed, color TV, a VCR, refrigerator, and a shower. You can stay there and make your crafts. You don't need to go anywhere. Get out of the van for a few days and stretch. If you want to stay longer than a month, I'll pay for another month. No problem."

Emmanuel has a heart of gold. He's always willing to help anyone who needs it. I thanked him and took him up on his generous offer. Right across the street from the house was a working-man's restaurant. Across the street from the restaurant was a video store with more than five thousand movies. What more could I want?

Every morning, I would get up early, walk across the street, and have breakfast. Then I would walk back to the cabin and work, making five to ten Dream Catchers. Go have lunch, come back, make a few more, and then have dinner. Usually by then Emmanuel was around, and we would go have dinner at a good restaurant in the area. At night I would watch videos. I was really enjoying myself. Local people would come over and say they had heard I was making Dream Catchers. I would show them what I had and sell one or two a day.

Twenty, thirty, or forty bucks was pretty good, when you didn't have any overhead. I was making money, making Dream Catchers, and it wasn't costing me any rent. I was a little lonely, but overall I was living pretty well.

However, one Sunday morning I got up and had a strong, strong urge that I had to get to Tucson. I have always been one to follow my intuition and to rely a lot on my senses and my prayers.

In a matter of minutes, everything changed. One moment I was almost completely at ease with myself and with my place in life. And then suddenly, the energy changed completely. Within twenty minutes I was ready to go.

Just as I was finished loading everything into the van, Emmanuel drove up and said, "Manny, what's going on? What are you doing?"

"I've got to get to Tucson."

"But, you're all loaded up," he noticed. "You don't have to pay any rent here. You don't have to take off."

"Oh, I wasn't going to leave until I saw you," I said, "I just want to get there."

"What's the urgency?" he asked.

"I don't know really, I just have to go . . . now."

When he understood I was serious, he shook my hand, and we gave each other a big hug. I told him I'd see him later. A few minutes after that I was in my van and heading down the road. About four hours later I arrived at my parents' house.

Things had improved with my parents. I had been in touch with my mom before Christmas, and she asked me to come home so I wouldn't spend the holiday alone. I told her that my hair was still long. My dad was on the extension, and she said, "Did you hear that?"

My dad said, "I don't care if your hair is down to the floor. Come home, Son."

Finally, my prayers were answered.

When I arrived at my parents' house on Christmas Day, my dad came out to greet me. My mom was crying with happiness that after five years her wayward son was finally home again. My dad was happy to see me. It was the first time he'd seen me with long hair, but he didn't make one comment about it. Later we visited my sister Norma, and as we left her home I heard my dad whisper to my mom, "He doesn't look half-bad with long hair, does he?"

My mom turned and gave him a shocked look, not believing what she was hearing.

They understood now that I was a Sundancer and what that meant. My dad seemed to have a new respect for me. He had heard from other people about the Sundance, and how hard and admirable it was to be a Sundancer. At some point, he mentioned what I was doing to one of his friends who knew about the Sundance from reading about it. He looked surprised and asked, "Manny is a Sundancer?" When my dad confirmed that I had danced several times, his friend explained that he knew about it and that it was a very difficult thing to do, that it was painful, and only very committed people follow that spirituality.

I believe the conversation had a lot to do with changing my dad's mind.

I spent another day with my parents. The next morning, I got up early, and Mom wanted to fix me breakfast. I declined. She asked me if I'd stay a few more days.

I said, "Thanks, Mom, but I can't stay. I've got to get to Tucson."

She said, "Why do you have to get? I've never seen you have to get anywhere."

"Mom, something is urging me to get there right away. I don't know what it is."

I reached Tucson at about noon that day and went to see my friend Anna, who is a promoter. She promoted a big show in Tucson and had a tent set up with booths inside and out. We walked around talking for a little while, but she was busy, so I left her alone and went my own way.

Little did I know that the next day I would find out why I was compelled to come to Tucson. It would prove to be a major turning point in my life.

Early the next morning, I woke up, had my breakfast, then headed back to Anna's tent. As I walked around outside I ran into Nan and Dave, a couple of people I knew, who were set up selling crafts. We talked for about an hour. I told them I was making Dream Catchers.

Nan pulled me aside and said secretively, "Hey, come here. Everybody's trying to make it on the native thing and trying to cash in on the Dream Catcher deal."

I asked her, "What do you mean?"

"Come here, I want to show you something."

So she led me inside and brought me to a table full of crudely made Dream Catchers! A short, little white woman was behind the table. Nan turned around and left, but I stayed there. I started scowling at the woman, and she looked at me with her innocent, hazel eyes and said, "Hi, can I help you with anything?"

I asked her, "Who made these Dream Catchers?"

She said, "A Choctaw lady from Arkansas."

"Well, true, authentic Dream Catchers are made by medicine people," I said angrily.

Taken aback by my aggressive tone, I could tell she felt

uncomfortable. She said she didn't mean to offend anyone, and asked me if I knew about them.

"Of course, I know about them. I make them. Did you know that . . . " And I proceeded to lecture her on how it had been a tradition from ancient people, and how only elders made them for people who had problems sleeping. I was really upset that a white woman, from God knows where, was trying to sell in my territory!

She said, "You make them yourself?"

"Yeah."

"I'd like to see them."

This had turned from a lecture to a possible business deal, and since business is business, I turned to her and said, "Well, I'll go get some."

"I can follow you out to your car," she said, "My girl-friend will watch the booth."

We walked out there, and, by now, I was trying to show off. I showed her all of my Dream Catchers, in all sizes and colors.

"Oh my God, you made these?" She asked.

"Hey, I make all of them, and I don't need anybody's help."

"I'll tell you what, if you make them for me, I can sell them by the truckload!"

I looked at her, incredulously, but trying not to show it, "You can?"

She replied, "I've got connections in Canada like you can't believe!"

She was telling me that she was going to buy Dream Catchers by the truckload from me. However, I found out later she really was quite a nervy young lady. She would commit herself to things financially, without a cane to hang on, all the while trying to think positively. As it turned out she didn't have *any* money to *buy* a truckload! Regardless, I had to admire her for her courageous and entrepreneurial nature. It was wonderful.

We walked back into the tent, talking and making plans. My mind was in a whirl. I was calculating how much money I would make and thinking that I'd have to hire people to help me.

We finally introduced ourselves to one another. Her name was Melody. We both felt pretty good about meeting. I told her that I was going to see some friends of mine but that I'd be back later.

So, I took off and found Thelma and her husband. They have stores in New York and Long Island and they did quite a bit of buying from me. In fact, they bought me out. Thelma asked me to make more Dream Catchers before the show finished. They wanted to have some to take home. When we finished business, Thelma said, "Manny, we're having supper at Carlos Murphy's. You want to join us?"

I said, "I would love to join you, but I just met this young lady. I was going to ask her if she wanted . . . "

"Heck," Thelma said, "Bring her with you."

"You sure you don't mind?"

"Not one bit, we can just write it off as a business expense."

I said, "Great! Oh, but Thelma, I don't even know if she wants to go or not. I'll ask her and see what she says."

I felt pretty good. I had an invitation for dinner, I had met a nice young lady, and my pocket was full from the sale. By now I had spent most of the day with Melody and discovered that I really enjoyed her company.

I went back to where Melody was and told her that I had to go to the post office to mail my son some money. It was his thirteenth birthday that day, and I always sent a bit extra on the kids' birthdays. Then I had to try to find a motel room to take a shower.

She offered, "If all you need is a shower, you can go over to my motel room. There's nobody there. Here's the key. Just bring it back when you're done. It's too hard to find a motel room in Tucson at this time."

Well, I was a perfect stranger, but I guess she felt she could trust me. I found the motel room where she was staying, and I went in and took a shower. It took me quite a long time to get ready, so when I got back to her booth, it was almost time for her to close.

Although she never said it, I think she was a little bit worried that she had given her room key to a person she didn't know. She must have questioned herself for being so trusting, because when I came in, I noticed a look of relief on her face.

Then I asked her, "Well, look, I've been invited to this dinner tonight over at Carlos Murphy's. Do you have any plans? Are you going out with Darren and Sheila?" By now I had met her friends she was with.

She said, "Well, no. They have plans, but I didn't want to go with them anyway. I'd love to go with you."

Thelma and her husband were already there when we arrived. While we had dinner we visited and talked shop. We had a good old time and ate some fine food.

Afterward, we drove back to her motel room, and, after parking our vans, we took a walk. We walked up the street to a fast-food place. As we sat there, we started holding hands and talking about Canada and the places I had been. I felt stupid. There I was, a fifty-two-year-old man, holding hands like a teenager. I felt ridiculous, but it didn't feel wrong. Though we had originally met to discuss business, our being together created a new chemistry.

I ended up helping her at the show. Then we left Tucson together and went north to Flagstaff. We traveled together for a couple of weeks, selling and making crafts. After a while Melody said she really had to get back to Canada.

By then, I was thinking, I really love this woman, and I enjoy her company. I really hated to let her go, so I thought, "Well, maybe I'll go with her to Canada. If things work out, I'll stay. If not, I can always come back." I talked to her about it, and she was delighted that I wanted to come.

It was quite an adventure going up there. We ended up at a New Age show there, which was quite interesting. It opened my eyes to many things that I hadn't encountered before. That show was my first introduction to a new way of life and a new circle of friends.

Once the summer was in full swing, Melody and I returned to the states to attend the Sundance.

This was the first Sundance Melody had ever seen. Just as her world had opened my eyes to many things, my world that is the Sundance opened her eyes to many different things. She saw how people prayed and suffered for their beliefs. It made her a believer. Since then she has accepted the native way and knows that it is a good way to follow spiritually.

Before she met me, Melody's own spiritual background was quite varied. She had had a lot of exposure to Catholicism as a child, evangelism as a teenager, then was lost for a few years in early adulthood. It wasn't until she was in her mid-twenties that she discovered esoteric teachings and beliefs. She had the right ideas; being kind to others, trying to heal the planet, thinking positively. When I met her, she had her own metaphysical crystal business called "CrystalEyes," which exposed her to many new philosophies and beliefs. She ended up with a mishmash of beliefs, and she danced to her own drum. She believed in one God and prayed to God regularly in her own way.

Ironically, a few months before we met, she had mentioned to a friend that she wondered why she was carrying so many native-oriented products. Now we know why: it led up to our meeting.

Melody's first Sundance was very special and inspiring for her. It was on the Rosebud Reservation, and she was quite overwhelmed and moved by the things she saw there. It was a very intense ceremony, but it had been especially tough on her because she was now five months pregnant. On top of that, we had just learned from the doctor that we were expecting twins! Melody was finally able to meet many of the friends I had been Sundancing with for a couple of years.

And two of Melody's friends, Joe and Mieke, made a fifteen-hundred-mile pilgrimage from Ontario, Canada, just to pray and to support us. They gave up their time, effort, and sleep to help any way they could. Mieke gave free psychic readings to everyone who wanted them. Many native people took advantage of her generosity. Joe was busy in the cook shack, helping out, washing pots and pans, and watching the front gate as security. It was a big comfort for Melody, having friends from home who could hold her hand while she watched me in the Sundance.

This Sundance began like all the others. The Sundance Chief followed tradition: we had sweats, did our prayers, and danced hard. But this was a special ceremony for several reasons.

The year before, I had wanted to pierce my back and drag buffalo skulls. I had wanted to do it for my children.

We strongly believe the buffalo brings us an abundance of spiritual energy, so that we can cope with everyday life and the realities of our world. This is the reason we pierce our backs and drag as many buffalo skulls as we can bear. The more there are, the more power we receive from the buffalo.

However, I didn't do it that year, because I had no one to help dress and take care of the wounds afterwards. This year, though, I had Melody with me. She told me she would care for my wounds.

On Saturday morning, they marked my chest and back to indicate where I was going to be pierced. Melody stood in the shade around the Arbor watching the dance. When she realized that I had marks on the front and back, she knew something was up. She was crying, and holding Mieke's hand. I hadn't explained anything to her about dragging skulls, and no one else had dragged skulls yet, so she didn't know what the marks on my back meant.

I knew if I told Melody what I was going to do ahead of time, she would get upset, and in her condition, I didn't want her to worry.

When I went to the tree to pray, I untied my rope and stretched it out to the northwest side of the Arbor. All my friends knew that was where I danced and prayed while attached to the tree, so everyone moved to stand near Melody. That Saturday morning, I was the first to pierce.

After my chest had been pierced, I was standing in my spot, dancing and praying. I looked across and saw my friend Harold. He had been pierced right after me. We danced back and forth to the tree, the traditional four times. On the last time, as I ran backwards, I saw Harold break loose one split second before I did. When I broke loose, a Sundance leader took my wrist bracelet and ran with me around the Arbor to the west side.

They had four buffalo skulls tied together waiting for me. The anticipation of feeling the weight and pain that come from dragging buffalo skulls actually becomes something good and joyous, rather than something to fear. At the same time, it is a way for us to give thanks in a special and sacred way.

This is also the reason I make my piercing bones out of buffalo leg bone. It seems as though every year this leg bone comes to me. I cut a section out of the middle of it. Then I split it lengthwise. I file and sand down the pieces of bone to the size of ballpoint pens. Then I sharpen the ends into points to make them easier to use during the piercing ceremony. I always give them away to people significant to me, whom I love.

They pierced my back and attached the four skulls. Using the sacred staff (our spiritual flag or symbol), I started slowly moving forward. The pain on my back was immense. I gritted my teeth and started praying hard, asking for courage and strength. Stopping to honor each direction as I reached it, I made one complete circle of the Arbor. On my second round, just past the north direction, the left piercing broke loose. I stopped, not realizing what had happened. I had felt a hard jerk on my back and some pain. But the pain seemed to center itself more on the right side now, and I didn't know why.

My Sundance brother Henry danced next to me. He leaned over and told me, "Keep going, Manny. One side broke loose."

I leaned into the other side, thinking it might break loose, too. Being out of balance like that made it much more difficult to pull the skulls.

I got them moving again and continued around the Arbor until I had gone four complete rounds. The right-side piercing had held the whole time. Finally, it was time to break loose. I backed up to the skulls. A few of my Sundance brothers sat on the skulls, and I took off running. I hit the end of the rope and broke easily enough. Though still in pain, I was thankful it was over. Melody had tears streaming down her face, and I could tell it had been difficult for her to watch. I had asked her before we started

Sundancing to be strong for me, and, all things considered, she was very brave.

Sunday morning, I didn't dance because the two piercings had taken a lot out of me, and I felt I'd fulfilled my commitment. Midday, I went to the Arbor, carrying my old pipe and another beautiful pipe I had just received from Todd, a pipe maker from Pipestone. The sacred pipe that I had had for five years was magnificent. It was fully covered with cut beads and the designs were geometric. My ex-wife had made it for me, and I didn't feel the same way about it anymore. It couldn't bring on the special feelings it used to. It was time to pass it on. I prayed the previous night and asked the spirits what I should do. The message came to me through thoughts.

When I got behind the Arbor, while the other Sundancers were resting between rounds, I called for Harold and Henry.

They were both happy to see me. As they walked up, they were smiling and laughing. Harold asked me, "What happened Manny, you feeling lazy today?"

I replied, "Come here, I've got something for you."

When they were standing in front of me, I presented my old pipe with the beading on it to Harold.

He gave me a puzzled look, as though asking me, "Why are you giving me this?" He couldn't speak. He didn't know what to say to this gesture.

"Harold, do you remember saying to me that if I ever wanted to get rid of this pipe, I should give it to you? Well, Brother, here it is. It's yours."

Henry was getting upset, and asked, "What's wrong? Why are you doing this?"

Turning, I held up the other pipe to him and said, "Henry, it's time for you to have a new *Chanupa*. Please take this, it's my gift to you."

I could tell by their faces that they thought I was leaving the Sundance for some reason. They had tears in their eyes and they shook their heads as if to say, "No, Manny, you can't do this."

Then I explained to them that it was time that I had a new pipe to go with my new life. I wasn't leaving the Sundance, I only wanted to honor my two Sundance brothers. Both looked at me and, not knowing what else to do, embraced me. All three of us shared tears together. It was a special moment for all of us.

Melody and I left the Sundance Monday morning and drove to Rapid City for a couple of days' rest and much-needed showers.

After we recuperated, we left Rapid City and drove south through the South Dakota Badlands on the road that goes straight to David Swallow Jr.'s Sundance in Porcupine. I had another three years with David and his people.

We were well received upon our arrival to the Sundance grounds. The people made everyone there feel welcome. I introduced Melody to everyone, and she made a lot of friends.

It wasn't long after arriving that we had to go cut down the Sacred Tree. Melody stayed behind at camp and prepared dinner. It was getting hard for her to move around, and it was extremely hot.

Everybody gathered behind David's pickup to follow him to the Sacred Tree. The convoy continued until we pulled off the main highway. David pulled the pickup close to the edge of a river and stopped.

Opening the door, he said, "This is it, boys!"

I saw him pointing across the river. I asked David, "Can't we get any closer than this? How are we going to get the tree here?"

He replied, "This is as close as we can get . . . and we're bringing it back on our shoulders!"

I said, "Oh."

I looked back and saw people getting out of their cars. David removed his boots before getting into the water. As I entered the water in my bare feet, I felt my connection with Mother Earth. Suddenly a common occurrence became a very special moment in my life.

Something triggered my sensitivity, something happened to my soul. A soft, intense feeling of peace and contentment came over me. I felt the warm water around my feet. I felt the cool, soft mud squish up between my toes. Both seemed to massage my feet.

It was as though Mother Earth was telling me that the next four days were going to be hard on my feet, and she wanted to show me that she could also be gentle on them. The river was about a foot deep, but it was very wide and had a slippery, muddy bottom. After crossing, we gathered around the Sacred Tree.

Once we cut down the tree, we placed it on our shoulders and began walking across the river. Fortunately, it wasn't very big. Everything went well, until we started slipping on the mud. Then it became very difficult to carry it without touching the ground or water. Slowly we made it across and started up the steep embankment on the other side. I slipped and fell, more than once, trying to get up the side. It was very difficult. Once when I fell, I used my body to keep the tree from falling on the ground. Finally, with strenuous effort, we got it on the trailer.

Two hundred yards from the Sundance grounds, we took the tree off and carried it toward the east entrance of the Arbor. By now everyone was hot and tired, and it was getting to be early evening. When we gently laid it down inside the Arbor, the base was lying right at the edge of the center hole. Melody was waiting along with many others. They had the prayer ties and flags that we were going to hang on the limbs at the top of the tree. It was such a beautiful sight: all those people walking up, saying prayers, and tying flags on the tree.

The Sundance Chief tied the traditional silhouette of a buffalo, a man, and an eagle wing to the branches. He did that so the Creator would recognize the men who were praying. The buffalo was on the tree because of its sacredness to us; the eagle wing represented the eagle that would take our prayers to the Creator. The man represented all humanity.

Sundancers started coming from all over to tie their ropes to the tree. Things got quieter around the tree. As each person finished, he or she would stand in a circle away from the tree so that other people would have better access to it.

Finally, the Sundance Chief announced, "Grab hold of your ropes, we're going to stand it up."

We started pulling, then some men got underneath the tree, pushing it up higher and higher until it was standing straight. Once the leaves were free of the ground, people remained still, waiting for the tree to stand erect before moving. The only movement was the vibration from the men who were struggling to stand the tree up. When the tree was straight, it was like a tension was broken. All the leaves started flickering and waving. There was a slight breeze that just made them dance. It was so beautiful and majestic.

The base of the tree sat in a deep, four-foot hole. After centering it in the hole, we had two or three men start shoveling in the dirt and tamping it down. The only thing holding the tree up was the ropes. They looked like spiderwebs branching away from the tree. Eventually the tree was standing alone in all its glory.

As each man walked up to it, he found his rope and tied

148

it down around the tree. By securing the ropes to the tree, they wouldn't be flopping around when we danced the next day.

Once the tree was up, there was a pause as though everyone was holding his breath for a minute. It was so impressive and awesome to see this magnificent tree and to watch it come alive. Now it stood alone like it did before it was cut down.

Melody and I returned to the van. We had a light supper, then I took off my muddy, dirty clothes next to our van and crawled in. The blankets were a welcome relief. I must have been tired because morning arrived quickly.

The next morning we did our traditional sweats and danced into the Arbor. It got hot very early that morning, but it was beautiful. Everyone was in great spirits. This was Melody's second Sundance in two weeks.

After we greeted the sun and placed our Sacred Pipes on the altar, we retired to the dancers' resting place. We were all sitting around visiting and introducing ourselves to dancers we didn't know. It was a good time to meet new brothers. It was a good time to encourage all the new Sundancers, to help them overcome their nervousness. We joked around, to alleviate the fears of the new dancers, because for some this is a scary thing.

Before the Sundance, Al managed to get a buffalo. It was bought from the tribal herd on the reservation. He had it butchered, and he had the skull lying back behind the Arbor.

Al asked, "Lionel, do you want that buffalo skull?"

Lionel looked surprised. "Really?" he said. "Yeah, I really like it, and it would look good in my living room. Sure, I'll take it."

I looked at Al and then at Lionel. I said, "Al, you're giving Lionel that buffalo skull?"

"Yeah." He was wondering what I was getting at.

I said, "And you accepted it, right, Lionel?"

"Yes, I am very grateful. I was secretly hoping this would happen."

"Well, Al, you realize what you have just committed Lionel to, don't you?"

A look of surprise and confusion crossed their faces. Then Al began to understand what I was talking about.

"That's right, Al," I said, "you gave it to him. He's accepted it. Now he's got to pierce his back and drag that skull."

Al explained, "I knew all this, but when I gave it to him, that is not the way I meant it."

I went on, "I know, and I realize you didn't do this to hurt him. I don't want to see him go through any pain, but that's the traditional way. He's got to earn the right to have that buffalo skull in his home."

Al looked at Lionel and said, "It's true, Lionel. I'm sorry, I forgot."

Lionel said, "Oh, man. Things are really serious around here!" Then he laughed, "If I had known, I could have picked one up for fifty dollars at the trading post!"

Everybody burst out laughing.

An old-timer listening to all this said, "Hey, Lionel, I'll drag it for you for fifty dollars! I'll pierce and drag it for you. You give me fifty bucks, and you can take the skull home!"

Then another guy jumped up and said, "I'll do it for forty!"

Then I chimed in, "Well, I'll do it for twenty-five. I don't mind getting pierced."

Everybody was laughing and making a big joke out of it because it had been so very serious at first. Then Lionel quietly asked, "Do I hear twenty?!"

Another round of laughter started.

150

Finally, after the laughter had died down, Lionel said, "Well, Al," as he shook his hand, "I accepted the skull. If I have to pierce for it and drag it, I'll do that."

Al said, "You think he should do it now?"

"It doesn't matter when, Al, as long as he drags it. You gave it to him, so it's up to you when."

Reluctantly, Al said, "What I mean is, it's really getting to smell bad. It's been dead for three days, and it still has the hide and everything on the skull. It hasn't been boiled or anything."

"Actually, it might be better this way," I said. "It's green and heavy. If the Creator wants him to drag it around all four times, Lionel will remember it well. If the Creator doesn't, he'll break loose before dragging it too far."

But in the end, they decided to wait until the following year for Lionel to drag the skull. He wanted to drag a skull that didn't smell so bad.

The dance continued all day. Later that afternoon Lionel came to me with tobacco while we were taking a break. He said, "Brother, I would be proud if you would do the piercing for me."

This was quite an honor, particularly since I had never pierced anyone before. His asking made me feel emotional. I took the tobacco and said, "Yeah, I'll do it for you. I'd be honored, Brother."

When you go to an elder to ask for advice or a favor, the traditional way is to go to them with a tobacco offering. Sometimes, when you don't have a bag of tobacco, you can use a cigarette. If the elder isn't committed to something else, he almost can't refuse to do the bidding.

So I explained to Lionel, "Whenever you take tobacco to an elder, first tell him what you want him to do. Before you give him the tobacco, give him the opportunity to refuse. If it's something he can't or doesn't want to do, that gives the elder the option of backing out if he wants." Lionel, like everyone else, including myself, was still learning.

The piercing song began. We placed Lionel where everybody could shake his hand as they went out of the rest area into the Arbor. I took him to the center tree and said, "Lionel, it's going to be a good one. It'll be okay. Don't worry, little brother."

He smiled nervously, "I'm not worried."

I let him pray for a while. I went to David and explained that I might have to put my glasses on. In recent years my eyes had been getting worse, and I needed reading glasses for anything up close. He told me to tie some sage on them, so the Spirits would accept them. When I brought Lionel to the buffalo hide and laid him down, he handed me his scalpel to pierce him. I closed my eyes as I put my hands on the tree. I asked, *"Tunkashila"* (Lakota for "the Creator") to give me compassion and to guide my hands. I asked for better vision, so I could see what I was doing.

When I opened my eyes, my eyesight was better than ever before, as though the brightness of the sun had increased tenfold. The whole world brightened up for me.

When I knelt down next to Lionel, I was on his left and David was on his right. David did the first piercing. I held the flesh while he did it, and then inserted the cherrywood piercing stick through Lionel's flesh. While David was tying the rope on, I grabbed and pinched the flesh together. David reached across to help me hold the flesh up. I took the knife and slowly slid it into his flesh. I felt a slight little pop as the sharp pointed scalpel broke through the flesh and then another pop as it went through. I didn't want to hurt my brother Lionel any more than I had to.

Slowly, slowly, I sawed and pulled the blade to my left to widen the hole that I had made. Blood sprang up imme-diately through the wound. It was hard to see what I was doing. David took Lionel's piercing stick and put it through the wound. Immediately we knew the wound wasn't big enough. Shaking his head, David indicated that I should cut some more. It would tear out if we tried to push it through his flesh. David pulled the piercing stick out, and I inserted the knife in and cut a bit more. Slowly, ever so slowly, I cut down until the opening was about a half-inch in length. Then David grabbed the piercing stick and pushed it through the cut, through the wound that I had inflicted on my brother's chest. This time it slid through easily.

I looked at his face, and it was expressionless, just a little pale. I knew the pain he was going through. I had felt it many times in the past. But I also knew that he was a warrior. When I tied his rope on, I made a figure eight around the wooden stick. Finished with our work, we picked him up.

I shook his hand and said, "Brother, you're on."

I could tell by the dazed look in his eyes that he was in pain and shock, so I kept him moving and talking. After a few minutes I could see that he was feeling better.

Many people can't take the pain and the shock that accompany the piercing ceremony, just as many people have trouble accepting an injection at the doctor's office. Piercing is done under the harshest conditions possible, as tradition dictates. It may seem crude to other people, but to us we are doing the very best for that person, the best we know how. We do it with the Creator's blessing and with as much compassion as possible.

I helped Lionel with his rope. I was trying to take it easy on my brother. I knew that he was in pain and hurting, but I also knew he was there by choice. Nobody ever told him he had to be there. I also realized he had found his spirituality, his road, and he was quite happy and content with it. That is what makes the Sundance so wonderful, the choice to be there is your own.

As Lionel backed up, his rope was tight. I told him to breathe deeply and pray hard—the harder he prayed, the less pain there would be. I kept telling him gently, "Pull back and stretch that flesh. The more you stretch it now, the easier it will break when the time comes. It hurts, I know, Brother, it hurts. Pull it back."

He pulled back until the rope was taut. It was bouncing then stretched tight. His chest was way out of proportion. I said, "*Ho ka*! Come on, go to the tree, and pray, Brother."

He danced toward the tree, then knelt on the ground and prayed to our God that we can touch, pray to, and cry with. He got up.

Lionel pulled back, stretching and stretching. The pierce on the right side suddenly popped off. He looked at me with surprise.

He said, "It fell off. It broke loose!"

"Hey, that's good, Brother. Now you only have one to break loose. The Spirits are smiling on you. Be grateful, be grateful that they are smiling on you. They are trying to make it easier for you. That's good."

He smiled at me. He was stepping lighter now, and with more vigor.

By now he had been to the tree three times. I told him, "This time when you go to the tree, run hard on your way back. Don't worry, I'll be here to catch you."

As the Sundance Chief, David controls when people go to and from the tree to pray when they are piercing. He waved Lionel on to the center. We went with him to the tree.

"You are ready to break loose. You only have one side to break," David softly spoke to him, giving him words of encouragement for the last round before breaking loose.

I saw David wave his fan at Lionel, telling him to break loose. I couldn't believe that little guy could run as fast as he could. He turned around and was running really fast from

154

the tree. As he hit the end of the rope, he started to fall, and I caught him under the arms and picked him up. "All right, Brother, you're loose."

He was so happy. "Manny, I did it!"

"You bet, Brother, it's done."

I led him around the Arbor back to his place, and everybody was touching him. Everyone wanted to feel his energy, that tremendous energy given to a Sundancer when he pierces that is so beautiful and contagious. It was good to watch him slowly, softly descend from his spiritual high.

Meanwhile, Melody was very tired and decided to lie down in the van to rest awhile. She had burned herself out from so many days of dancing, first over at Rosebud and then at Porcupine. Slowly, she climbed into the van. Leaving the doors open to catch any faint breeze that might happen by, she stretched out to rest, and, though uncomfortably hot, she dozed off.

After sleeping awhile, she woke up and could hear the drums. Suddenly, she felt something move. It was her babies, moving inside her for the first time. Then she felt them again. She got up and couldn't believe it. It was the thrill of her life. She was so excited she couldn't restrain herself and started to cry, wishing she had someone there to share her miracle. She got up, came over to the Arbor, and asked me to come over to where she could talk to me. "What's wrong?" I asked. I was confused because she was crying, but she was also smiling.

She said, "The babies moved for the first time. They were listening to the Sundance drums and started moving." Then she continued, "I've felt them move a couple of times already. It almost feels like they start dancing every time they hear the Sundance drums."

Naturally, I was thrilled. It was such a beautiful thing and even more special because it happened at the Sundance.

I believe that where children are when they hear their first sounds is important. I can't think of anything more wonderful that could happen to a person, to have the first sound one hears and responds to be the sound of Sundance drums beating.

BELOW — GREEN

"Mother Earth"

GIVER

OF LIFE

After the Sundance was over Melody and I headed back to Buffalo, New York, and Niagara Falls, where we had a storage shed. We had just started renting a three-bedroom house in the town of Richmond Hill, just north of Toronto. We continued exhibiting at shows and selling our crafts all over Canada. As life went on, things got a bit easier for both of us.

One morning we were preparing for one of the biggest New Age psychic fairs in Canada, if not North America, when the phone rang. It was an old friend of mine from Oklahoma.

I asked him, "How did you get my phone number, Bob?"

"It wasn't easy, I called all over California. My friend, are you sitting?"

"What do you mean?"

He says, "It's about your ex-wife. She got killed in a traffic accident last night."

We had been separated and divorced for a while now, so it really didn't bother me emotionally. I felt absolutely nothing toward her. My first thought was how the kids were, and I asked Bob about them.

"They are fine, just fine. They're here at my house. What do you want to do about them?"

Still in shock, I tried to gather my thoughts and said, "Look, I don't have any money right now. I have a four-day show starting tomorrow. If you could watch them, I'll pick them up after the show."

He said, "Okay, wire me permission to accept responsibility for these kids or the welfare department is going to come in and take them. If they do that, you will have a really difficult time trying to get them back when you get here. By then, they will have them placed in foster homes."

I pleaded with him, "Don't let anyone touch my kids, Bob. Please, keep them together for me. I appreciate your concern and your friendship. I'll call you when I get ready to go."

You really learn a lot about your friends in times like these. I thanked God for Bob's intervention and prayed I would have a good show so I could afford to get my children.

The world that Melody had introduced me to showed me things I didn't know existed. The first show she took me to, she was selling her crystals and gemstones, and I tried to act

as though I saw that sort of crowd all the time. Melody just laughed at me. She knew I was uncomfortable around some of the people. We saw some rather odd individuals, including UFO abductees, palm readers, astrologists, and hypnotists. The show really opened my eyes to things that I was familiar with in some way, but not in the way I was seeing them there.

After that introduction I told Melody about how, for thousands of years, our people had been consulting the Spirits for guidance. Some older medicine people used different methods to help people. There were those who used feathers, sticks, small bones, and even stones. Others would use the "hands on" way of healing and helping. Much of it was done by drumming and singing while they contacted the Spirits for advice.

So this was not a strange world for some of us First People. We just don't have a name for it, that I know of. A good native friend of mine, Ted Silverhand, calls himself a seer and does "readings" for people. I heard he's very good at what he does.

For myself, it's something I've had all my life. I always had people asking me for advice and telling me their problems. It seemed I always had words of comfort for them and knew what to tell them in their times of need. I helped a few couples resolve their problems when they were at the point of breaking up.

It was so much a part of me I didn't realize that I had a gift. I'm very grateful for it. I never realized anyone would be willing to pay me for the advice I had to offer. I was so wrong. People pay counselors and consultants for advice everyday.

The Creator brought me a way to help people and feed my family. It's a fair and good exchange. That's what Melody showed me. I now know that I am a seer, interpreter, adviser, and counselor, and very good at it. I have a great deal of experience and have received testimonials of my ability to predict people's futures and advise them how best to use that information. I'm proud to be a part of this old and honorable practice.

So now that my children were alone, I would be faced with a major expense just to go get them. Out of the blue, our friends Barry and Carol called and asked if they could give us some money. Another friend, Georgina, offered a financial gift. Ted Silverhand gave us money to help. Then Carl, Shawna, and Melva offered their financial help. This generosity from everyone really choked me up. There weren't words to thank them. I was very grateful and thanked the Creator for bringing me such special people in my time of need.

It is hard to give everybody credit who deserves it, because so many people do. People I didn't even know came from everywhere to help us. Everyone who gave money gave it unconditionally, without strings or a time limit to pay it back. Without their help, I don't know how we would have done it. It was a lot easier to get my kids.

Right after the show, Melody saw me off at the airport in Toronto. After everyone's help and what we had earned, I had three thousand dollars to take with me. By evening I was in Tulsa, and my friend Bob met me and took me to his house.

When I got to Bob's house, my four daughters and one son were there waiting. My twin girls, Mary and Becky, had just had their tenth birthday. The accident had happened right before their birthday. Some friends of the family, Barbara, Mildred, and Sherry, bought them a couple of presents. I was very grateful.

Seeing my kids for the first time in two years was an emotional event for everyone. I had missed them immensely and done many prayers for them. I pierced for their protection and safety. I prayed to get them back someday, but I sure didn't expect it to happen this way.

That was why the Spirits told me at the Sundance the year before that I had to dance and pierce every day for my children. They were trying to see if I was worthy or willing to sacrifice for my children. My red chest was swollen, inflamed with pain, and it burned from so many piercings. God now knew that if they were with me, I would make sure they were protected in all ways.

I strongly believe the Creator warned my ex-wife to stop neglecting our kids, as I understand she did for quite a while, leaving them alone for long periods of time at the condemned house they lived in. Perhaps, the Creator warned her that if she didn't stop, drastic steps would be taken to protect those children.

Although the kids didn't like being so overprotected from the curious neighbors, I hoped that one day they would understand that Bob and Dee Dee had done them and me a big favor by picking them up at school before the news of their mom's accident spread throughout town. That protected them from the so-called friends and neighbors—from the gossip and stares, and from pointing fingers—until I got there.

I picked up my children and took them away from all that. All of my ex's friends had gone through the house like tornadoes. They had taken my guns, silversmithing tools, clothes, chainsaws—everything my ex-wife and I had together, even the kids' clothing. Luckily, some friends who used to work for us had been able to save a few of the really personal items that belonged to my wife, things she wanted to leave the kids. That was good, and I appreciated it.

161

All this time I had a sick feeling in my stomach, wondering how I was going to deal with having my kids back in my life. Though Melody said to bring them up and we'd manage, how would it be when reality set in? Melody had no experience with children at all; she'd been an only child. How was she going to handle all the kids, especially when she was pregnant for the first time?

I knew it would be difficult for all of us and would change our lives, but my heart ached for my children every time I thought about how their whole world had been turned upside down, overnight. I wondered how they felt to be suddenly in the care of a father they hadn't seen in two years—to find themselves with no home, no mother, no clothes, and no creature comforts. The only thing they had to hang on to was faith in their dad. I felt so sorry for them, for their losses and confusion. They were all clinging to me, their only hope for protection from the storm in their lives.

Bob took me to the town of Claremore, and we bought a station wagon just the way it was sitting in the car lot. I didn't even know if it was in good or bad shape. In my state of mind, the only thing I could do was depend on *Tunkashila*, God, to help me. So, I bought the station wagon, put the kids in it, and left for Canada. I hadn't even been in Oklahoma for twenty-four hours.

On the drive home, all five kids wanted to sit by me in the front seat. It was as if the backseat was too far from me. I was all they had now. The first stop we made was in Joplin, Missouri. We stopped at a motel room, and all the kids took showers. We stopped at a store, and I bought them each two new sets of clothes. After everyone had dressed and cleaned up, I took them out to dinner. They couldn't eat enough! They looked so thin and undernourished. I wondered what life had been like for them while I was gone. It broke my heart just to think about it.

We worked our way slowly, steadily all the way north to Canada. When we reached home, naturally Melody had embraced the change in her life. She had taken our house and turned it into a home for the new arrivals. She found bunk beds, mattresses, sheets, pillows, and pillowcases for the kids. It was quite a job for a woman who was seven months pregnant, and it was a big job for anybody to go from an only-child family atmosphere to caring for five children she had never met before. I was very proud of her and always thanked God and the Spirits who brought her to me. It was all in preparation for this. Melody had prayed for someone to share her life with, and her strong prayers called me from California to Tucson. The call was powerful. God knew that eight months later, I was going to need her and so would my children.

When the kids arrived, friends from everywhere came to help Melody get ready. Bags and bags of supplies arrived everyday—clothes, shoes, toys, books, everything they could possibly need. The generosity of people overwhelmed me. News traveled fast about what had happened to the children, and everyone was supportive and helpful.

Shortly after the children arrived, Melody and I got married. Although she was seven months pregnant, I wanted Melody to be married and have everything legal when she gave birth. My son Rockie gave her away at a civil ceremony, and all my daughters stood up with us. They were just beautiful. They had accepted Melody and her love from the first moment they walked in the door. I was very happy about it.

Perhaps planning for the wedding and adjusting to Canada helped the kids keep their minds off the trauma they had gone through. I think it made them feel more secure in their new home and environment.

We had a wonderful reception at the house of Melody's mother, Lynne. There were many tears of joy and laughter.

A couple of months after the wedding, in late December, Melody started to experience some pain one night after dinner. We called the hospital, and they suggested a warm bath and a beer, to make her relax, which she did. However, the pain was getting worse, so we called the hospital again. Now Melody was lying down and the nurse asked me to put her on the line. When Melody described the pain she was having, the nurse told us to bring her in, she was in labor! They said they'd be ready for her.

There were about six inches of fresh snow on the ground and our driveway had a slight incline. I shoveled and cleared it as best I could while my daughter Stormy helped Melody get ready. It was hard for her to walk, but we got her in the car. I still had trouble backing out and worried that we might get stuck in our own driveway. Again, Grandfather was watching over us.

We headed to the hospital, and by now it was snowing heavily. The flakes were large and wet. The wipers were having trouble keeping the windshield clear. York-Central Hospital was only eight miles from where we lived, but because of the snow it took about half an hour to get there.

At the hospital, the nurses took Melody directly into the labor room. Stormy and I went in and stayed with her through her seven hours of labor. We heard that wasn't very much for a first birth, but to me it felt like days. It hurt me to see Melody in so much pain. I wished there were some way I could take it from her. Stormy, who was only thirteen, was helping Melody breathe and holding her hand through it all. She had attended a couple of prenatal care classes with Melody. Being the oldest daughter, Stormy had been responsible for all the kids when her mother was gone, so she was mature beyond her years.

We had found out a couple of months before that there was really only one baby, not two as we had thought. The delivery was completely natural. No drugs, no cut, the baby just arrived. Melody gave birth so fast that Stormy ended up holding one leg while I held the other. Of all the children I have fathered in my life, this was the first one I ever saw being born. What an amazing sight it was.

At the Sundance the previous summer, I had prayed for a healthy baby, and she turned out beautiful and perfect in every way. I made a commitment to Grandfather to pierce my back and drag buffalo skulls, to thank him for bringing her to us in good health and complete.

We named her Oriona (Or-ee-on-ah) after the constellation Orion. Her middle name is Estrella, which is Spanish for "star."

After the birth, they took Melody and the baby upstairs to a room, so Stormy and I left. It was about six o'clock in the morning. As Stormy and I walked out, the first thing I saw on the ground were three small snow sparrows, pecking away at some crumbs on the hospital steps. The Spirits had brought me a native name for my little daughter, Little Snow Sparrow.

After Melody and the baby got home we all settled into a routine controlled, of course, by the whims and temperament of the baby. It took that little baby's energy to unite us as a family, and the kids instantly fell in love with their new little sister.

Spring was upon us before we knew it, and we started thinking about the Sundance. It was getting to be time for me to go and give thanks, to show my appreciation for all we had received in the past year.

The Sundance season arrived and we got ready. Money

just appeared, it seemed, when we needed it. We bought a pop-up trailer that could sleep eight, we loaded up the car we had from Oklahoma (which was miraculously still running), and headed toward South Dakota, camping out along the way.

This particular trip was really special to me. Although my children attended all four Shoshoni Sundances in Wyoming with me, this would be their first Lakota Sundance. They were finally going to see the piercing that terrified their mother.

We traveled along, and stopped in Pipestone, Minnesota, where I buy my pipes to take to the Sundance. We met with some of our other friends who were coming to the Sundance from Maryland. We went down to the quarries and saw Todd, Ray, and other guys I knew who were carvers.

Commercially, there are many versions of "peace pipes" sold throughout the country. However, a pipe from Pipestone has a card stating its authenticity, and the pipes are made only by native people. Sometimes I buy several pipes and give them to the Sundance Chief, so he can give pipes to those Sundancers he deems worthy.

The giving of a pipe is very important, and something to be thought about carefully. When the Sundance Chief gives a pipe and makes someone a pipe carrier, the Sundance Chief becomes responsible for whoever carries and whatever happens with that pipe. Traditionally, you can't buy yourself a pipe, it must be given to you. To be a pipe carrier is a sacred responsibility, and not to be taken lightly.

I don't believe a pipe should be considered a sacred object until it has been in a Sweat Lodge and has had a medicine person breathe life into it. When it is given the breath of life, the power to cure, then I believe it is sacrilegious to buy or sell that *Chanupa*. It becomes a living entity, and you don't sell living beings. This is why I will not buy or sell any part of the eagle and will not sell a Sacred Pipe. There is quite a bit of dissention about what's right and what's wrong. I personally believe a pipe is just an object, just like anything else, until it goes through the ceremony. Many tourists buy pipes at the center at Pipestone.

I believe that the natives who have been there for generations quarrying the pipestone are the only ones who should be able to sell those pipes. It's a gift given to them by the Creator. This is the way they feed their families. In the old days, although they didn't sell them, they used to trade them for ponies. They traded for pemmican or dried buffalo jerky. They traded for deer skins or beads. Everything that was tradable. So, if anybody should be able to sell the pipes, I think it should be those people. They are the only people from whom I will buy a pipe. I will trade for a pipe, if the occasion arises and the trade is fair. As far as I am concerned, that is acceptable and makes me happy.

After meeting the other Sundancers in Pipestone, we headed toward South Dakota. Before we arrived, something remarkable happened. One of my girls, Rebecca, who was ten years old at the time, told me, "Daddy, I want to Sundance. I want to be in there with you and share. I want to experience it."

I sat and had long talks with her. My son Rockie, who was fifteen, also said he would like to be in the Sundance with me. It humbled me, my two children honoring me like this. That they should choose to follow me in the Sundance and the way of the *Chanupa*, and the Red Road. We sat and talked and I asked them questions—why they wanted to dance, what the Sacred Pipe meant to them, and so on—to understand why they wanted to do it. I felt their answers were appropriate, so I allowed them to dance with me. I also explained that they had to dance four years before they really made up their minds about piercing or not piercing. I think my son was glad of that. He felt he wasn't ready for piercing yet. He just wanted to be with me in the Sundance.

We reached the Sundance, and there was quite a controversy because Ironwood Hilltop Sundance had broken apart. A family argument about whose property the Arbor was on had been the reason. Our Sundance grounds had moved to Hollow Horn Bear. The Sundance Chief from Hollow Horn Bear had given permission to us to Sundance on their grounds until we found a permanent place.

The year before, I had asked the Creator to give me a healthy, normal baby. If my prayer was answered, I would commit myself to honor the Creator and my baby by piercing my back and dragging buffalo skulls. The Creator had answered my prayers, and now was the time to fulfill my commitment. The Arbor in a Lakota Sundance circle is not big, but it feels that way if you are dragging buffalo skulls. Melody told me later that when people around the Arbor realized I was going to pierce, at least fifty of them ran to stand behind me and my family. It was as though everyone knew something special was about to happen and wanted to be a part of it and support me.

First I was pierced in the front, once on each side. When I broke loose and danced around the Arbor, I immediately returned to the Sundance leaders and asked that they pierce me on my back. When I was getting pierced, I asked Lessert to make this a special piercing. I did not want to break loose until I had done my four turns around the Arbor.

He said, "Okay, it's up to you." When he finished, he leaned close to me and whispered in my ear, "Manny, that's guaranteed to hold till Christmas!" He had made the piercing deep.

Sometimes they don't want to hurt you, so they don't pierce too deep. But because of the weight of the skulls, men break loose before they have finished what they came there to do. I wanted to make sure they pierced me deep enough so the flesh wouldn't break before I was finished.

While standing there being pierced, my mental state was high. It felt good to be giving back something for all the Creator had given me. Henry came and stood in front of me to give his personal energy and support. He looked right into my eyes and held both of my biceps with his hands as the blade cut me. He watched to see if I was all right and had the courage to see this through.

After Lessert pierced me, he said, "*Ho-ka.*" He smiled at me, "Okay, Manny, you're all right."

They tied me to the buffalo skulls. I was fortunate, I believe, because there were only four skulls, and they only weighed twenty to thirty pounds each.

I asked for my baby daughter to be brought to me. I told them, "I'm going to carry her around with me."

They brought Oriona, my Little Snow Sparrow, to me and I held her in my arms. It was quite a sight to see: me, an older, tanned native man; and my daughter, a blonde wistful baby, a blonde dressed in a white outfit for the ceremony. (At times I called her my Little Jellyfish.) It felt so wonderful, the experience of carrying my child, whom God had given to me with all her limbs and as normal as any child could be.

Afterwards Melody explained to me, as best she could, what was going on while I carried the baby around. There wasn't a dry eye anywhere. Men, women, and even some Sundancers were crying. My girls, Stormy, Dory, and Mary, were crying and holding on to each other. It must have touched people's hearts to see a man suffering for his daughter. Maybe they felt I was carrying a part of them. As though the baby represented every person who witnessed the special ceremony.

True to my request, and true to the friend who pierced me, both places where I had been pierced hung on as I danced around the circle. I could feel the gravel under my feet. I could feel gentle breezes. I could smell sage. I started slowly from the west, stopped first to the north to hold my baby high to the Spirits of the north for their blessings, and then continued.

With the skulls dragging behind me, I had to lean forward, sometimes almost parallel to the ground. As the skulls tumbled around, they landed on their foreheads and teeth. When the teeth hit the ground, they dug down and yanked me backward. The pain was excruciating.

I danced on. I offered my baby to the east, and when I got to the south I offered her to the south. Each time I stopped and offered her to a direction for blessings, it was difficult to get started again. Usually, when dragging skulls, you are given a sacred staff for each hand to help pull you along. However, when I took the baby and was offered the staff, the Sundance leader said, "You're not gonna need this." He took it out of my hands as though he knew I would have the strength to pull without it. Finally, I went around and stopped, and I offered my baby to the west. Now I had to do my four rounds.

I was yanked back and forth, back and forth. I started moving forward and then I started going a little faster. I felt so good, but I was tiring out quickly. My mouth and my throat were so dry, yet I still felt full of energy. I felt as though I were pulling the whole world behind me, yet I had the energy of everyone in the Arbor helping me.

The baby was quiet, looking around. She played with the feathers on my eagle-wing fan. My blood from the two piercings on my chest had stained the white outfit she wore. Melody would later decide to keep the outfit so that one day she could explain to the baby what it was all about.

I went around my second time, trying to catch my breath. I started going around the third time, and I suddenly felt stronger. I believed the baby gave me energy. The support of everyone watching and praying for me gave me strength. The courage from the Creator helped me to keep going.

Everyone was feeling my pain. As I reached the west side of the Arbor, they stopped me. I thought I had another round to go, but they said, "That's it, Manny. You have gone around four times."

I stopped. I was feeling very exhausted, and my heart was pounding. I wasn't perspiring because I was so dry.

Someone took the baby from me, and then Henry said, "Okay, Manny, it's time to break loose. Its time for you to break from the skulls."

A big friend of mine from Olympia, Washington, a red-headed, freckle-faced Sundancer named Don said, "Manny, I'm with you, Brother. What do you need me to do?"

I asked him to sit on the first skull. Smiling at him, I said, "Hang on, Don, I'm going to take you for a ride." Smiling in return, he turned and walked toward the skulls.

Then my children Rockie and Becky sat on the second and third skulls, anchoring them so that I could break loose. After everyone was in place and ready, I stood as close as I could to the skulls. Another Sundancer was waiting to catch me.

I took off running at a full gallop. I was running fast and low. I wanted to make sure that I broke the first time. If a person doesn't break the first time, he has to try again and again until he succeeds.

At the last instant, right before I broke loose, I looked

over at Lessert, who had pierced my back. He was standing there looking, but not at my face. He looked at my back, and as I broke loose, I saw a look of disbelief on his face. He was surprised that I broke loose as easily as I did.

I had fulfilled my commitment to Grandfather. I had carried my baby around four times, as I had asked the Creator to help me do.

My job was done, and I had done it with honor, respect, and many prayers. The Great Spirit saw no reason for me to be hooked up to those skulls any longer, so he allowed me to break out on the first try.

We finished out the day with much joy and good wishes from other people. That day was a long and hot one, but a good one. It had been hard on me.

At this Sundance we were allowed to return to our camps. When I got back to mine, it was not quite dark. Many people were visiting each other, talking about the day. I sat by our camp in the shade.

Another Sundance Chief had come to support me. He sat down, and my girls brought him a cup of coffee and a sweet roll. "Manny, when are you coming to my Sundance?" he asked quietly.

"I'm doing this Sundance, then I have to go to the other one that asked for my help."

Disappointed, he said, "You could do the same with me. You could come help us. I would really like to have you there. You've got powerful medicine."

I started to feel swayed, because he was the man I had felt so good with the first time I did my piercing. He was persuading me to go with him. Then I thought of the controversies that surround the Sundances. And this Sundance Chief runs one of them. He doesn't want anyone but Lakota people or Native Americans to Sundance with him.

There are mixed feelings, egos, and politics involved in

certain Sundances, because they are becoming accepted by people from all over the world, people with different cultures and beliefs. Among the native people, there are arguments about whether to accept these outsiders or not. In some Sundance circles, the native people want to keep the Sundance exclusively a Native American ceremony. It depends on the Sundance Chief.

Although I'm not a Sundance Chief, I do have my own opinions, and I've been to the Sacred Tree enough times to feel that I can express them. Some Chiefs allow outsiders into their Sundance, to dance and worship with us. Yet others don't want anyone except Native or First Americans in their Sundance. Then there are some Sundance leaders who don't want anyone except Lakota (Sioux) dancing in theirs. I've heard some say, "We don't want any white people," or, "We don't want any Mexicans here." I'd like to ask them, "What is a Mexican? Isn't it a mixture of European and native? What is the blood line of the so-called full-bloods?" I'm sure that if there are any pure-bloods left, there are very few. Most people are of mixed heritage, whether we accept it or not. That doesn't make us love *Tunkashila* and the Sundance any less than the so-called full-bloods.

Then there is the matter of money. Who has the money to give us so that we can have a Sundance? The white people do. We native people certainly do not. The white people are the ones willing to help us, and all they ask in return is to be allowed to pray with us. Granted, there are people that use our way to profit and abuse our spirituality. But Grandfather can handle them. We can't blame all white people for the acts of a few. They don't like to be categorized any more than we do.

One Sundance Chief, Norbert, expressed it well when he said, "The Sundance flag has four colors in it. It doesn't belong just to us, it belongs to everyone who is willing to honor, respect, and sacrifice for our beliefs. If anyone is willing to learn, we should be willing to teach and not to judge other people by their color."

During my talk with the Sundance Chief, I explained that I felt I had committed myself enough for the year. Possibly in the future, I would Sundance with him.

He gave me a message that the Spirits told him to bring me. They told him that because of the way that I Sundance, and how often I've been pierced, that I was now ready to help people. I would be given two special stones as a way to help people. They would not be crystals, just ordinary stones, special healing stones with powerful medicine in them.

This was ironic to me because, unknown to him, I made a good part of my living making "Stone People Medicine." The process of creating these small stones was also brought to me in an unusual way, and now I was selling them all over the world. What he was telling me seemed quite a coincidence.

He told me I would know when they came to me, it would be under such unusual circumstances that I would know. "Manny, I don't know why I am saying this to you or doing this. I was told to do it, so there it is."

I replied, "I don't know anything about healing. I wouldn't know what to do or say."

He said, "No, none of us do. We all have to learn. When it comes to you, you will know and you will be shown the way. The same way you were told to come to the Sundance and pierce. You will know what to say, what to do. It's going to be very good for you. Remember, it's not you doing it, it's the Spirits helping you do it. With the stones, you will help people."

Here was the message that the spotted eagle had given me in the Shoshoni Sundance: that I will be shown how and when to help people. Just as the eagle had given me the message, now it was brought to me again by a medicine man. This message could not have come from a stronger source. I had to believe this Sundance Chief's message was from the spirit of the spotted eagle.

I have always had problems with words like "healer," "healing," and things related. There are too many people claiming they can heal, sometimes with profit being the only intention, so I use these words carefully. This message telling me I was to heal people was told to me by a Sundance Chief who had received the message from the Spirits, and so I believed it wholeheartedly. Neither of us had anything to gain from this, because there is never any charge for spiritual healing of this kind. I never hold out my hand for money for what I do.

It is also known that once you have suffered at the Sundance for four years, you have earned the privilege and the right to give blessings to people in the name of the Creator. To cleanse houses, cleanse people, give names, whatever people ask for you to do, you can do. You have earned the privilege and the right.

We left the Sundance. My brother Henry from Maryland was having a Sundance two weeks after that, and I told him that I couldn't make it. He asked me, "Come over. I really need you."

I said, "Henry if I can, I will, and if I don't, it's because I'm not supposed to be there."

We headed south to Oklahoma, so my kids could see some of their old friends. From there we went to Arkansas to see some of Melody's friends, and then on to Memphis, where we stopped to have breakfast with some dear, old friends, John and Betty.

Something very interesting occurred after breakfast. Taking me aside, John told me he had something for me. It was my first sign since my conversation with the Sundance

Chief. John honored me with a beautiful, smooth stone and explained that he knew I needed it for something—he wasn't sure what. It was quite an honor and exciting to receive this gift so soon after being told it would come to me. I hadn't seen John in years. He knew nothing about what the Sundance Chief had told me, yet here he was giving me a stone. After he had given it to me, I told him everything. He just gave me a knowing smile.

Then we headed north toward a powwow in Ohio. I was honored when they asked me to do the blessing of the grounds. I did it in an unusual way: I used four veterans because we as natives have always respected and honored the warriors. I put one in each direction to guard that entrance. When the prayer was over, I brought them back in. It was a beautiful ceremony and a fantastic powwow. We were there for three days.

During the powwow, another interesting event happened to me. A non-native woman set up next to us and approached me with a gift: a stone. She explained that she'd been carrying it for about two months and didn't really know why. She had picked it up at a Sundance in Northern Ontario, near Manitoulin Island. Her son had been in the Sundance, and while there she was told by the Spirits to bring this stone with her to Ohio. She had no idea whom it was for or why she was bringing it, but she was told it was for someone.

When she presented it to me, she felt good and became very emotional. She knew that it belonged to someone else, that it wasn't hers. Her only job was to carry it to the person it belonged to, and she realized who that person was the minute she saw me. When she gave me the stone, I knew instinctively that this was the second of the two stones I had been waiting for.

That's the way things happen when you are in this spiritual world or are communicating with the Spirits. The Spirits create a drama, so you remember that it is not you, but they, who are doing the healing. They teach you how to use the signs they send in the right way. It might seem unusual, but it is very real.

Right after the powwow we stopped at a campground. We checked our messages from home and found out that one of our customers from Baltimore had called and said she needed a large shipment of our crafts. When Melody returned the call, she took the order, and it was quite substantial— enough for us to drive there to deliver it. We still had a couple of weeks before the kids had to return to school.

We would also be able to visit my Sundance brother Henry and some of our friends who lived in the area. Melody was happy to go there because she knew that Henry's Sundance had been the weekend before, so I wouldn't be tempted to participate.

When we got to Baltimore, it was hot and humid. We paid for a motel room and just kicked back for the rest of that day. The next morning we went to our customer's store. During our conversation, she mentioned, "There's a woman I know who always dances at Henry's Sundances. She told me that they're getting ready. In fact, they start today."

It was Thursday. Henry's Sundance must have been rescheduled. I looked at my wife.

Melody said, "I can't believe this. It was supposed to have been last weekend."

The store owner said, "It was. They changed the date for some reason or other. I don't know why."

Melody did not want me to Sundance again because of my sunburn and because it would be my second Sundance in a couple of weeks. It was getting a bit hard for this old man. We called on another customer, then headed out to Henry's place, where the Sundance was.

When we arrived, there was already quite a crowd singing and dancing. They'd gone in that morning.

When Henry and Harold saw me, they were very happy. We all got emotional. Here I was, needed, and I didn't know it. The Spirits had again manipulated my life to take me where I was needed, and where I had to be. After their greeting, I told them, "Look, I've got my trailer over at a campground. We'll get here early, and I'll dance with you tomorrow."

Everybody was really happy, except Melody. She was a bit upset because she knew it had been Henry's prayers that had brought us here. She was worried about my health after the previous Sundance.

That evening, while we were having dinner together, Melody dropped a bomb. "I'm going in to Sundance with you tomorrow. I want to be there with you and for you," she said.

We both started to cry. I felt like the whole dining room had gone quiet. It was the last thing I expected to hear from Melody. Once, shortly after meeting in Tucson, Melody said that if there was ever a time I couldn't Sundance for health reasons, she'd go in my place. It humbled me that she would consider going through it, especially now. My daughter Becky also wanted to go in.

The next day, we brought our trailer and set it up at Henry's. Becky, Melody, and I went into the Sundance later that morning. My son Rockie didn't go in. He wasn't ready for another one so soon.

They took us to a sweat lodge, then we entered the Arbor from the east and started Sundancing. It was wonderful to have Melody there, and to have Becky with me again. This was a small Sundance, but a good one, a powerful one.

The day before, we saw a young native man named Jim

178

lying on the ground. Since the morning before he'd been suffering with a severe migraine headache. Melody had asked me to try to help him.

I said, "No, it's not time. He's paying some kind of Karma, or he's suffering for a reason. It's not time. If he's like that tomorrow, I'll help him."

The next day, I saw Jim again, still very sick. I went right to him and told him, "Come on, get up."

He said, "No, I can't. I'm too sick. My head hurts bad."

I asked him to come into the Sweat Lodge with me. I called some others, to make four warriors. I felt I needed them to form my healing circle: one warrior for each direction. We took him inside for about half an hour. (What the spirits bring to a person in this ceremony is not for public knowledge, so I cannot divulge it here.) Coming out, we took Jim and laid him back down where he was before. He lay there for a while. During a break, I went over and visited with some friends. Not long after, Jim came up to me. His eyes were as clear as could be where they had been full of pain and anguish before.

With a big smile, he said, "Manny, I want to thank you for doing whatever it was you did. I don't know what kind of medicine you have, but it is good. You're gonna help a lot of people."

He shook my hand and went back to his spot under the Arbor. He was really grateful, and I was surprised that I had done something so positive. The Spirits brought Jim to me to help me see how this healing worked.

After that, I found out that I was there for several reasons. First was because Henry wanted to be the first to be pierced at his own Sundance. He had never been pierced because there had never been anybody qualified to do it. He asked me if I would, and of course, I couldn't refuse him. We danced the next day, and I pierced him.

That morning, Melody and I rested on separate blankets between rounds. When I got up to put my sage crown on, my piercing bones fell out. I had inserted them in the side of my crown, so they'd be handy. Melody looked at me, but I didn't say anything. She knew that I felt they fell out because I should use them again. She had a sick look on her face.

The next day, I told Henry I wanted to be pierced, last piercing round. During the break, Harold came up to me and said, "Manny, I want to pierce for you in your place. You've done enough for us already."

Very moved by the gesture, I said, "Harold, you don't have to do that for me. It's my obligation."

"Manny, please, let me have this privilege."

I looked at him for a long, long time, thinking and asking myself if this was something that could be passed to someone else. Harold wouldn't give me a chance to think it over any more. He asked me for my piercing bones.

By this time, Melody was crying and thanking Harold. She was really worried about my health. Melody honored Harold with a special gift, to give thanks. She gave him something that meant a great deal to her. It was a large obsidian arrowhead necklace that I had made for her when we first met.

My brother Harold's gesture moved me deeply. It created a stronger bond between us. Strangely enough, when Harold was pierced, halfway through the song the piercings on both sides suddenly fell off. It was amazing. Neither Harold nor I could believe it, but both of us were happy.

That Sundance was beautiful. Many people came and honored me, and brought my family many things. I was humbled by the experience. It was my second Sundance in one year and I thought, "I may be getting a bit too old for this. Past the half-century mark and still dancing like that?"

My wife said that it served as an inspiration to the younger people coming up. Seeing a guy like me who's diabetic and has high blood pressure, dancing and suffering, encouraged them to go on.

We finished our commitment to Henry's Sundance, packed up our trailer, and headed back to Canada.

INNER — PURPLE

"Spirit Within"

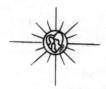

SPIRITUALLY FULFILLED

Life in Canada was beautiful. When we arrived, though it was early in September, a blanket of autumn was already starting to cover the landscape of rolling hills. The trees looked happy to be shedding their green leaves of summer. They seemed to be dancing with joy as they displayed their new fall dresses of golden and crimson leaves.

Later that same year, we had another tragedy strike our family. While coming back from a show in Montreal, I was beginning to have severe pain in my abdomen. I kept passing it off as indigestion, but it grew progressively worse. On the drive back, I was complaining about my weight and said to Melody, "Wouldn't it be nice if I could just go to a hospital somewhere and lose weight!" That taught me to be careful what I ask for.

After four days of constant pain, I felt I couldn't handle it anymore. I was hesitant to go to the hospital because I didn't have any medical insurance. In Canada, every resident has free medical coverage, but I did not have access to it because I was an American.

One evening, I was lying down and didn't want to get up. Melody and the kids were worried. While I was lying there, it occurred to me that I should try to heal myself using the stones I was given. I started praying with them. I asked God, if they really worked, to heal me—not just for my own purposes, but also for my family. Shortly after that, the pain forced me to give in to Melody's wishes and go to York-Central Hospital.

When we arrived at the emergency room, the doctor told me that I was a very sick man and would not be able to leave. When they told me how much it would cost per day, I started to get up to leave. The doctor told me to wait, that something could be worked out financially. He also secretly told me that I could not be refused medical attention and surgery if needed.

After being admitted, I remained there for ten days. During that time I contracted pneumonia, and the infection meant they couldn't remove the gallstones they had found in my gall bladder. I was on intravenous fluids and antibiotics my entire stay in the hospital. No food or water. I lost twenty-five pounds.

The pneumonia was so persistent, they decided to release me for a couple of weeks until the infection cleared up and they could operate to remove the gallstones. The last day before I left, they put me through several more tests.

 184

When the doctor in charge of my case came in with the X rays, he had an astonished look on his face. He couldn't believe what he saw. The gallstones had dissolved. They simply weren't there anymore, but they knew I hadn't passed them. He said that in all his years as a doctor, he had never seen anything like it. I tried to explain to him about the healing I had given myself, but he seemed to dismiss it entirely.

Maybe this form of medicine is just too intimidating in this day of advanced technology? Perhaps it is lack of belief? Personally, I knew it was the healing I did on myself that dissolved the gallstones. It didn't really matter whether he believed it or not; I knew my medicine had helped me cure myself. It's like the old expression "Physician, heal thyself," meaning, the true doctor or man of medicine should be able to heal himself in order to offer methods of healing to others. I felt the Creator brought me a way to heal myself, to make me realize that I also could help others. It helped me to build confidence in the new way of healing I had received.

I went home to recuperate. The entire ordeal put a tremendous strain on my family and our finances. We mulled over what to do for most of the month.

That winter the Canadian economy started a slow downward slide. Our customers were wary of buying more stock because of the way things were going. Our business was in trouble. Sales were way down. Everywhere we went the story was the same. "Your things are beautiful, but we're not buying now." This worried me. No sales and the price of food inched higher and higher every day. It was a sickening feeling to go out day after day and come home with little or no money.

I started praying hard to Grandfather and asked him to bring me direction, to show me a way to get my family into a better situation. As if by a miracle, I started receiving in my thoughts an answer to my prayers. At first I didn't want to say anything to anyone. I didn't want to build their hopes up if I couldn't fulfill what I was thinking. My thoughts kept saying, move back to the States.

On the afternoon of November 30, when I finally mentioned it to Melody, a look of delight came over her face.

"If only we could," she cried. "It could be the answer to all my prayers."

The next day was a Friday, and we were going to go out again to try to sell. We were facing a pretty slim weekend if we didn't sell anything. We made several calls without success. In desperation, I thought about a store that had called me the year before. At the time, the owner had asked me to stop by with my crafts. I don't know why, but I never went to see him. Now I was desperate and searching for an angel.

We pulled into Upper Canada mall parking lot in Newmarket where his store, "Nature's Yard," was and called him from the car phone. Michael came on the line and was really glad to hear from us. He asked us where we were calling from, and when we said from the parking lot, he told us to come right up.

Taking one look at all the crafts we had, he paused for a minute. Then he took everything we were holding, put it to the side, and said, "I'll take all this, and triple it for my other two stores as soon as possible." He asked us to balance it out so there would be an equal amount for each store.

My head was spinning. We started taking inventory of what we had on hand. It was quite a substantial amount. Tripling it answered our prayers for a way to move to the States. Melody was amazed!

After that day, we gave notice to our landlord, and an interesting thing started to happen. People came out of the woodwork to buy our crafts. Everything fell into place for us to go. That is usually how you can tell if you're on the right track about something. If you find most things keep going wrong, and there are obstacles everywhere you turn, rethink what you're doing and try something else. You'll know it's right if everything goes your way. When you're on the right path, obstacles disappear. We knew all this money coming in wasn't to keep us there. It was Grandfather's way to get us going.

On December 19, exactly twenty days after deciding to move, we were on the road to Arizona. In that short time, we had packed, sold all our furniture, closed our lives in Canada, and headed out. It was an emotional time for Melody. She had always wanted to move to the States, and now it was happening. She was leaving her friends and family behind to make a fresh start.

On Christmas day, we arrived at my mom's house in Ajo, Arizona. It was a wonderful Christmas. Most of my children had never met or known their grandparents. After losing their mother, it was good for them to have a sense of family. My sisters and brother all made them feel welcome and loved. It was also the first time Melody met my mom and dad. After visiting for a couple of days, we headed for Phoenix to find our new home.

It took us about a year to get situated and get our business off the ground. Unfortunately, when Sundance season came about that summer we didn't have the money to go. Perhaps Grandfather was keeping us from going, for whatever reason. This really depressed me. It was the first year I would miss the Lakota Sundance since I had started. It was a difficult thing for me to face.

The remainder of the year was spent growing our business and expanding our product line. I found myself on the road a lot. Phoenix couldn't support us the way Toronto had, so Melody had to hold the fort by herself often. We were careful not to be separated for longer than three weeks in a row. We didn't want what had happened in my previous marriage to happen to us.

That February while set up in Tucson at the gem and mineral show, we received word of my dad's passing. We immediately packed up and prepared for the funeral.

By the spring of 1994, I had made the commitment to go to the Sundance no matter what the expense. Even if I had to go by myself, I was not going to miss another one.

As an elder, it was my responsibility to help organize things, so on the first weekend in July, I had an orientation meeting at Marge and Mario's house in Altadena, California, for anyone who wanted to attend. At the meeting, we found out there would be another Sundance in Colorado, being put on by the same Sundance Chief, David Swallow. The South Dakota Sundance was scheduled for the middle of August, but the one in Colorado was slated for the middle of July. This made it a better time for us to attend, and financially easier, so we decided to go to Colorado.

We had two weeks to prepare. In order to raise some cash for the Sundance I had to make a quick sales trip to northern California. The trip was tough. Everywhere I went, people said they were worried about the economy and didn't have any money. I found it very hard to make a sale, but I was determined to go to the Sundance. Slowly, from a small sale here and another one there, I gathered and saved the money we needed.

On the day we left Phoenix, the temperature was 115 degrees. We took two vans and pulled our pop-up trailer. My son stayed home, and our five girls came along. What an adventure! Their energies and temperaments are so different from each other, it made for an interesting and challenging trip—to say the least. I had to handle the reins of that team with one iron fist and one kid glove.

We stopped in Albuquerque to pick up Rose Marie, who wanted to attend the Sundance with us. She was a healer I had met at a Whole Life expo in Albuquerque (it's a combination psychic fair and alternative-healing exhibition), and it was her dream to go to a Sundance. So she came with us and helped with the driving.

We arrived at the Sundance grounds, near the town of Buffalo Creek, the next evening well before dark. The natural beauty of the camping grounds around the Arbor was absolutely breathtaking. Yet it appeared that Mother Nature had manicured the area just for our benefit. The Arbor was big and had fresh-cut evergreen boughs lying over it, offering a wonderful shade. With the Rocky Mountains surrounding us, it was an ideal camping spot.

The Sundance Chief, David Swallow, was very happy to see me with my family. He asked me to set up in a spot next to his camp. There was a clear brook running nearby, lots of trees, and a beautiful landscape. Nature had been busy, making the meeting place for the Spirits and the humans a place to remember.

Sunday was tree day. Rose Marie and Melody had driven into town for supplies and groceries. When it came time to get the tree, excitedly the people in our camp got ready to go. There were a couple of my adopted nephews from California. They had come to pray and offer their support to all the other dancers. There was Big Jon from Los Angeles, Little John from Benecia, and Mario, who had come to dance and pierce from Pomona with his girlfriend, Taran. (Another nephew, Paul from Cerritos, didn't arrive until the following day.)

By this time a large crowd was gathering. I called my girls and started following the others. I felt something in my stomach. Some people call it "butterflies." To me it was more like a restless spirit within me. A spirit that wanted to be noticed, not just with indifference, but with emotion.

Of all the tree ceremonies I have mentioned so far, this one touched me the most, and I don't know if it was because of the loss of my dad, or if it was the pain that I felt for my mother. I hadn't shed any tears since my father's passing, but now I cried for my mother's pain and anguish. They had just celebrated their sixty-first wedding anniversary before he died.

Somehow the words David said at this tree moved me as no others had. Somehow I related the tree giving its life so we could Sundance, to my father giving life to four other siblings and me. Suddenly, I felt as if the spirit of my father was within the tree, talking to me. As the first axe strike hit the tree, I felt a profound sorrow for that tree. Perhaps I felt that it was passing on to another life just as my dad had done recently. I know deep inside there was a relationship between the two events.

For the first time since his passing, tears came to my eyes that were just for him. A part of my sorrow had to do with unresolved differences between us. There would be no other opportunity to talk things over. There had been so many feelings, thoughts, and experiences I wanted to share with him. Now that wasn't possible. Through the years it seemed that every time I went home, things would be fine for a couple of days, then our relationship would begin to feel strained. I truly would have loved to find out what it was about me that made him react the way he did. Regrettably, we never had that opportunity. The chance for resolution was no longer there, and for that reason I was mourning. In my mind and heart, I dedicated this Sundance to my dad's memory.

The tree went up as beautiful and as proud as all the others. Many people tied their ropes and prayer ties on it.

There were many things being asked of the tree. The energy was high around the Arbor. We all returned to our camps to prepare for the next day. We left the Sacred Tree alone at last as if to give it the respect and time it needed to prepare itself for us and the next four days.

Monday morning, Grandfather blessed us with a warm and cloudy day. Long before sunrise, Sundancers from all over gathered around the fire pit, getting ready to go into the sweat lodges. Melody and I got up, grabbed our towels, and headed down to the same place.

The smell of dust was already starting to make its presence known. It mingled with the wood smoke rising from the fire pit. I could see a few Grandfather rocks poking their red-hot faces through the mounds of hot coals. The coals and ashes also were giving us their pleasant and distant smell.

Crawling in on my hands and knees, I felt something almost like an embrace from the sweat lodge. What a comforting feeling. As we sat there quietly, waiting for the Sweat Lodge ceremony to begin. I felt a tremendous sense of relief as one of the dancers started softly singing the "Four Directions" song.

I ran into an old Sundance brother and leader, Bo from South Dakota. Everyone was in a jovial mood. When enough guys were ready to fill the sweat lodge, we started the first sweat. It was good and hot.

Returning to camp, I started getting ready. When Melody returned she got all her things, including her bedding, and moved to the woman's tepee. She was going to be dancing for four days and couldn't return to camp for any reason. There was a pain in my chest for her because I knew the ache of hunger and the deep knife thrust of thirst that she would soon be enduring.

My heart went out to her, but she wanted to pray and was determined to do it. All I could do was be there, be strong for her, and help her pray. She was praying for me—that was important to her—and in turn, I would pray for her. There was nothing personally to gain from being there. Only others to whom the prayers are directed would gain anything.

As I look back on it, day one passed rather swiftly, but at the time it seemed long and slow. It's amazing how quickly we forget the pain and the thirst. Several people pierced that day, and we all danced hard.

The second day I received word that my good friend Dick Smith, his wife Connie, and her father had arrived from Burbank, California, to support me. This day was harder—everyone was thirstier and hungry. I had a commitment to drag buffalo skulls and was going to do it on the last day. However, when I thought more about it, I decided that I should do it on the second day, while I still had the strength.

That morning, I picked up my baby girl, Oriona, and she nuzzled me with her nose and gave me a kiss on the cheek. "Daddy, can I dance with you today?" she asked.

I'm not sure if she remembered the time I carried her in the Sundance two years before, but it was almost as if she knew I was going to be dragging skulls. It really touched me. As I embraced her I said to her, "Sure you can, Honey. You're gonna dance with Daddy."

So after going in, we put our pipes on the altar and the dancing started in earnest. The very first piercing round was the round for me to drag the skulls. Right away I got my back marked to show where I wanted to be pierced. I told David and Bo that I wanted to stay pierced and drag the skulls. They needed to pierce me deeply, so I could try to drag the skulls all four rounds. There were eight, fairly large skulls.

They took me to the tree to pray. After a couple of minutes, a Sundance leader asked me if I was ready. I nodded yes. I walked over and stood on the buffalo hide. With David on one side and Bo on the other, I handed them my piercing bones. I felt David grab the flesh on my back. I felt the knife cut into my back, but my prayers were so deep and intense there was very little pain. By the time it was Bo's turn to pierce my right side, my prayers for strength had been answered—I didn't feel a thing.

Suddenly, as if awakening, I felt both of them grab my arms and lead me toward the west side of the Arbor. Melody handed me Oriona. She was smiling and looking around at everyone with curiosity on her face rather than fright.

There were eight warriors carrying the eight skulls behind me. David believes that each man dragging skulls should at least make one complete circle with the skulls attached to his back. Therefore he had the skulls carried by the warriors one full circle around the Arbor. While we were dancing, I heard someone say, "*Wamblee*, eagle!" I raised my head and saw two beautiful spotted eagles circling the Arbor directly above us. Since I was dancing, I couldn't keep looking at them, but I was told that they disappeared into the sun. I was really honored to have their presence while I danced and pierced. It meant that all my prayers would be answered and anyone praying with me would have their prayers answered.

Getting back around to the west side, the warriors put down the skulls. It was my time to move them by myself. As I started leaning into the rope, at first I felt like I was trying to pull the world. Ever so slightly I felt the skulls start to move. Then suddenly the left side broke loose. My thoughts were that I didn't want to break yet. I wanted to drag the skulls, so as carefully as I could, I continued pulling with my other side. The weight was too much, my right side broke loose as the skulls started to move again. I suppose Grandfather didn't want me to go through the pain and suffering required to move that kind of weight.

When I broke loose, I yelled with joy and ran around

the Arbor, holding the baby. This was my third time dragging skulls, and I was happy to have made it through again.

I returned Oriona to my wife and went to the center of the Arbor, the Sacred Tree. After praying and giving thanks at the tree, David and Bo were waiting for me to finish my prayers. When I was through, they turned me around. The pieces of flesh that were hanging off my back were cut off and placed in small pieces of red cloth. They were my flesh offerings and were tied to the tree.

Many people ask me, "Why do you pierce? Why do you mutilate your body like this?"

It's not mutilation or self-torture. It is our way, our very sacred way of giving a small piece of the only thing we truly own, our bodies. We feel that anything other than the body is something material that we can live without. Flesh, blood, and pain is all we truly own. It is the flesh of the body that houses our spirit and soul. Piercing is a way to give our living flesh to the spirit world, so the Spirits will listen to our prayers and pleas.

More men pierced and prayed and broke loose. It was a beautiful Sundance. The singers' voices were still strong, and we had two drums singing all the sacred songs for us. Again we were blessed with a partly cloudy sky. When the sun was out and hot, Grandfather would always bring us a cloud to cool us off a bit.

I had been on blood pressure pills for several years and diabetes medication since 1991. My wife was very concerned about this because we had accidentally forgotten the high-blood-pressure pills. At high altitudes my blood pressure would rise, my head would start buzzing, and I'd get very sick.

When we were dancing, Melody and several others were praying I could overcome this illness. All their prayers for me have been answered. Since that Sundance, I haven't had to take any blood pressure pills, and I am down to one diabetes pill a day (quite a drop from the three I was taking before.)

On the third day, one of my twin daughters, Becky, joined us in the Sundance Arbor. She had wanted to dance all four days. As an old experienced Sundancer, I knew how hard this was, so I convinced her to dance only the last two days.

The third day was the healing ceremony. It seemed like all the people who were there to support us gathered around the Arbor for healing from the Sundancers. We believe that within the Sacred Circle, every Sundancer who willingly goes in to suffer and give of himself or of herself has the right to be a healing tool. That Sundancer earns the right, during that special day, to offer healing with the Creator's blessing. Every dancer slowly proceeded around the Arbor, doing their best to help the people who were lined up. The ceremony lasted about four hours, and many people cried when the Sundancers prayed for them.

When we were getting our pipes from the altar, Melody looked up and saw a cloud. It was in the exact shape of a buffalo skull. When she pointed it out, several other dancers also saw it. It was clear; there was no doubting that it was a buffalo skull. It was a good medicine sign that meant strength and abundance for everyone. The day was longer than usual. We didn't get out of the Arbor until long after dark.

Day three was over, and everyone was tired. I could tell the thirst was taking its toll on all of us. I could see Melody suffering quite a bit. Incidentally, it was Melody's birthday, and she was happy to be helping others and to be at the Sundance on her special day. Becky was having a very hard time; she hadn't realized how hard David's Sundance would be. By the end of the first day, she was glad she had committed to only two days.

The final day arrived, and it was the hottest day since

the Sundance had begun. The morning was beautiful, bright, and sunny. We were told the day would be shorter than the others. Everyone was happy. They had all undergone a very challenging trial and had made it. Many others who had only made a one-day commitment joined on the last day to dance.

The Sundance leaders and helpers (including me) had to be pierced on the last piercing round. When the time came, we all gathered in the center. One by one, all the Sundance leaders were pierced.

I wanted Melody to be with me when I was pierced, so I asked the women's Sundance Leader, Pansy, to bring Melody to the tree. She brought Melody a couple of minutes early and told Melody to get on her knees. When Melody knelt down, her knees landed on the small, hot pebbles. Her knees blistered and burned.

When they pierced me, we all moved to the southwest side of the Arbor. I was happy to see Rose Marie; my daughters Stormy, Mary, Dory, and Oriona; my nephews, John, Jon, and Paul. They were all there supporting me. We danced until it was time to break loose. There were four of us piercing this last round. We all broke loose. Al and Bernice's son, Richard, was called in to do the piercing on David. He danced strong and hard while dragging the skulls. It's very difficult to drag skulls far when they are so heavy and there are so many.

During the last couple of rounds, your mind races frantically. Who still needed prayers, or whom may I have missed? You realize that the time to Sundance is ending until next year. Although you can pray to the Creator anytime, it's as though your prayers are stronger during this sacred ceremony. I'm sure everyone goes through this experience before the four days are over.

Since it was David's last time to Sundance in the Arbor

in Colorado, it was a very special year for him. You could see he was leaving a part of himself behind, as others had before him. The people had lost their previous Sundance Chief to the Creator and had asked David to run the Sundance. It was his fourth and last year. His commitment to the Denver people was complete. They would have to choose another Sundance Chief.

We left Buffalo Creek the next morning and stayed around the Boulder, Colorado, area for the next couple of weeks. We were recuperating, making crafts at the campsite, and wholesaling to native craft shops.

The remainder of 1994 was spent selling our crafts and getting ready for the next Sundance. As 1995 began, some changes occurred. My son Rockie turned eighteen and decided to move out, to test his wings and perhaps grow up a bit. That made it a lot easier on Melody. Now all she had were the girls to take care of.

Our business was growing and getting better all the time. We were very fortunate to have become so successful with our spiritual crafts—the Stone People Medicine, Medicine Circles (Wheels), Spirit Crystals, Dream Keepers, and Dream Catchers.

It seems the spirits were pleased with my willingness to give of myself. They rewarded me with a way to make a living that not only helps people, but helps me feed my family. With my health affecting my work, I was grateful to have a creative method to make a living that didn't take its toll on me physically. Everything is created in an assembly-line fashion at home. All the girls, including Oriona, help out in some way. Everyone has a job. It teaches the girls a way to make a living and helps develop their creativity.

Our Stone People Medicine has become incredibly popular, and we now have customers in Israel, Japan, Europe, New Zealand, and the U.K. We have so many letters from people thanking us for our Dream Catchers, Medicine Wheels, and Stone People Medicine. They are testimonials that we are doing the right thing.

On several occasions, people have approached me and pointed at the Dream Catchers, and said they don't work. They said that their child's sleep was more disturbed and that the child was not sleeping well at all. The Dream Catchers do work, but what most people don't know is that only the ones made by medicine people will work. Dream Catchers made by others, people who don't know their significance, are just decorations. They have no spiritual medicine to work the way they are supposed to.

If you're thinking of buying one, find out who made it and what kind of person they are. Ask about their spirituality. Ask if they have earned the right to make spiritual items like that. Yours or your child's well-being is at stake. Be sure the person you get one from is someone you're comfortable with. Every Dream Catcher we make has a card on it saying the following:

THE DREAM CATCHER

A very old native belief, that as you sleep and dream, the dreams good or bad, leave you to come true. They are attracted to the Dream Catcher's web by the Dream Spirits. The web permits the good dreams to escape through the round hole in the web and become reality. The bad dreams get stuck in the web and vanish with the first rays of the new sunlight.

The dates for the 1995 Sundance were August 9th for tree day, with the actual dance occurring from the 10th through the 13th.

There were several people who had told me they wanted to go to the Sundance to either support or dance. This amazed me because it was such a distance to journey. Most people only have to travel within their own city to pray, and now these people were willing to travel great distances to join us in our prayers.

We were glad to be going to South Dakota, where the Sundance in Porcupine is very traditional. I hadn't seen Al, Bernice, and Richard Tail since 1991, so I was happy to be going there again. A lot had happened in four years.

As the time grew closer, we had decided to make some changes in our lives. I went east for a month to set up at four native arts and craft shows. While I was gone, Melody and the girls got ready for us to move. They had yard sales every weekend and sold all our furniture and other things. We decided to move into a trailer for a few months. This was a fairly last-minute decision, sparked mostly by the high cost of living where we were. Melody also decided to home-school the girls because she was unhappy with what public schools offered. This also allowed us to be mobile and spend more time together as a family. The way things were, I had to do a lot of traveling alone.

Melody managed to fly up to Chicago to do the last show with me at Notre Dame University campus. It was very successful, but the whirlwind of activity really started when we got back to Phoenix. We had to rent a storage space, sell the rest of our things, pack what was left, and get ready to move. We bought another comfortable travel trailer (after selling the pop-up) that slept eight.

During our yard sales, the heat was unbearable. It was as though the Spirits were angry with Phoenix. It seemed the very ground itself groaned with the blistering waves of heat. It was miserable.

The day to leave the house had finally arrived, and it

was the hottest day of the year. Phoenix was having record-high temperatures, and the peak that day was 125 degrees. We left that home for the last time at around 3:30 in the afternoon. Melody didn't have air conditioning in her van, and I couldn't use the a/c in mine because I was pulling the trailer. So we were hot and anxious to get going. Then disaster hit.

Melody had gone on to check the mail and would meet me at the gas station. I was about six blocks from our house when suddenly the radiator hose blew, and I had to stop. I managed to pull into the parking lot of a gas station. After all that we had been through, this single obstacle almost made me have a nervous breakdown. It was rush hour, and road service couldn't get to me for at least two hours, since there were so many cars breaking down because of the heat. We still had to drive about three hours to my mother's house in Ajo, and we were stopped short.

Both Melody and I believe that everything happens for a reason, and as hard as that philosophy is to take sometimes, it was all we had right then. Gratefully, I called my sister Virgie's husband, Jerry, for help. I was thankful that he was there to help us. He helps everyone in the family with their vehicles, and he got there in about an hour. After much running around to get the right part, we were finally on the road again around eight o'clock. Everyone was exhausted, hungry, and ready for bed, so we decided to stay in Phoenix that night and leave the next morning. No one really noticed Melody's face.

The next day, we had some more running around to do, and we were on the road by noon. The heat was up to 115, and it was getting worse. None of us realized that with the windows open, driving in the heat was similar to putting your face in front of an oven for a couple of hours. By the time we got to Ajo, Melody's face was bright red and very badly burned from the heat. She also had sun stroke and was pretty sick. Her face had actually blistered from the heat and wind burn.

We decided to spend a couple of days in Ajo at my mom's, before setting out for South Dakota. It was just the medicine we all needed. My mom's house is the only place on earth where I feel I can truly relax and rest.

On Sunday I discovered that my piercing bones had been left in storage in Phoenix. As much as I hated to go back, once I'd started out on a trip I had no choice. My piercing bones were too important to be left behind. I suppose I could have made other ones, but these were special, and I had worked long and hard getting them ready for the ceremony.

Early Monday morning, we headed for South Dakota. Our first night on the road was spent in Truth or Consequences, New Mexico. Melody's face was a swollen mess. She was in agony, and I didn't know how to help her except to treat it as a severe sunburn. We were putting sunburn lotion and spraying cool water on her face. The burn was so deep that it remained hot. The only thing we could do was keep it cool.

When we reached Albuquerque, Melody went to a pharmacy and was very relieved to find a cream that completely eased her pain. Within hours she felt and looked a lot better. She was sensing that maybe the Creator didn't want her to Sundance, and she didn't want to meet all the people coming to the Sundance looking like a creature from *Star Trek*.

We arrived in Rapid City on Friday and set up at the KOA Campground. It was the same weekend as the motorcycle rally in Sturgis, South Dakota, that turned South Dakota into Motorcycle State. There were bikers from all over the United States and Canada. I was a little nervous about my girls going anywhere alone, but we made it to

Sunday without incident. All of the bikers we encountered acted respectful. Many were family men, and some had their ladies with them.

While there, we shopped for our giveaways. It was Becky's fourth Sundance, and my fourth with David Swallow Jr. We wanted to honor the Sundance and all those people we Sundanced with. It was also Lionel's giveaway, so he met us in Rapid City and bought the things he needed as well. The people who danced with me—drummers, singers, the Sundance Chief, the Sundance leaders—all had to be honored. We wanted to give some of the Sundancers' families things they may not have otherwise been able to get.

The people on the Pineridge reservation have the highest unemployment rate in North America, and life is very difficult for them. The government supplies them only with starchy foods and commodity cheese. Unlike so many other underprivileged cultures, the Native American people by nature are not complainers. They have a lot of pride. It's like the old adage, "The squeaky wheel gets the grease." Perhaps if they complained and lamented more about their plight, like so many other cultures, there would be more help available. What a tragedy that in such a rich and diverse country as the United States a lifestyle of poverty and deprivation has been left to the original people of this land.

The winter months are especially hard. It's hard to imagine what these people do when they run out of propane or need warm clothes. They are always getting hand-me-downs or, worse, nothing at all.

It was important to Melody that they receive some new things, so we did what we could. We also arranged for watermelons to be picked up on the last day of the Sundance. We wanted to get at least fifty watermelons—covered with ice and ready to be eaten—for the hungry and thirsty Sundancers when they came out on the last day.

Driving on to the reservation Sunday afternoon, I had a mixture of anticipation, nervousness, and relief. We had made it again. It was my time to give thanks to the Creator, and I was grateful that the Creator allowed me to come again to pray.

The Badlands were spectacular in their beauty and colors, but unyielding and harsh in the heat. The glorious sunsets and sunrises reminded us of the work of the Great Spirit. Yet Sundancing on this land was excruciating when it was hot and the ground was full of stickers.

At times I envy the quiet relatives who live on this wonderful land. They seem to absorb the quietness of the land into their souls. Then I think about the hard life they endure day after day, and I realize I'm glad that I am where I am. Still my heart aches for them. I wish I could have them all with me always.

Arriving on the Sundance grounds, several people who had come on my invitation were already there. Snowy and Conrado from San Diego had arrived a few days before to help any way they could, and Billy from Texas was there to do the same.

We set up camp, then Melody and I walked around to see who was there. The grounds were so quiet. Everyone seemed to be in their own separate worlds preparing for the days ahead. There was a lot that needed to be done before the Sundance started, and David Swallow Jr. had not arrived yet.

Bernice and Al Tail were welcome sights. They were the first people we saw as we started visiting.

Soon others I had invited arrived: Jon and Jodi from Las Vegas; Phil from Hemet, California; Mario from Pomona, California; Arthur from Searchlight, Nevada, with his nephew Mike; Bert (an herbalist and natural healer) and Big Jon from Los Angeles; Dale and Terry from Ontario, Canada;

Suzanne from Woodland Hills and Judy from Santa Maria, California; Karen from Missouri; Jason from Landers, California; Gil from Riverside, California; his sister Thelma and her husband, Raul, from Silver City, New Mexico; Rose Marie and her husband, Marshall, from Rio Rancho, New Mexico; and Lauren (the first editor of this book) from New York City. They all honored me by coming to help or to Sundance. All of them arrived at our sacred ground as though pulled by invisible strings tied to their hearts and souls. It was touching that the Creator had given me the gift of knowing to invite all these beautiful people. To see this group of selfless individuals make this incredible journey to suffer and pray truly warmed my heart.

It is important for me to mention these people, especially because they all traveled a long journey at great personal expense. They became relatives and part of my spiritual journey just by offering to pray and suffer with me and all the rest of the people on that sacred ground. Also, their contribution made my thirteenth Sundance the most memorable and interesting of all my Sundances.

The tree from the year before was still standing with all the prayer ties and flags on it. For some reason, Sunday night before David arrived, the tree was taken down and cut up for firewood. In all my years Sundancing, I had never seen this happen. Several Sundancers were very upset about this, including me. To my knowledge, the tree was to be taken down in ceremony during the day with the Sundance Chief present, and it was never to be cut up for firewood. Perhaps this was a sign of things to come.

On Monday, with Snowy's encouragement, Conrado approached me with sincerity to ask if he could Sundance for his father. He wanted to fulfill a promise he'd made some time ago: that if his father's health improved, one day he would Sundance for him. His sincerity and concern for his father brought tears to our eyes. I told him I would ask David. This was the first time Conrado had been to a Sundance, and he needed to be made aware how serious this commitment was.

Also, Arthur said he wanted to Sundance for his father, who had a tumor in his head. Then Suzanne told me that she had to Sundance, Jason wanted to dance, and Gil asked if he could dance! Even Rose Marie asked if she could dance. I had never been asked by so many people before. I sat with each one individually and had long talks. I wanted them to understand the seriousness of what they had asked me to help them start. It was a wonderful feeling to introduce them to such an incredible journey.

This was when I truly realized that my job wasn't to be a Sundance Chief, but to introduce individuals to the Sundance and set them on their journey. Often I had wondered what the Creator wanted of me, and it had now become very clear. Perhaps with my experience and with David Swallow Jr.'s leadership and spiritual guidance, many others could benefit from the spirituality and selflessness the Sundance offers.

That Monday afternoon, Melody and I went to the community center to pick up a package. We had asked a friend of mine, Neill, to send us some flat boughs of cedar from Washington State, and he had shipped me a forty-pound box of flat cedar clippings. They were clean and freshly picked. He had included a note and artwork engraved on a hand-split cedar board. It was addressed to me and to the people of Porcupine. I was very moved by his gesture, and we were all very grateful to have them.

On Tuesday, while we were in Rapid City getting more supplies and water, Sean and Jim arrived from Ohio. Jim was so anxious to Sundance that he didn't wait until I got back to approach David and ask his permission to Sundance.

He'd been a firekeeper and doing Sweat Lodge ceremonies for six years, and now felt he was ready to Sundance.

Sean and Jim had driven from Toledo, Ohio, and I suppose when they got there Jim wanted to find out right away if he would be allowed to dance. So without me there to take him, he went straight to David and was met with a disappointing answer. David told him he must help with the fire, security, or whatever is needed at the Sundance for four years before dancing. Jim was devastated, and his friend Sean was sad for him. He knew why Jim wanted to Sundance and how much it meant to him.

Melody and I came back from Rapid City and heard the news. I had a long talk with Jim. I told him I didn't understand why, but it wasn't my place to question David. I also told him that now he had found out not everyone is allowed to Sundance. Apparently, David had seen something in Jim that made him refuse the way he did. I don't know what it might have been.

The rest of the day and on Wednesday, Jim walked around helping, but he seemed lost. He helped others make their piercing bones and helped them get ready to Sundance. At about noon, Jim came to me with tobacco and asked if I would please talk to David again on his behalf. I explained that I would do it, but if David refused him again, he would have to carry out David's wishes.

I called the people who had come with me and wanted to Sundance. There were seven of them. They each needed to learn how to put tobacco in their pipes, as it is done in ceremony every time they fill them. At this time I also told them that mine was not the final word on whether they would be allowed to dance. David had the ultimate say. If he refused any of them entry into the Sundance, they must give him their pipe, to be used by someone else who needed it to go into the Sundance. The reason, I told them, was because

David can sometimes feel when people are not sincere or not ready to do what they're asking to do.

After everyone had their pipes ready, we walked to David's camp. David and Gerald Ice, one of David's Sundance leaders, were waiting for us. Everyone who wanted to dance sat on the ground in a semicircle facing David. I sat on his right side, and we placed a chair in front of him. Leaning close to David, I said, "This young man, Jim, who I'm bringing up here, told me that he's already been to see you, and you refused him to Sundance this year. He's asked me to speak to you on his behalf, and if you could please reconsider his request. Yours is the last word, and I've explained to each of them that if you refuse any of them, they must 'gift' their pipe to you so you can use it."

David nodded his head and said, "Okay, Manny, bring him up."

I motioned for Jim to come and sit on the chair. For a long moment, David sat there looking at Jim, as though receiving his guidance from the Spirits. Then David said, "Usually when I say something like this, I have a very good reason, and I don't change my mind. Usually, people don't come back to ask the second time. You're a smart man. You came back a second time, and you brought one of my Sundance leaders with you. You are sincere, and your heart is good."

As he leaned forward to take Jim's pipe from him, he asked, "How many days are you going to dance?" Nervously, Jim also leaned forward—not knowing whether to give him his pipe, shake his hand, or what—and almost fell out of his chair. David and I had to suppress a laugh, so as not to take away from the seriousness of the situation.

Everyone else was also accepted into the Sundance. Relieved that they didn't have to give up their pipes, they headed back to their camps.

Melody and Jodi had gone into Rapid City while all this was going on. They got back just in time to go to get the tree with everyone else. There were nearly thirty cars and vans lined up on the highway, heading out to get our Sacred Tree. It was about 5:30 in the evening. By the time everything was finished it would be dark. It would be hard to put the tree up in the dark, but that is the way things were going.

We drove about thirty minutes and pulled off the main highway onto the land where the river was. Everyone had to climb down a steep bank and cross the river to get to the tree. The river had only about a foot of water in it. Melody, Stormy, and Lauren stayed on the side where the trailer was because they didn't have shawls, and all the women attending had to wear a shawl over their shoulders. That was the traditional way to show respect to the tree and the Sundance Chief.

David said some prayers, then asked a young girl to come and swing the first chop at the tree. A native girl around four years old assisted in taking the first swing, then a small boy took his turn. Next, an elder was asked to take a swing.

Finally, all the Sundancers were cutting the tree down. Maybe it was my imagination, but it seemed that everyone was chopping at the tree too fast, and too aggressively. Maybe because it was getting late, but it seemed that all the men were almost angry while cutting it down. It was different from any other time I'd witnessed the tree-cutting ceremony, and I was a little uncomfortable. I wondered if anyone else noticed. It was time for the tree to drop and for us to catch it. Then something terrible happened. The tree started to fall and broke in half! Many people openly wept. Everyone was shocked. Everyone looked at everyone else, wondering what was going to happen.

David said to all who could hear, "Traditionally, when something like this happens, the Sundance is over. However,

I know that many of you have traveled long distances to Sundance, so we are going to try again. Everyone will suffer for this tree, and I will have to drag buffalo skulls for this tree," he continued. "If this second tree breaks or even touches the ground, that will be it. The Sundance will be over for this year."

My emotions were running high. How could this happen, I wondered. Why did it happen? Right then I decided I would do everything physically possible to keep the second tree from hitting the ground. Even if it meant I had to put myself under it, I wasn't going to allow this one to hit the ground. Apparently others had the same thoughts as I did. Maybe we were all being tested; every Sundance seemed to have some special lesson involved. This was just the beginning, I thought, and wondered how it would affect the rest of the Sundance.

The second tree received the same ceremony David had given the first tree. Soon it was time for it to come down. This time everyone was on their guard so that the tree was caught and didn't touch the ground. The tree was about fifty feet high and perhaps two feet in diameter. It was a big tree, and it took everyone's strength to keep it off the ground. Slowly it was carried across the river and up the muddy banks to the trailer that was waiting to carry it. For the first time since I'd begun Sundancing, all I offered in help was encouragement to the younger people.

By now the sun was slipping behind the western skyline. What a magnificent sunset. Remarkably, in the eastern skyline sat the moon, just as full as could be.

With tremendous effort and struggle, they managed to get the tree on the trailer and secure it with ropes to ensure it didn't fall off. Everyone else who had been watching was getting ready to drive out and follow behind the trailer.

Silhouetted against the western sky, with the oranges,

yellows, and reds mixed together, were the black figures of Sundancers standing guard over their Sacred Tree. The tree's branches looked black against the brilliant colors of the August sunset. I couldn't help but hold my breath for a moment at the sight of it, knowing that the next time we saw the sun, we would be in the Arbor, praying.

By the time we got back to the Sundance grounds, it was pitch black. Many vehicles drove up to the Arbor and put their headlights on so the Sundance Chief and the Sundancers could see. Carefully the tree was lifted off the trailer and carried into the Arbor through the east gate. There was a hole prepared and ready so the tree could be put up. The Sundancers placed the tree on the sacred ground with the base close to the hole.

David said some prayers and everyone was asked to attach their prayer ties and flags. Then the Sundancers tied their piercing ropes to the tree and pulled the rope to prepare to raise the tree.

With tremendous strength, the Sundancers and other men there helping out pushed the tree toward the hole and started pushing it up. All the Sundancers who had their ropes extended were moving around the Arbor to balance the tree, while others filled the hole with earth. Soon, the tree was in place and swaying in the darkness.

The full moon behind the tree gave it an eerie look. Lights from the cars reflected the glorious colors of the flags and prayer ties. Silently the tree stood, regally waiting to fulfill its destiny. The leaves shimmered in the light, as though shivering, anticipating the next day, when the tree would become the Creator.

Exhausted and spent, I headed back to camp with Melody. She had to get her things together now because she needed to spend the next four nights in the women's tepee, close to the Arbor. It worried me because she had just recovered from the severe burns on her face. I wished she would dance only two days, but she was determined to go the distance, and I couldn't stop her.

It was almost 11:00 p.m. when I finally got to bed. My mind had a hard time shutting down for sleep after all that had happened.

My internal clock woke me up at 5:00 a.m., and I jumped up and got ready to go to the first sweat. I woke up Lionel, then headed for the sweat lodge. I was the first of the men to arrive, so I started yelling, calling all the Sundancers to get up, to come to the sweat lodges. Someone always has to do that. It seems even though the Sundancers know they have to get up, they want someone to tell them when to do it. I was surprised to see Melody was already up and waiting by the women's sweat lodge. (She has a really hard time waking up in the morning.)

Before I knew it, we were lined up for the Going In ceremony. The sun came up over the sandstone cliffs, east of the Arbor. Because of my diabetes, I was wearing moccasins and couldn't feel the ground under my feet. But the air was warm and beautiful. The low murmurs of the Sundancers standing around talking and the smell of burning cedar were calming. I'm sure it made wonderful memories for a lot of people that morning.

As with all my other Sundances I felt a tremendous sense of pride as we lined up to enter the Sacred Circle. I felt an exhilaration course through my body and goose bumps popped up all over as I heard the drum and the first high notes of the singers' voices.

Once inside the Arbor, the time for self-sacrifice was once again before us. I couldn't help but think about how grateful I was to be there to give thanks. We had had a very good year and had many things to be thankful for.

Melody hadn't noticed that I'd had the clay marks put

on my back. I was planning to drag buffalo skulls the first piercing round. My health problems dictated that I should do it right away. It was important for me to make sure I was strong enough to drag the skulls before I got too weak to do a good job at it. This would be my fourth and last time to drag skulls.

My piercing round finally arrived. Lionel took me into the center, and Melody stood near me while they pierced my back. I wanted her to know that it was okay. The only thing I could do was smile at her. I knew it was hard for Melody to watch me. She had tears streaming down her cheeks. She knew I had asked them to pierce deeply, so I could drag the six skulls all four rounds.

The sun was getting hotter, and it was still mid-morning. They tied the skulls to my back, and six Sundancers carried the skulls to the west gate of the Arbor. My right piercing broke as soon as we moved. This meant I would be dragging the skulls on one piercing.

Melody handed Oriona to me. She was wearing a special outfit that she had picked out herself for the occasion. Oriona asked Melody why she was crying and told her to be happy for her daddy. She showed a lot of wisdom for a three-year-old.

Once more I was carrying Oriona. She would give me strength while I danced around the Arbor. After honoring the four directions on our journey around the Sacred Circle, we reached the west gate. The dancers set the skulls on the ground while David prayed with me.

All the people from my camp, and those who had come on my invitation, fell in behind me while I pulled the skulls. Many of the men and women around the Arbor were weeping for me and at the sight of carrying Oriona.

Grasping Oriona tightly to me, I leaned forward. The weight of the six skulls stopped me in my tracks. Slowly, ever so slowly I started leaning and pushing forward. I was scared that my other piercing would break and that I wouldn't be able to drag the skulls. I wanted to have the chance to suffer and pray. I had waited all year for this and wanted to go through with it. Slowly the buffalo skulls started moving for me. As we were moving, I felt overwhelming gratitude to the Spirits for allowing me to drag the skulls. First I prayed that I wouldn't break loose and would have the strength to do this. Then I prayed for all my relations and the tree that we had lost. By the beginning of my fourth long trip around the Sacred Circle, my mouth was very dry. My energy was almost gone. I had been carrying around Oriona the first three rounds, and I couldn't carry her anymore. Putting her down, I asked her, "Honey, can you dance with Daddy?" Bo, the Sundance leader fanning me with his fan, whispered in my ear one word, "Run."

"Run?" I thought to myself. "I'm having trouble walking!" Bending over, I spoke to my little girl and said, "Honey, Daddy needs your strength. Daddy needs your help. Daddy needs to run."

Looking up at me and smiling, Oriona said, "Okay, Daddy." And she started moving forward pulling on my fingers as if wanting to run. I started moving faster. I ran about five feet and suddenly the other side broke loose. What a wonderful feeling: that my prayers would be heard and answered. I had completed my four years of dragging skulls. I felt a sense of pride, a sense of spiritual accomplishment at having completed my commitment.

The rest of that day went by slowly and was extremely difficult for everyone, it seemed. It was hard to believe that so many would be so exhausted and drained when it was only the first day. Rumor had it that several women were around the Arbor on their moon time. If that were true, it would explain why so many Sundancers were so weak.

The rumors were justified. A couple of the women went around asking the women near the Arbor that very personal question. Several women answered that yes, in fact, they were on their moon. They were firmly asked to leave the Sundance Arbor area. Most were good about leaving after learning what it does to the Sundancers in their weakened condition. All Sundancers, including the women, suffer from the high energy that women on their moon put out. It has a dramatic effect on Sundancers because of their weakened condition.

The next morning was much like the first. Mario joined us this morning and committed to three days. Then one at a time, Jason (who is sixteen years old), Arthur, Conrado, and Mario came to me to tell me they wanted to pierce that day. Then one by one as the day progressed they fulfilled their commitment to the Creator. What a beautiful sight it was to see those young warriors giving of themselves for all their relations.

I don't remember what round it was when Mario wanted to pierce, but we took him to the tree, and, after he was pierced, we carried the skulls for him one round. When he started the second round, he broke easily; the Spirits were smiling on him. When he returned to the sacred tree, one of the Sundance leaders reached for the eagle staff and Mario, thinking he had a hold of it, let the staff go. It fell to the ground. I never saw it happen, but David told me about it and told me that because Mario was my nephew, he had to drag the buffalo skulls again for having dropped the staff. After that round was over, I told Mario about it. I explained that if he didn't want to do it, I would drag the skulls for him because he was my nephew and I had introduced him to the Sundance circle. As I finished saying that, Bo walked up and said he would drag them if Mario didn't want to because it was his eagle staff that Mario had dropped. Mario, surprised that two men were willing to drag the skulls for him, said he would drag them and couldn't leave that responsibility to anyone else. He agreed to drag the skulls the next day, but he wouldn't get the chance until the last day.

David decided to have the healing round halfway through the second day. Melody told me she was glad to have the healing round then. She was having trouble coping with the heat and had been resting when the Sundancers were called to the healing round. She told me she was grateful to be thinking of helping others when she was immersed in her own exhaustion. The healing round actually made her feel better, thinking of the others who needed healing. It was a good round.

Shortly after the healing round, without telling me, Melody left the Sundance. She had started her moon time, and to show respect for the other dancers, she left the Sundance grounds right away.

On the third day, Gil from Riverside joined us. He works for the California prison systems, and for years he has been helping inmates. Both native and non-native men and women have the Sweat Lodge available to them with Gil's help. It was Gil's turn to dance and pierce. He did it with pride and courage.

A very good friend of mine, Bert from Marina Del Rey, California, was a very much appreciated member of our camp. Being of traditional Filipino descent, a lot of his ancestors' medicine ways are the same as ours: they sweat, they pray, and they heal. Bert is a very experienced healer who uses acupuncture and herbs. He danced and prayed with us and beaded medicine bags for people. He used herbal medicine to heal many of the Sundancers right after they had been pierced. Both Sundancers and supporters expressed their gratitude for his being there. Every year, Bert makes a pilgrimage to South Dakota and attends

Sundances to help any way he can, using his special medicine and experience.

On Sunday, everybody looked better and stepped lighter. It was the last day. Even Bob, a man who had been pierced every day since the first day of the Sundance, started lifting his feet higher.

Phil and another Sundancer, Rose Marie, joined us. She had made a commitment to pierce once on the last day. The whole day was hectic because many dancers had waited to pierce on the last day. All the helpers and Sundance leaders also had to pierce for the privilege of having helped.

That afternoon a cold wind had moved in from the north, so the hungry, thirsty Sundancers weren't too interested in cold watermelons. We almost had to beg people to take them.

The Sundance ended late that night. I was honored and privileged to have danced with so many strong and dedicated people. I am proud and honored to know each and every one of them.

When we left the Sundance, we headed for California. We had to be at a Native Arts and Crafts show in Glendale at the end of August. We stopped in Casper, WY., and bought a laptop computer and printer to edit the new edition of the Sundance book. Disney's Hyperion Publishing had purchased it to be released in July, 1996.

At times it was like a traveling road show, with all of us in the small, 24' travel trailer. With six females, it wasn't easy - the shoes alone, boggle the mind!

From Glendale we traveled north to San Juan Bautista. There we had some time to visit Lionel. Those days were wonderful. Spending September in northern California was great. We'd go for walks along the wharf in Monterey, ate calamari and watched the sun set in the west over the Pacific Ocean. We would often have artichoke feasts in the trailer, with mayonnaise to dip. Visiting the fruit and vegetable markets, for just picked, fresh food, was wonderful. It created a lot of great memories for the kids, Melody and me.

We heard about a book show in Denver the middle of September, so we packed up and headed out. It took a few days to get there, but we made it in time.

We set up, I signed books, and we sold some Stone People Medicine stones, Dream Catchers, etc. as sidelines to all the bookstore buyers.

Around this time, we decided to head to Ontario Canada to stay at my mother-in-law's house. Recently widowed, Lynne was away for a month and said her house was empty. So we decided to stay there for a while, get off the road and out of the trailer. So we headed for Ontario.

That Christmas was so typical Christmas - lots of snow, a traditional tree, more presents that any of us needed. It was a time to celebrate, because I'd sold the rights to my book to Hyperion, and it looked like things were going to get better for us. Melody had traded in her white Safari van, she called, "White Cloud" to get me my dream vehicle, a brand-new burgundy, GMC Suburban. It was more than we could afford, but we felt sure better days were coming, and Melody wanted me to have it as a present for all the work I'd done. Driving that beautiful vehicle is like heaven. Nice gray leather interior, all the bells and whistles, now I was set for Christmas for a few years.

In January, Melody and I took the train to New York City. We wanted to meet with the publisher, to see if they would do more to promote my book. That was an adventure in itself. We had to get up at about 4:00 a.m., and we were so excited about the trip we were singing, "New York, New York" while getting ready for the taxi to pick us up. The kids thought we were crazy, but we were anxious about the trip. Melody and I were on the train from Toronto, for 11 hours. We stayed in a Howard Johnson's, and took a cab to the publisher's offices the next day. There we met Bob Miller, the president of Hyperion, the associate editor, our editor, head of publicity, etc. We all met in the boardroom, to discuss the potential for the Sundance book, and my next project, the Stone People Medicine book. They were all anxious to see how the Sundance book would do.

When we got back to Toronto, we packed up and got ready to head back to the south west. We wanted to be at the Tucson gem and mineral show.

We got there on time, as the show started the next day. After setting up camp, Melody called my agent, BJ Robbins, and she told us that Hyperion was really interested in my next book, Stone People Medicine. She said they wanted to know how soon we could get a book proposal together, and that they could give us an advance just on the proposal. We were so excited, especially because it was a result of our trip to New York. BJ was saying that the advance should be really great, because they were so anxious.

So we had to make a decision. We originally intended to move to New Mexico, and use what money we had left to purchase some property. But with this opportunity, we decided to drive to Las Vegas, NV., camp out at Circus Circus Casino RV Park for a month, and use the time to write the book proposal.

We decided that if we waited a while to buy a home, it may be better, because perhaps the advance would enable us to buy a nicer place. So we remained homeless, on the road, in the trailer - with hopes that this would be the "big one" and maybe things would get easier for my family and me.

After the gem and mineral show, we started to head to Las Vegas. We stopped at my mom's house in Ajo for a few days. It's always so great to see my mom, sisters and brother. We always eat beans, chili, homemade tortillas, tamales and all the traditional food I grew up with. We play cards until we fall asleep at the table, or someone gives in or runs out of quarters. We tell jokes and reminisce about the past and who was mom's favorite. My sister, Rachel always has one of those jokes that she tells in Spanish. Before she finishes, she is always laughing, before she can get the punch line out, which makes everyone else laugh before they hear the end.

After a few days of relaxing and good times, we headed for Nevada. Melody seemed to come down with something, she was complaining of feeling sick all the way to Las Vegas. She could only eat cup-o-noodles. She thought it must have been the water in Ajo, as we'd taken some jugs of water in the trailer with us.

When we got our spot at the RV park at Circus Circus in Las Vegas, Melody and I got busy with the book proposal. We sat at the table with the laptop, and wrote every day for almost a month until we were finished. The kids had a ball. There was a huge recreation area with a pool, playground, arcade and store near the campsite.

Melody continued to feel ill, and was also complaining about how it hurt to walk, like her pelvic bones were sore. She suspected something was wrong. She continued to lose weight on that medication. One afternoon, she called all of us together in the kitchen of the trailer. She showed us one of those tests you get at the drug store, and sure enough, she was pregnant. I just can't figure out how that happens.

It was a huge shock to all of us, especially because we didn't have a home, or the prospect of one in the near future. I didn't know what we were going to do. We were happy, but nervous about how we were going to look after another child. Melody stopped taking all medication right then and there, she didn't want anything at all in her system that would affect the baby's health.

So with that news, we tried to get really busy finishing the book proposal for the Stone People book. We had it complete, ready to send to Hyperion by the end of February, and got it in the mail to my agent. Then we waited, and waited and waited.

We headed to northern California, back to San Juan Bautista, CA. This time we stayed for about a month at the K.O.A. campground.

Melody was starting to show. She'd visited a clinic in Hollister, and had all the necessary tests, to be sure the baby was okay. The trailer appeared to be getting smaller.

We had to be in South Bend, Indiana by Father's Day weekend. So by the beginning of May we started heading east again, towing the trailer. We drove to Phoenix, Tucson and on through New Mexico. We stopped near a place close to Silver City to see this house for sale. As we imagined our advance would be a good one, we looked at this beautiful home, northeast of Silver City. It was such a great house, and Melody got tears in her eyes when she saw the master bathroom. I dreamed of being able to give my Melody this home. So we told the real estate agents, as soon as we found out about our advance, we'd let them know.

We got to South Bend a few days before the show at Notre

Dame University. We were camping at another K.O.A. campground. After the craft show, there was the huge Book Expo in Chicago. So we drove in for that to meet with my agent and see how progress was going with the Stone People book. Hyperion was having trouble figuring out how to market my little book about stones. They wanted to include the stones with the book, but didn't know how to do it, without it being mass produced in China and still being cost effective for the consumer. It was a dilemma, but we figured, Disney's marketing geniuses should be able to figure something out.

We received the first hardcover copies of the new Sundance book, 2nd edition at that campground. It was so awesome to see the new book. They did a great job of design and editing.

After South Bend, there were three other shows to attend: Madison, WI. , Davenport, IA., and finally, St. Charles, MO.

From Missouri, we headed for Arizona. We all had to be in Las Vegas by July 19 for the beginning of a book signing tour for the new edition of the Sundance book. Hyperion decided to send me on a 6-city book signing tour, and Melody was able to come with me.

The first signing, was remarkable. There were more than 100 people there, and the back wall was covered with my books. Jodi had done an incredible job promoting this signing. She said the book was very close to her heart, and she put everything into making it a huge success.

Next day, Melody and I flew for the rest of the book tour. The kids went back to Phoenix, with our friend, Marlene. At every city we would be met at the airport by an escort. It was so funny to watch Melody waddle from gate to gate at airports. She was getting bigger, making it more difficult to walk. Our last stop was at a bookstore in Phoenix. This book signing was particularly close to my heart, because as a surprise, my whole family came up from Ajo to attend.

They hadn't really shared this success with me. To have my mom, brother, sisters and in-laws there for support, was almost too much. It made me very emotional. When I saw, my mom walk in, sort of bent over, it brought tears to my eyes. I only wish my dad had been there to see all this too. After the last book signing, we all went over to the Olive Garden for dinner. It coincided with Stormy's 18th birthday, so we had a dual celebration.

Well, it was getting close to Sundance time again. So the day after the book signing tour, we all piled in the car and headed to Colorado where we had the trailer in storage. We picked it up and headed for the Sundance.

This Sundance started pretty much the same as any other. All my old friends were there to greet my family. After so many years of attending David's Sundance everyone becomes family, some closer than others, but all family.

The first person I saw was Al Tail. He waved, dropped what he was doing and came over to greet my family. We stood there awhile and caught up with the things that had happened since the last time we had seen each other.

I asked if Lionel was there yet, he said he wasn't or at least he hadn't seen him. Lionel was his adopted son. Bernice and Al had formally adopted him and given him the native name, "Scarlet Eagle." This was something that Lionel held in high regard and with honor. I asked about Bernice, and he said she had just left for their house, we just missed her.

Al went back to work and we set up our camp. We parked our trailer and set up our shades, etc. More people arrived.

Our camping spot is right next to the road so we were where we could see everyone driving onto the grounds. The beauty of where our Sundance is held, is that though the temperature can get really hot during the day, it cools off to a comfortable level at night, making it much better to sleep.

Next thing I knew, Tree day was finally here. There seemed to be a quiet electricity in the air. The ground itself was vibrating to a different energy.

Lionel drove in some time during the night, so we didn't see him until that morning. When I got up to fix a cup of coffee, I saw his van sitting where he usually camped, next to Al and Bernice's camp.

The next day we went into the arbor early in the morning. The morning was a little on the cool side but pleasant. The Sacred fire had felt really good on our skin as we stood around it and waited for Bo to call us to get ready and line up. It was a great feeling to be there, smelling the wood smoke. Once in a while, I'd get a faint whiff of cigarette smoke mixed with it. I had smoked for 37 years before I quit about six years before and I suppose I'll always remember it as a friend.

Anyways, all the smells, noises and sights together made some beautiful memories that morning. All the handshakes and hugs from my brother Sundancers, felt really good. There is a special bond formed by all of us. We all come together willingly to offer ourselves as sacrifices for the people. We feel a strong, brotherly pride to be doing what we are doing, as relatives. The feeling is akin to soldiers being in combat together.

The Sundance leader, Bo, blew on his eagle whistle, and said, "Let's line up." Everybody was waiting, so he didn't have to say it twice.

We all lined up. At the head of the line was, Lionel carrying the huge Buffalo skull for the altar. Behind him was David, Bo, the Sacred Staff carrier. The rest of us followed each other as we walked around the north side of the arbor.

Slowly, we danced around the arbor to the beat of the Sacred Drum, as we stopped to honor the four directions. The people, standing around the arbor facing us, were very quiet and they hung their heads in respect.

The last man was followed by the ladies. They looked so beautiful and dignified. Their dresses were bright, colorful, yet simple. Like the men, they chose to look humble and as good as they could for the Creator and the Spirits.

The first day went by like a fast-moving creek. There were a few guys that pierced. They are the ones that have pledged to stay pierced the entire four days. This takes a lot of courage.

Between rounds, many of us would stand around the sacred fire. Don the fire keeper, supervised and organized the shifts to make sure the fire was kept going continuously. Every year he would travel from New York State, getting there a few days early to cut wood, and prepare the Sweat Lodges for the Sundance. He's a tall man, in stature, but always humble in his manner, always trying to follow traditions as best he could. Sometimes, I feel that it was harder to be a fire keeper than to Sundance. A good fire keeper could mean the very success of the Sundance. So we were grateful for Don, and all those that tended the fire.

It was truly amazing how the Sundance had grown. We couldn't help but notice how many people were there that I had invited, or that had read my book and made their way there. It felt good to know the Creator had guided so many people to experience the Sundance.

It seems when I had the vision to write this book, the spirits had many things in store for those that read it. There were probably about three hundred people there that year, and by the end of the 3rd day about ninety dancers had pledged. I'm not saying everyone there was a result of my book, but a number of the attendees were people I'd invited.

Due to the fact so many more people were attending David's Sundance for the first time, a security problem was beginning to develop. Many people attending for the first time weren't ready to be there, and didn't like witnessing the piercing. We also were aware that some undercover (they do not identify themselves) F.B.I. agents were there, checking things out. Anytime a large number of people gather for spiritual reasons, the government has to step in and check things out.

I was also feeling this was the beginning of pulling away from this Sundance. Almost every year, after the Sundance, I would say this is my last time. I'd fulfilled my commitments, and beyond. And it was a huge expense for my family. The cost of traveling, food and general expenses for a family of seven people, would be close to $3,000, depending on where we were coming from.

When the Sundance was over, we stayed behind for an extra day to make sure the campsite was clean, and to pick sage. We always tried to leave it better than before we got there. Many times through the year, I need the sage for ceremony and to give to others. We packed up and headed back to Lynne's house. Melody wanted to give birth in Ontario.

Melody and the kids were watching the news one day at the end of August. They found out that the medication Melody had been taking could have killed her. It was being taken off the market, and was dangerous, especially for women Melody's age. We realized right then that the baby, had literally saved Melody's life. I don't know what we would have done if something had happened to her. Melody became pregnant just in time to make her stop taking those pills.

Every business day, since the beginning of March I had checked for a call from Hyperion about the advance. So by early September, we finally got the word. They had decided to pass on the book altogether. We were very upset that they had kept us hanging for so long. So I decided to finish the manuscript (which was almost done anyway), and publish it myself. I had published the original Sundance book with no money - I figured I would do it again.

So Melody and I set out to try and raise the funds. We sent letters to all the people who wrote about the Sundance book. So many people prepaid for their copy, with the promise it would arrive by Christmas. The response was phenomenal, and it wasn't very long before we had the money necessary to get the down payment for the printing. Then I finished up the manuscript and Melody helped with the editing and final touches.

It was getting really difficult for Melody to work on the computer as she was so big, and really ready to have the baby. But I spoke to the baby, and said very strongly that it couldn't be born until the manuscript was done. We worked on it until, October 18th, then the manuscript was put in the mail to the printer.

Like an obedient child, Melody went into labor around 12 noon the next day. My son, Stone was born October 19th, 1996 at 4:07 p.m. He weighed in at 8 lbs. 14 oz. and was beautiful. Melody was fine, and truly glowed after giving birth. She said on the 2nd day of his birth, when she was feeding him, she was looking at him thinking, "How are we going to do this?"

She was worried about our future, especially because we didn't have a permanent home, and the HUGE advance didn't come through. Well, Melody said while she was thinking these thoughts, Stone put his hand on her arm, as though he was saying, "It's going to be all right, don't worry."

224

I gave him his native name, "Medicine Hawk" because when I was driving to the hospital to see Melody. I saw a hawk flying near the hospital, right over the van. He landed ahead of us on the power lines, and sat there watching me intently, as I drove by. And he was medicine for Melody, as he saved her from taking those pills.

As promised, we had books in hand by late October. Stormy and I decided to make a trip to California, pick up some of the books at the printer, and try and sell some there. We were gone for about a month. We got into a minor car accident near San Jose. This woman-admitted fault at the scene. Her slick lawyers for her insurance company ended up paying very little for the physical damage to Stormy and I. We got back in late November, and prepared for some sales calls.

We heard about a Native gathering in Hull, Quebec the first week of December. It was called, "The Sacred Assembly." The reason for the gathering was initiated by Elijah Harper, to bring together Native people and many of the religious leaders. There were several seminars and workshops arranged to try and bring about a healing.

Many representatives of the Native people in Canada were there, because their parents, and in some cases the children, were severely abused and stripped of their heritage. Growing up they were taken from their parents, had their hair cut and beaten if they spoke their native language. They were called residential schools. In many ways, this was meant to be an apology from the administrators of the schools to the Native families that were affected by the injustice inflicted on them. It had caused so many generations of abuse, alcoholism and drug addiction. Many of the children from the residential schools were not only beaten regularly, but were also sexually abused by the teachers and priests that ran the schools.

We went there to set up a booth, sell books, stones and Dream Catchers. It was a powerful weekend, because of the emotions that had risen to the surface.

There was this awesome efficiency, hotel room that we stayed in. It was just below the ground level, so when you looked out the windows, the snow would cover half of the window. It gave it a warm, cosy feeling. Melody would cook breakfast and dinner there.

One of the attendees, was the Grand National Chief of the First Nations, Ovide Mercredi. He would pass by our booth, and there were always lots of people around him. One time as he passed, I asked him if he wanted a copy of my book, as a gift. He looked at the book, then me, then asked me if I was the author. When I told him I was, he said, he'd read it, and it had inspired him. He wanted to come back later to talk to me about it. Melody and I were excited someone in his position, had read my story.

The next day, unexpectedly, Ovide came behind our booth, put his jacket on the chair and joined us to talk.

We hit it off, right away, and a new friendship was born. He sat at our booth for a while, and one customer, not noticing him sitting there, asked him the price of a Dream Catcher. It was funny, and really gave us a lift. Ovide said my book had made him more proud to be Native, he began search for his own spiritual path. He also said he had a lot learn from me. I was honored, as he is highly respected as a leader for the Native Peoples.

We had a great four days in Quebec. We spent the next couple of weeks getting ready for the holidays.

On Christmas eve, we were heading for the mall to take the kids to meet Santa. We were only four blocks from the house, and got into a really bad car accident. I checked to see that everyone was all right. Emergency crews were on the scene really fast.

The next couple of months were spent in treatments with a chiropractor and physical therapist. My back was very badly damaged.

This couldn't have come at a worse time, because the end of January is the Tucson gem and mineral show, and we always do well there. Financially, I didn't know what we were going to do. We would have done really well with the new Stone People book at the Tucson show, and it is difficult to prove what you "might" have made.

So I would say that the first four months of 1997, were one of the worst periods of our life together. Without money coming in, we were under a lot of stress.

As we approached Sundance time, it occurred to me that we may not be able to go. The money situation was tight and we were trying to play catch up. The new Stone People Medicine book was doing really well, and we had finally paid off the printer. They had given us a bit of time, because of the circumstances.

In early May, I left for an arts and craft show in South Bend, IN. Becky and Mary came with me. On our way, I stopped to make some sales calls in Cleveland, Ohio.

While I was making a sale at a Native store, I met a woman who had read my first edition of the Sundance book. Her name was Pat, and she was very excited to meet me. She said the book had changed her life, and in some way had saved her. She wanted to get to know me and wondered if she could come to the Sundance. We ended up staying the night there. She paid for our hotel room, so we could have dinner with her. She was thrilled to meet the people from the book, and was very connected to Native traditions. She was also a Mixblood. We gave her the information about our Sundance and said we'd keep in touch as it got closer.

By the beginning of July we had to make the decision whether we were going to the Sundance. Usually, money comes in from unexpected sources or from some sales. Though we had a bit of money to go, it wasn't enough for us to get there and back. Our new friend Pat, offered to give us money to get there. She had an idea on how to raise some money and sell lots of my books. She said she knew a lot of wealthy people in Cleveland, and felt many of them would want to help us out. So we gratefully, accepted her help, and prepared to go.

Before we knew it, it was Sundance time again. This year we had a small pop-up trailer, our 24-foot travel trailer (in storage in Niagara Falls), and our new addition, Stone, who was nine months now. Stormy helped Melody out so much. Being that we had two trailers and both had to drive, Stormy would watch Stone while Melody drove. We stopped in Cleveland to meet up with Pat. She gave us the money, and said she'd meet us there. She would fly to Rapid City with her doctor friend, James and they would rent a vehicle there and come to our Sundance.

We parked in Shawn's driveway in Toledo. He needed a ride to the Sundance, and would help with pulling the pop-up trailer. It worked out well for us, because Melody did not want to drive with the trailer. The rest of the trip was really great. We looked forward to seeing our friends again.

When we arrived at the Sundance grounds, it had been raining for a few days before. The bridge over the creek had washed away, and the creek was quite high. They had to build a bridge, which enabled us to finally drive over with both trailers. We set up camp at our usual spot and settled in. Our camp was the hang out for a lot of people.

This Sundance will probably be known as one of the most memorable, because so many things happened. Lionel brought a special guest with him this year. In a rented motor home, Princess Erena from the Maori tribe in New Zealand came. She was accompanied by two women from Italy, who were, sort of, her "ladies in waiting." She appeared to have a lot of money and wanted to help Lionel's dream come true by helping the people of Pineridge, SD.

She was a very large woman, with black frizzy hair. She had these tatoos on her chin and lips that signified her royal lineage. She really caused quite a stir, as she said she was deeply spiritual, and wanted to experience our Sundance.

We picked up Pat and James at the airport. We were all excited about our new friends, and grateful that they had helped us get to our Sundance. We drove right into Rapid City for groceries, and supplies at Sam's Club and Wal-Mart. They always got so much business from us. Everyone we brought to the Sundance we'd take to those stores to get virtually everything they needed. We got back to camp, and helped them set up near to us.

There was a ceremony brewing, because we found out the Princess had to be presented to us, to meet us officially. So we all lined up waiting for her to come and meet us. As she came out of the motor home, she would start to sing. She had flowers in her hair, barefoot and walked a few steps, then she would sing. It was strange to say the least, but fascinating. She'd walk a few more steps, and sing some more. It seemed like a "Four Directions" type of song.

When she got to me, she put her gift for me on the ground. In her tradition, she believed that everything must come from the earth, not from people. So all gifts were placed on Mother Earth first, then the receiver picks it up. So I picked up the gift, and she put her nose up close to mine and breathed. It was a Maori custom, as a way of sort of "inhaling" your energy. It was very strange. I had to try to keep from laughing. I was all right, until the nose thing. We were all quite fascinated by the strange customs. Seeing David's face when she put her nose up to him, really was a funny sight. He didn't know how to take it all.

Word got out about the Princess, and native people were starting to line up at her motor home door giving her gifts, with the hopes she would help out financially. She had promised Lionel that she would adopt 20 families in the area and support them with a monthly check. She had purchased a used car for one elder, bought a washer and dryer for another family. While in Nebraska, she bought Pendleton blankets, household goods, pots, pans etc. for another family. She must have spent more than $20,000 over the course of the Sundance. To say she caused an uproar, would be an understatement.

Melody, Pat and the Princess drove to get some supplies. While they were gone, we had some trouble at our Sundance grounds. Apparently there was a dispute over who owned the land we had our Sundance on. Our Sundance Chief had been having trouble before the Sundance. There had also been a rumor started that our Sundance was armed. So our Sundance was raided by several Alcohol, Tobacco and Firearms officers and tribal police. Of course, it wasn't true, it was only started to try and disrupt our Sundance. A couple of years before, they had shut down the Fool's Crow Sundance, right in the middle of the ceremony. Many of the dancers from that Sundance came to finish at ours. Now they were trying to shut ours down.

The problems seemed to stem from others who were jealous at the large number of people that attended David's Sundance. This year there were easily 500 people camped on the land.

Also the fact that David allowed nonnative people to dance,

caused some problems. Many traditional Lakota believe that nonnative people should not be allowed to Sundance. I suppose that people have a right to their opinions, but to my way of thinking, the Sundance is for the people. I don't think the Creator said only a certain race of people could Sundance. But the controversy was building to a huge problem.

There was one instance during the Sundance when two black helicopters flew over our arbor. And we heard there were several FBI agents in the hills, watching what was happening. All this controversy really caused some people to become frightened and leave, worrying over being involved with something the government didn't want.

Even I was a bit concerned for my family, because I knew other instances where the government got involved, and violence and gunfire broke out. But like David, I had faith that the Creator would take care of things.

Pat's friend, James had got right in there and offered his help tending fire. He was eager to help the fire keeper, and would pull some of the night shifts watching the fire. Both James and Pat were enjoying their experience. It was such an unusual year. It would probably stay in many people's memory for years to come.

My daughters, Stormy, Mary, Becky and Dory were dancing, so Melody wasn't able to finish her 4th year as there was no one to watch Stone and Oriona. I was very proud of my daughters, honoring me by following these ways. I never told them they had to, and it was always on their own terms.

The Princess took tobacco to David, to see if she could Sundance. She was given permission, though this was her first Sundance. Her spirituality in New Zealand, had many similarities, and she said she had a vision to Sundance and pierce. I had gifted her a pipe, from Pipestone, MN., so her vision would be complete.

The night of the 2nd day, the Princess was on top of her motor home on the roof. She was singing to the moon. We were sleeping, but her singing woke us up. It was such a strange melody. We found out the next day she was praying to her spirits, to please allow her to Sundance.

Stormy began her moon and had to leave on the 3rd day. This

gave Melody the chance to finish her 4th year commitment. The Princess hadn't been able to dance for the same reason, until the last day. So on Sunday, Melody and Princess Erena joined the procession into the Sundance.

There was a fine mist of cold rain that day. The Princess said, "The People of the Mist," and their spirits were there to watch over her.

Melody had given tobacco to Pansy, the night before. She wanted to pierce on her wrist. Pansy allowed her. Melody wanted to pierce and suffer for all the abused people of the world, young and old.

Princess Erena's vision was to be pierced seven times in a V-shape of eagle feathers on her back. Now that was going to be difficult. When those she had picked tried to pierce her, it was difficult because they were nervous and the mist made her back wet. So I helped, and we finally got all seven feathers in. She danced a few rounds with her back pierced that way. Then at the second last round, she had the feathers ripped out, so she could complete her commitment.

Lionel was so happy she was there. He loved and respected her, like a spiritual sister. But Lionel made the mistake that we all do, and put her on a high spiritual pedestal. He also felt this tremendous relief, that her coming into his life, would be the fulfillment of his prayers. It had been his dream to be able to help those on Pineridge. He dreamed of building a community center and clinic for the young people and elders there.

Our Sundance ended in the dark, and it was very cold. We were all relieved that things had ironed themselves out.

It seemed to be an infringement of rights, of a different sort. Some of the traditional Lakota people objected to the Mixbloods, Sundancing. Like reverse discrimination, they objected to non-Lakota practicing this spirituality. But they don't own the Sundance. Other tribes also practice the Sundance, so it isn't just for the Lakota. So with prayer and determination, our Sundance continued, in spite of the F.B.I. watching, in spite of the A.T.F. raiding, and in spite of objections from the traditional Lakota.

The next day, we began saying goodbye to everyone. Pat and

James left, and said we would see them in Cleveland on our way home.

It was always hard to say goodbye to everyone, knowing we wouldn't see many of them for another year. With reluctance, and sadness, we started to pack up to leave that Monday. We couldn't stay an extra day this year, as Shawn had to get home, and we had to get to Cleveland. Pat had some plans for us there.

So by about 12 noon, we were all packed up and ready to go. We said goodbye to everyone and thanked the Princess for all her gifts. By Wednesday afternoon we were back in Shawn's driveway. We didn't stay, we hoped to get to Cleveland by that evening.

Pat had booked two rooms for us at the Embassy Suites. They were very luxurious, and really welcome after roughing it at the Sundance. Pat said that she had planned a huge benefit at some wealthy woman's house and we would all attend. She said they'd invited about 80 people.

The night before the benefit, Pat said the woman that was having it, took ill and would not be able to do it after all. So they decided to move it to the Hunt Club. So we continued to stay at the Embassy Suites.

Meanwhile, Pat was trying to arrange for me to have a book signing at Harrod's in London, England. Melody and Pat went to a travel agency and spent three hours with a travel agent making arrangements for a European tour.

Pat said there were two women traveling to Cleveland from Spain. One of them was Dame Williams, a wealthy woman that was very sympathetic to Native Americans. Pat said they were old friends and Dame Williams and her friend, could be huge benefactors.

I was beginning to think I just may be able to buy Melody that house in New Mexico. So we called a real estate agent there, and asked him to look into the current price.

The day before the event at the Hunt Club, it had rained heavily in Cleveland. Pat called us early the next morning and said the room we were supposed to be in at the Hunt Club had been heavily damaged by water. So, Dame Williams would be in the lobby to greet those that had been invited, to explain why we weren't able to have it in the room. Pat still didn't want me to go there, but took some books to try and sell to those that attended.

Melody was beginning to get very suspicious. So she started calling around to find out the number to the Hunt Club. I got mad at her for doubting Pat. After all, she'd put us up for seven days now. Two rooms at around $145.00 per room, per night - this was an expensive trip. Things just weren't adding up, but I still had faith. Most of it was wishful thinking, and dreaming that things were going to finally happen for us. Melody called some of the people Pat had mentioned. They didn't exist, or at least their numbers weren't available.

Pat said that she expected Dame Williams to send us flowers, to apologize for all the trouble we'd had getting things together. We never got any flowers.

Then Pat said, that Dame Williams was going to contribute $279,000 toward helping me get several book projects written. She said that the money was being put in Pat's bank account, and they were waiting for the wire transfer from Europe.

It was kind of like being in a beautiful prison. We were being held captive, in these luxury surroundings. The kids swam, and Melody and I went in the Jacuzzi. They had this huge breakfast buffet every morning. It was incredible. Melody just felt there was something wrong.

As it turned out, we were set to do a Native show just outside Cleveland for two days. Pat came to shop, and said that she was expecting Dame Williams any time to drive up in her limousine. By this time, we were all going along with her. We were getting anxious to leave and go home. I was still hoping, in the back of my mind that it would all be true.

It finally came time to leave. We'd been at the Embassy Suites for ten days. The cost was easily $3,000. We thanked Pat for everything, and she said she would be in touch as soon as the money was transferred from Europe.

The whole experience was very strange. But when we looked at the overall picture, we had a wonderful holiday, she'd helped get us to our Sundance. And we got to dream for a while. Nothing ever came of it. But it baffled us for a long time. We never saw Pat or heard from her again.

Now Lionel had things happening with Princess Erena. When they all went back to California, Lionel said the Princess wanted to bring him and me to Italy for a couple of weeks in October. It sounded really exciting too, and what a great opportunity. Besides I'd get to spend some time with my brother.

So I decided to drive out to California to make a sales trip, and to get there in time to leave for Italy the beginning of October. It was so great to be traveling with my brother.

The Princess paid for everything. As it turned out, the Italian edition of my Sundance book was released around the same time I got there. So we were trying to get copies to sell to the people we saw on the tour.

It was coming to our attention that though Princess Erena was married, she was very attracted to my brother, Lionel. All the things she'd been doing for him, was because of this. Lionel didn't feel that way about her at all. He cared for her, and respected her spiritually, but didn't feel the same as she did.

The real problem was that Lionel had held her in such a high regard. It never occurred to him that her motive to help him, depended on their relationship.

But we enjoyed the tour anyway. We stayed at different people's places, had several events in Italy, then moved onto Switzerland. It was there that I asked to go to Germany to meet my daughter, Sylvia. We had just been in contact recently and I'd never met her. She was conceived while I was in the army, stationed in Munich. She had three children, now my grandchildren. So some of my friends in Switzerland called her to see if we could meet. Things just fell into place to make it happen.

Lionel was a bit disappointed I was leaving, but the Princess was quite pleased, as now she'd have Lionel to herself. I said I'd fly back from Germany, if changing the ticket wasn't too much trouble. Lionel stayed an extra week.

Taking the train to Munich, was wonderful. When I got to the station, I knew Sylvia right away. She looked a bit like my daughter, Becky. It was a wonderful time. I stayed in a hotel, and visited with them. We got to know each other in a few days, and I was feeling like a piece of my life was fulfilled. Sylvia was a wonderful young woman, and I was very proud of her.

We finally had to say goodbye, and next thing I knew I was flying back to California. I'd left my Suburban in the driveway of a friend there, and would now need to drive back to Toronto.

Back home, we got busy making crafts to get ready for the busy Christmas sales season. Stormy and I planned for a trip to New York State to sell at a couple of Native arts and craft shows in the middle of November. When we set out, we were just west of Toronto, and I had to stop and pick up some papers.

I was at a stop light, when a small van in the other lane, lost control of their car, and slid right into the side of my Suburban, right behind me. This was my third accident in a year, and I don't think my back has ever recovered. The next few months were spent in therapy again, trying to correct and put my back in place. I was in constant pain. Stormy and I were in rough shape.

In January, Melody and I were at a book signing, in Erie, at Navajo Corner. It was an excellent turn out, with TV coverage and everything. At the hotel at night, Melody was looking at the real estate guide for the area. We were getting ready to settle down and find a home.

The following Monday, we met a real estate agent, looked at some homes and found one we liked. By mid-June we were taking possession of our new home in Erie, PA.

We had some delays in getting Melody immigrated, so Mary, Becky, Dory and I went to move our stuff in. Melody, Stormy, Oriona and Stone would follow in August.

So the girls and I tried to set up our house. For the first while, the we all I slept on the floor, and used a card table in the kitchen.

After getting things set up, I took the girls up to Toronto to be there while I went to the Sundance. I probably wouldn't have even gone this time, but there was a family flying in from Italy just for the Sundance. We'd met them when I was in Europe with Lionel.

When I arrived there, quite a few people were already there. Everyone was happy, shaking hands and hugging me. It was another year with my extended family.

The next day, the family from Italy, arrived in a nice motor home they had rented in Denver, CO. Barbara was the only one I knew, but she had her husband, son, and daughter with her. She also brought her sister, brother-in-law, and children. They were such beautiful people. I was happy they made it in time, because the next day was Tree Day.

Thanks to David we had the whole day to relax. It was great to have time to visit with my Italian friends. I spent the day teaching them how to make prayer ties, and explaining the things that were going to happen and why.

We didn't go after the tree until late in the day. We finished getting it in the ground by dark. I was so exhausted, I went straight to sleep, first light came really early.

Next morning, I woke up about 4:00 a.m., and quickly got dressed and ready. Another job had been given to me, to get everyone up.

"Sundancers, Sundancers," I yelled. "Time to get up, the Sweat Lodge is ready and the stones are hot, time to get up, this is NOT the Holiday Inn!"

Slowly, the Sundancers would come out of the dark. They walked through the smoke of the sacred fire, like ghosts from the past. Some of them were having their first cigarette for the day, while others stretched and tried to wake up. For the first time that morning, I saw my brother, Lionel. He was smiling, hugged me and asked how I was. Seeing Lionel really picked my spirits up, and made the Sundance seem more complete.

As soon as I had enough dancers ready, I crawled into the Sweat Lodge, and would call them into the first lodge.

I returned to my trailer, got ready and headed up to the arbor. Time just flew, as I looked around everyone was ready and starting to line-up. David came over, went into the lodge and sweated himself in. When he came out, we were all lined up waiting.

He waved at the drummers, and the slow, "Going In" song began. We slowly, danced into the arbor, and put our pipes on the altar. Then we got our first break of the day.

People were relaxing on the west side of the arbor. I could see Barbara and her family, sitting with her family on the north side of the arbor. I felt funny, because every time I went by them, they would wave. All I could do was smile at them, after all this wasn't a parade. I guess they finally figured it out, because after awhile they would also just smile when I looked at them.

Looking around the arbor, the dancers looked well spirited and happy to be there. Lionel's daughter, Monique, was trying to pace herself. She'd committed to pierce this time. Lionel was a bit nervous because she'd asked her dad to do the piercing on her. I can certainly understand how that feels. I've had to take (cut) flesh from a loved one before, and it's not easy.

Pansy was beginning to show signs of wear. She was trying to train others to take her place. Just like the rest of us, that time in our lives, of needing help, was here.

The first day a few people did pierce, but the majority of the people that are piercing spread themselves throughout the four days.

Next morning, "Sundancers, Sundancers, it's time to get up. The stones are ready, let's go, let's get going. First Sweat is starting now!" I was yelling, but of course that was not quite the truth, there weren't enough Sundancers to start it yet. It just got them going a lot faster.

The rest of the day, went really fast. All the people that were dancing were really enjoying themselves. I could tell by the feel in the air that they were putting all their being into their prayers.

Finally, the long day came to an end. The dancers were starting to feel the thirst and hunger. It was getting dark as we danced out of the arbor. We circled the arbor and when we reached the west side, we all hurried to get into a Sweat Lodge to sweat ourselves out. I was so tired, I headed straight for my trailer, and fell fast asleep.

On the third day, it started out as a beautiful, warm and vividly clear day. We sweated in and entered the arbor. Everyone faced the east to welcome the sun.

There were long, stringy, thin clouds stretched across the horizon, just above the bluff that lifted off the ground, straight in front of us. The sun was still low enough that the clouds were painted purple. As we danced, they changed to pink, then they changed again. This time the color was a breathtaking, brassy, orange. Just before the sun peeked over the bluff to bless us, the thinning clouds turned to a beautiful golden lace. They thinned even more, and disappeared, as the sun finally looked at us, and sent us its blessings.

People started piercing again, both men and women. Right after the noon break, another piercing was announced. There was only two or three people piercing this round.

My niece, Monique was taken to the tree, escorted by Pansy. I was there with Lionel, and went to her. We told her to kneel down at the base of the tree and pray. That's when Lionel told me he had to do the piercing on his daughter. He was quite pale looking, because he had never pierced anyone before. Then he said she wanted him to pierce her just on top of her collar bones. This was a difficult place to pierce, because of where it was. She was very small and a little on the thin side. I thought that it might not be so hard. The flesh can be picked up very easily.

Both Lionel and I walked her around the sacred tree to stand on the buffalo robe. She stood there, bravely, smiling at us. She looked at her dad, and said to go ahead, it would be all right. Lionel held the scalpel I had given him. He got really close to her so he could see what he was doing, and started to cut. He tried to control the scalpel, to try to keep it from going very deep. With his inexperience, it was as though he couldn't control it, it went deeper than what he wanted it to. We inserted the bone into the cut, and tied it with a small eagle feather on it. Then we did the other side. This side went a little better than the first, but it was still a little deep. Monique thanked her dad and all of us there, and Lionel took her back to her place.

The dance continued for another half hour or so. The other two dancers, broke from their piercing, and it was now time for Monique to break loose. She had asked Lionel to help her. The only way to do this is by grabbing the bone underneath with two fingers on each side, and yanking it to tear the flesh. I was standing right there in front of her, and Lionel put his left arm around her. He grabbed the piercing bone, and pulled as hard as he could. It didn't break. So he said to her, "I'm sorry, Meja."

Bravely, she said, "It's okay, Dad, go ahead." He grabbed a

hold again, as hard as he could, and yanked it hard. Again, it didn't break. By now, Lionel is starting to panic, and feeling nauseated that he was hurting his daughter. Then he yanked it again, and again. It still wouldn't break, and Lionel had tears in his eyes for his daughter's pain. By this time, Bo saw that Lionel was having such a hard time, he asked him to move out of the way. He grabbed a hold of her and with a terrific yank, he broke the piercing bone loose. He quickly moved to the second one, and broke it on the first pull.

Then Bo took another scalpel and removed the two pieces of flesh that were hanging from her piercing. I held the red cloth, as he put her flesh into the cloth. I tied it up and hung it on the sacred tree. Lionel noticed that Monique was getting faint, so he held her up and took her to the tree. She sat down with her head and arms on the tree, it looked like she was going into shock. So Lionel and I stood there and fanned her, talked to her. She wretched a couple of times, but nothing would come out. She was too dry.

This was one of the most difficult times I've ever seen someone pierce, and one of the hardest times I've had at any Sundance. My heart went out to Monique, and Lionel.

That Sundance ended late on Sunday evening, with everyone feeling they had completed their commitment. I got to a phone, not far from the Sundance grounds, and called Melody. I found out that on August the 10th, she had finally been approved to come over to the U.S. I had been praying very hard that she would be home in Erie, by the time I got back from the Sundance. I got back home around the middle of August. I spent the next few weeks, recuperating and trying to furnish our home.

Around Christmas time, we got the bad news that my Sundance sister, Bernice Tail had passed on. It wouldn't be the same without her. She had a good heart, but was feisty and strong. Her spirit would be sorely missed.

In March, of '99, I met a young man at a workshop near Boston, MA. He was a LaStone therapist, and had read both my books. He'd driven up from New York City to meet me. His name was Bruce, and we became quick friends.

Meeting Bruce, would turn out to be a real turning point in my life. He has become a nephew, friend, and in many ways, a son to me. He is one of the people that the Creator has brought into my life to make it better.

In May, Melody and I drove to Illinois to see Rockie graduate from Navy School. I was very proud of how far he'd come. If he stuck with it, he'd do really well in the Navy.

With that taken care of, we got ready for our busy summer season. I decided to make a trip to California. I had a part in a movie. Thought I'd make a sales trip along the way, then go on to San Juan Bautista.

My brother Lionel wasn't his usual self. He'd been so disenchanted with Princess Erena. When things didn't turn out as she'd hoped, she had disappeared in Europe.

Many people felt let down, as they had hoped for financial help from her. The whole situation left my brother in a deep depression. It was like part of his spirit had left. It hurt me to see him like that, and it didn't seem to make a difference, what anyone said, nothing would bring him out of it.

It made me respect my brother Lionel more, because he stuck to his beliefs and morals and wouldn't allow himself to be bought. He simply could not do something that was not in his Spiritual heart, regardless of how many it would hurt. It had devastated him spiritually and physically.

It was around this time, I decided to start an organization. I had tried in 1993, but circumstances at the time, prevented me from getting it off the ground. It was called "The United American Metis/Mestizo Society" and it was to unite and help all the Mixbloods. All those of us that were part native and part other races, had been left in the cold. We didn't seem to belong in either world. And I wanted to do something to help. So I formed U.A.M.S. and began taking memberships. There were conservatively 30 million, Mixbloods in the United States alone - so I had some work to do!

EAST — YELLOW

"New Beginnings"

R I S I N G

S U N

I got back from my trip in mid-July. And it was time to get ready for the Sundance. But again, we were without the funds to go. My nephew, Bruce came through this time. He lent us some money to go, because he wanted to attend with his wife, Angelika. And he didn't want to go without me being there.

So once again, we were heading to the Sundance. This time we only brought the pop-up trailer. All the girls wanted to camp in their own tents. This made it a lot easier to travel - and a lot less cost for gas too.

Arriving at the Sundance, we went to set up at our usual spot. But right over our camping spot, was this huge teepee. Apparently, there had been a group from Italy, there to have a "native" experience. They had been taken through the Black Hills, the Devil's Tower, and a teepee had been built for them. Part of the group wanted to stay and be in the Sweat Lodges, and even Sundance. A few of them had read my book, in Italy.

The girls basically scattered to see if their friends were there. Melody started getting coffee ready. That was always a priority as soon as we got there, as there was always someone ready for a cup of coffee.

I was telling Monique, Robert, Lesley and the others, as they arrived, about U.A.M.S., and most of them wanted to join. Melody was making membership cards right there in the trailer. I'd even had T-shirts made up, so lots of them wanted the shirt to go along with the membership.

There was something very different about this year. We couldn't put our finger on it, but things just weren't the same. It was the first year without Bernice. Al Tail seemed lost without her.

Next day was time to pick up Bruce and Angelika at the airport. So Melody and I set out for Rapid City to meet them. It was always so great to see people make the trip to our Sundance. With uncomfortable living conditions, extra expenses, and eating food they're not used to, was a sacrifice in itself.

The security problem this year was nothing. All the problems had been resolved, to the point the security consisted of a couple of young teenage boys. We would always try and bring them something to drink. They would have to sit there for hours stopping cars as they went in, I guess, just to show some semblance of security. They were very committed young warriors, our future Sundancers, to carry on the traditions.

We got Bruce and Angelika to set up their tent close to us. We put up our shades, and started getting visitors from other camps on the grounds.

At one point, I even asked David if he would consider becoming our spiritual leader. He said he'd have to give, being our spiritual leader some thought. He said that he had just turned in his tribal card. He also said that he was now like us, because he no longer had an enrollment card. But he thought what I was doing was a good thing. He never gave me an answer so I took that to mean no. I didn't bother him anymore. Melody wanted me to ask him again, but men don't beg. It's a man thing.

There was a problem brewing, and Melody had taken it on as a personal mission to resolve. On the day before the Tree Day, we had purchased a new toilet seat for the outhouse. The one they had was cracked. Well on tree day, one of the Sundance leaders had the outhouse removed and taken over to his camp, for his mother to use. He had built it for the people from Italy. This left all those around our camp, and my family without any place to go. For a couple of days, people were going in the woods, near an open pit.

On Tree Day, David was sitting, taking tobacco from people

that had questions, or that wanted to Sundance. I was sitting next to him. Along came Melody, with tobacco in hand, straight up to the front of the line to hand David tobacco. She said, "David, I'm sorry to interrupt, but this is really important. Can you please have some sort of outhouse made? We have no where to go. The only outhouses available now are for the Sundancers." David promised that he would look into it. We both sort of chuckled at the intensity of Melody's request, but I guess it was important.

This was the first year I decided not to go with everyone after the tree. Bruce, Angelika and my daughters all went. I just wanted to relax this time. I always went and helped take the tree down.

We still hadn't seen any sign of Lionel. It seemed as though many of the "cast" members were there, but one of the main characters hadn't shown up yet. We were all getting worried about him, especially because of how he'd felt for the last year.

They all finally came back with the tree. Some cars would always come ahead of it, beeping their horns, and letting us know the tree was coming soon. Everyone that was still at the Sundance grounds, would all start heading up to the arbor, to wait for the tree to be brought in. Once again we finished putting the tree up way after dark.

The first day of the Sundance began, without my brother, Lionel. He had driven all night long, and got in around 4:00 a.m., so we didn't expect him for the first day. But at least he made it, and was safe.

There was a couple that had come in from Oklahoma. They really brought some wonderful energy to our Sundance. Keith and Karla had read my book, and after meeting up with me in St. Louis, they decided to come to our Sundance.

Keith jumped right in helping with the fire, staying up all night and doing whatever was needed. And Karla was always busy at camp, sorting things out that they brought to give away. She also did a lot of cooking, and always had coffee ready for anyone that came by.

The first day of the Sundance was interesting. One of the pledgers, had asked to pierce just about every way he could. He originally came to our 1996 Sundance with Snowy's husband,

Conrado from Florida. So his first Sundance wasn't until 1997. But it appeared that he was going to make this year, a year we would never forget. He committed to pierce all down each arm. Then he hung from the tree, pierced on his back and front. He also dragged buffalo skulls. Then he pierced and broke loose from the tree. Some of us were worried what would happen when he had a drink of water!

For some reason, this year there was so much hanging from the tree, dragging of the buffalo skulls and piercing, the supporters didn't know where to go. If you wanted to support and stand behind more than one Sundancer, it was difficult. They were doing all the piercing, or so it seemed, at the same time.

Bruce was watching all the piercing that was going on, and he said it kind of took away from the sacredness of the ceremony. He felt it was almost like a circus, the way it appeared everyone was trying to out do the other.

By the end of the Sundance, I was exhausted. I had been busy helping to pierce people, and take flesh offerings. This Sundance had been really hard on me. There were a number of Sundancers that didn't want to be pierced by anyone else but me. Though I was honored, I didn't really have much of a chance to watch all that was going on.

By and large, it was a really good Sundance. Melody finally got somewhat of an outhouse by the 2nd day of the Sundance. Mike a Sundancer, who opted to help out this year, dug a slit-trench, you know, one that you have to straddle when you use it. But he put a plastic chair over the trench, cut a hole out of the chair seat and fashioned a tarp around the whole thing. It wasn't the greatest, but it was a place to go, and Melody was very grateful. What she noticed though, was that it didn't come from David or any of the other leaders. She told me she didn't think she would be coming back again.

We had all gone to Tony and Diane's house for a shower, early the next day. We were so grateful to have a place to become human again. There was going to be a big memorial for Bernice. So many people had left the Sundance grounds already. People packed up and headed home pretty fast. Bruce and Angelika had already taken their flight home. Keith and Karla left early that morning. But we wanted to stay and honor Bernice. After the memorial, there was a giveaway.

My brother, Lionel was still not himself. He was distant, and appeared removed from the Sundance and all the people there. There were still some people from Pineridge that hoped the Princess would come back. It had been two years now, since anyone heard from her. We heard a rumor that she was on television in Europe and was showing her pipe that I gave her. To our knowledge, she never finished her commitment. Lionel was still very depressed over the whole thing.

We left the next day, and in saying goodbye, it really felt like we wouldn't be back. We had made some wonderful friendships over the years, but the time was coming to move on. I didn't know how or why, but the pull away from this Sundance was getting stronger.

On our drive home, something was beginning to form in my mind. I started thinking about having a Mixblood Sundance. I had certainly danced enough times in my life, to be able to run one. I never wanted to be a Sundance Chief, because I didn't want the responsibility. But the more I thought about it, the more I realized that there were so many people out there that wanted to Sundance, but felt they were infringing on those people in South Dakota. This would be a solution.

I don't know where all these thoughts came from, but as I was driving along, I seemed to be guided toward a brand-new direction. The more I thought about it, the more excited I got. Melody and the kids had their reservations. And true to form, Melody had a lot of questions - questions that I couldn't answer, yet.

We got home around the middle of August, and I got right to work, selling crafts and getting new members for the Metis Society. The second week of September, I was home with a terrible back problem. My friend, Sue had recommended a chiropractor in Erie. But something unusual happened at the session. He did an adjustment, and he also did sort of a reading on me. I was telling him about wanting to have a Sundance, only I didn't know where. He told me that someone was going to donate land, and it would be close to Oil City, PA. I didn't think much of it at the time. I'd just met Brian, and really didn't know his track record with psychic impressions. Nor did I expect it.

At the end of September, we got a call from Lionel's daughter, Monique. She was crying, and said that her dad was really sick, and she thought he may be dying. We were all crying before long, and could not believe that Lionel was so ill.

Stormy and Melody immediately got on the phone to network with people, and let them know that Lionel was sick. We were going to try and raise some funds for me to fly out to see my brother. Well the support was amazing. All our Sundance brothers and sisters were worried, and the calls to Monique started flooding in.

Apparently, after the Sundance, Lionel was asked to take someone on Vision Quest. Some strange things happened on their walk up the hill. A huge swarm of mosquitoes landed on Lionel, and bit him many times. Maybe that was part of the reason he got sick. He got back from the Sundance, and became weaker and weaker. He'd been to a clinic in Hollister and it was determined he had diabetes, and an enlarged heart.

It was unbelievable to me, that my brother had become as sick as he had. I knew he was disheartened with life, but I never dreamed he would get sick like he did. He was five years younger than I, but looked 20 years younger!

I was devastated. Lionel was the closest man on earth to me. We often said we'd die for the other, in a heartbeat. I could talk to Lionel, in a way he understood. Many times he gave me spiritual advice that helped me along the way.

Somehow, with help from some generous souls, I managed to get the money to fly out there. I flew out mid-October for about two weeks. Paul picked me up at the airport in San Jose, and I stayed with him, until he could drive me to San Juan Bautista, CA.

By the time I saw Lionel, four days had passed. Paul lent me a car and I went straight to see him. He'd lost some weight, and seemed to be weak, but he said he was getting better. He was watching what he ate, and was learning to adjust to all the medications. There were a lot of side effects that were making him lose his appetite, or feel nauseous. His spirits seemed to lift when he saw me.

So I took him out to eat, then we went to the wharf in Monterey and walked around there. He would tire easily, but was happy to be getting out. I also took him on a couple of sales calls in the area.

We talked about things, and I wanted to help him, but he didn't ask. He really felt David would be able to heal him. I couldn't push myself on him. He needed to ask. Instead I just accepted being his friend and brother.

He wanted to know how I managed to live with diabetes, high blood pressure and pain all these years. I didn't know how to answer, I only wished he didn't have to deal with it. David told Lionel he felt that a woman he had scorned, may have put some bad medicine on him. This played on his mind, and in some ways, I think he believed it.

Time came for me to go back to Erie. I hated to leave Lionel, because there was a part of me that wondered if I would ever see him again. We had some really good, quality time together this trip, and I was sorry to leave.

That December, I decided to make a trip to St. Louis to see Rod and the crew there, then Oklahoma to see Keith and Karla. It was mostly to drum up members for the Metis Society, but I managed to mix some sales calls along with it.

When I was in Oklahoma, something amazing happened. Keith and Karla gave me tobacco, and asked if they could offer their land for the Sundance. They said they had 80 acres, and could build a nice arbor. Keith said he had all the equipment to bring in the trees around the arbor, and he would build it however I wanted. Keith and Karla also asked if they could Sundance.

This offer made me very emotional. I had gone from an inspiration in August, to this. It seems the Creator wanted me to go ahead. The signs were all there.

Since I was already there, we went to look for a Grandfather Tree. Let me explain how this particular tree was chosen. There were quite a few trees, so I walked around to the ones that looked like they might fulfill our Sundance needs. I narrowed it down to three beautiful trees. I went to each one and prayed, and asked if they would be willing to do this for us, in prayer. The one I chose brought tears to my eyes, I felt very emotional around it, and I took that as a sign that it was agreeing to be our Sacred Tree.

Without saying anything to Keith and Karla, I asked them to go to all three trees. Without hesitation, both of them returned to the same tree. They both said they got goose bumps and tears in their eyes. They had to tell me individually, how they felt. They had a right to help choose the tree, as this dance was for the people, and they were two of my future Sundancers. We found it, prayed to it and gave it tobacco.

It was my desire to have all live trees. And I wanted there to be two fruit trees at each direction. It was going to take a lot of work to get the arbor ready. Keith decided to do all he could to make it happen in time for June 21, 2000.

On the drive back to Erie, I was thanking the Creator for making things fall into place. So many things were going through my mind. How many dancers would come, what songs would we sing, who would be drumming, were all questions I was asking myself. The Creator kept telling me in my thoughts not to worry, that every thing I would need would be there when I needed it. This was one of the times when you learn to have faith, big time. This is when you find out if the dreams and visions you have been having are real or just beautiful thoughts.

My friend, Sue had asked me two years before to build a Sweat Lodge on her property. That April, we finally got to build it. It was the first time I had a Sweat Lodge near my home. I had one in Missouri, at Rod's house, but it was a long way to go for a sweat. Later on that month, we had another Sweat Lodge to attend, at Dave's house. Being asked to pour water at these Sweat Lodges was a big honor to me. The extended family in Erie was starting to expand, and it was nice to come home and have a place to purify. I was grateful to both of them for allowing us to have our spiritual ceremony at their houses.

In May the weather was nice and warm in Oklahoma, so Stormy and I drove there. All the trees around the Arbor were planted including the Grandfather Tree. Keith and Karla had worked very hard to make things happen. It was as though they were driven by some unseen force.

We had a ceremony around it, on May 5, 2000. That was a special day, because all the planets were aligned, and the celestial significance would give the day a special energy.

Before we knew it, it was time for my First Annual Mixblood Sundance. This time we took the pop-up trailer. It was a lot easier to pull. I was thankful to have it, even if it was falling apart. I hoped it would make the trip one more time.

As we drove up to Keith's place, I felt a funny sensation in the pit of my stomach. You can't for a second know or even understand what was going through my mind. "What are you doing here?" I'd ask myself, "You're not a Sundance Chief!" Then in defense I would say, "Why is Grandfather bringing me all these things to do." As I looked around, I remembered what Grandfather had said to me, that everything I need would be there. I had to have faith in the Creator. After all the work that Keith and Karla had done, it was too late to turn back.

Keith and Karla greeted us with happy smiles when we arrived. The arbor looked beautiful, but there was still a lot to do. As the pledgers and their families started arriving, our work force grew larger.

We still had to build Sweat Lodges, put up a teepee for the Woman Nation, put up a flag pole, a shade for the drum and build a cook shack. And I still didn't have my drummers and singers. But the Creator said they'd be there, so I had to have faith.

Hawk, Pam, Sandy and their family arrived, with John. Bruce and Angelika flew in, with Jim and Liz from New York City not far behind. Barbara arrived from Texas, with her teepee, and soon after Susan got there from Oklahoma City. Bruce's mom, Eddie and her friend, Nancy had just arrived from New York City, as well. The air was starting to get charged up with excitement, and nervousness with anticipation. The arbor already had a special energy around it.

It was great to see everyone coming to my trailer to see me and say hello. They were also letting me know that their words had not been empty. They were here to Sundance.

Bruce needed to be shown what he had to do to Vision Quest. Bruce had brought me tobacco in Florida, when we met on one of my selling trips, earlier in the year. He needed to learn to make prayer ties, and all he needed to get ready for his ceremonies.

Bruce and Karla asked to be put on a Vision Quest. When both of them returned after two days, we had a Sweat Lodge for them, and they got ready to begin the Sundance preparations.

Our dear friend, Sharon from Ontario, and her friend Nancy from Philadelphia arrived by taxi early Thursday afternoon. What a sight that was! I don't think Nancy had camped recently, because she was dressed in these slip-on heels, and the Capri pants with a bead fringe around the edge. As she stepped out of the taxi, her heel dug into the mud. She just laughed at herself. They were both a welcome addition, and Nancy had this wonderful sense of humor.

It was all starting to come together, like I'd envisioned. A lump was in my throat, looking around at everyone, sitting in groups, getting ready for the new traditions.

Late that afternoon, after a heavy rainfall, there was an incredible sight in the sky. A double rainbow had formed from north to south, right over the arbor. At the same time, a huge flock of white birds flew back and forth over the Sundance grounds. It was such a spectacular sight, and a good sign of things to come.

Jackie had also arrived and was helping others tie the four directions' ribbons all around the arbor. It seemed as though everyone was working together.

We were expecting a big drum from Andy in Ohio. He was building it especially for our Sundance. But it was late in coming, so Keith let us use his drum. Andy's drum did finally arrive on Saturday afternoon.

The Sundance grounds were certainly different from anything we'd been in before. It was originally a cow pasture on Keith and Karla's farm. And when it rained, it flooded the terrain, as there wasn't anywhere for the water to go. It also caused many of the tarantulas and other insects to come to the surface. This made some of the ladies a bit squeamish, but we all managed to try and live together for a while, in peace.

As we got closer to the time to begin, I looked around and

realized I still didn't have any drummers and singers.

It had finally come time for us to prepare to go in. After all the Sweat Lodges for purifying, and preparations to get ready, it was time to go in. With butterflies in my stomach, I called everyone to gather around so we could start the ceremony. And still I had no drummers and singers.

A friend of mine from Wyoming, said he would be there to sing and drum for us. I must have looked at the gate, a thousand times, waiting for him to arrive. And still no one was there.

Before we all lined up on the west side of the arbor, we were standing on the east side of the arbor. I asked the Creator, "Where are my singers? Where are my drummers?" Suddenly, it felt like a jolt from the pit of my stomach to my head. And a slap in the face, the Great Spirit told me they were standing in front of you and around you. I finally realized that he was talking about the people that had come to support the Sundance. This would be a great way for everyone to feel involved with the ceremony.

Once on my way to St. Louis, a song began to come into my head. By coincidence I happened to have my tape player next to me. I picked it up, turned it on to record, and started to beat on the steering wheel. I began to sing the words the Creator was bringing me. I didn't realize at the time how important this song would become to the Mixblood Sundance. It was the only song we had to sing at that first Sundance. It was meant to honor the four directions and the Creator. And the best part, was that it was in English, so we could all understand what we were saying.

I walked into the crowd of support people, right to Jim and I told him, "You're going to be my lead singer on the drum." At first he didn't want the job, as he felt he had no experience drumming. But he could tell by the look on my face, no, was not an option. So he relented, and I showed him what to do. Then I pointed to three other ladies to help us. They also tried to get out of it, but I said, "You came to help, this is what I need you for." They agreed if I showed them what to do. At the drum they stood and listened and learned. I had my drummers.

We lined up. The drummers were told to begin a slow, steady beat. All the Sundancers started moving. There was a total of eight dancers, I led everyone in, followed by Keith, Rod, Hawk, Bruce, Karla, Susan, and Rebecca was the Woman Sundance Leader. John, the elder, was asked to be my outside helper, and he smudged us all in.

It was now very dark, and everyone had found their place inside the arbor. Then I called for everyone to get their bedding, because they would be spending their first night, sleeping inside the arbor. And they would stay in the arbor until the end of the Sundance.

Early next morning, before the sun came up, I asked Melody to make some coffee, while I got ready to begin the first day of the Sundance. When I got there, everyone was all ready to start. We still had about an hour before sunrise. The drummers were starting to assemble, and a blessing done on the drum, with prayers and tobacco, before beginning.

We all stood facing the east, and blew on our whistles as the drummers drummed. We stood there for about 45 minutes, when a small spot of sunlight began to rise over the horizon. Everyone showed their happiness at the sun's appearance, in different ways. We continued dancing, until the sun was well above the horizon. I waved at the drummers just then, so they knew it was time to stop.

The dancers brought me their pipes, and I put them on the altar. They each went back to the spots where they had slept. Joking with them, I told them it was a breakfast break. They all moaned and groaned.

I went out to the drum, and people that I had selected as singers were there waiting with John, the elder. We sat down, and I quietly started leading them through the "Four Directions Song." Everyone picked up the words and music really fast.

By the time the break was over, everyone was ready to begin the first round. All the supporters had assembled around outside of the arbor, near those they were supporting. There was a total of about 30 people that first Sundance.

Through my directions, I showed the men how to rush the tree, and the women would follow slowly after them. It felt like we were in a dress rehearsal at first. As the day wore on, everyone fell into place to do what was necessary for a successful Sundance. The First Annual Mixblood Sundance, had officially begun.

We decided to honor the passing of Rod's father, and Sharon's son, Tony. There were empty chairs inside the arbor, and each chair had a picture of each one that passed, with a blanket on each one. In Rod's case, he was absolutely devastated when his father died. For a year he was unconsolable. Honoring his father at his first Sundance, meant a lot to him. And Sharon's son Tony, died suddenly from heart failure the night before his sister, Dina's wedding. Sharon had to act like Tony was sick, and unable to attend the wedding, the whole day of her daughter's special day. Can you imagine the heartache and mixed emotions she endured that day? We were glad to be able to do something to help them both honor the memory of their loved ones.

On Saturday, the sun was high in the sky, and the Sundancers were beginning to show signs of wear. Today would be the day that three of the Sundancers had committed to pierce. Originally I was not going to have this Sundance be a Piercing Sundance. I never wanted it to get like it was at my last Sundance in South Dakota. I wanted it to be a Thirst Sundance, similar in some ways to the Shoshone Sundance.

But two days before the Sundance began, Keith, Karla and Hawk approached me with tobacco to pierce. They said they had a vision to pierce, and they would honor me if I didn't want them to pierce, but they would have to fulfill that vision at a piercing Sundance. I was humbled by their request, and told them I would pray about it. In my prayers to the Creator, I was told, that I wasn't in control, that the Creator was. And my job was to enable the Sundancers to fulfill their commitment. So the answer came, and I told them they could pierce. The only condition I put on it, was that they could only pierce once a year. That way, there wouldn't be any grandstanding at my Sundance, and they could do what they felt they had to do.

Our drumming circle was expanding. The drummers and singers would change every day. Poor Jim, had been so into his job, that he had blisters on his both hands, with bandages wrapped around them. One of the drummers, Nancy had become so involved with the drumming, that it was hard to get her away from it. What was so great about that, is that she had never experienced any native ceremonies at all. At the time, she lived in Philadelphia, drove a 2000 Mercedes convertible, and lived very comfortably. So it was quite a change for her to be there.

Sharon and Nancy had also designated themselves to help cook, and wash dishes for everyone at the makeshift cook shack that Larry built. Larry had been helping Keith with a lot of the labor involved, running security and tending to all the things that were necessary, while Keith was dancing.

The "Four Directions" song, was now sung repeatedly throughout the whole Sundance. It was the only song we had, but like Grandfather told me, I ended up having what I needed. And it worked out wonderfully.

After the noon break, I got everyone ready for the piercing round. Keith wanted to be the first to pierce. The drummers started singing. In our Sundance I had been told to only use one rope for piercing. So to maintain a good, sanitary way of doing it, I had made each piercing Sundancer their own separate harness. Not having a buffalo hide, I used Bruce's large elk hide, to lay the pledgers down to pierce them.

Keith laid by the tree to pray, then laid down to be pierced. The other dancers all stood around to share this with him, and fan him as he went through this most sacred ceremony. I pierced him quickly, and had him on his feet dancing for his personal time in the sun, connected to the Sacred Tree. He danced very strongly, like the tree gave him more strength and courage, while connected that way. He danced four times to the tree, then three times back to his spot. Then it was time to break loose, on his fourth time he lunged backwards running strong and hard, breaking clean and with joy that he had fulfilled his vision.

Hawk was next to pierce. When Hawk was pierced and pulling back on the rope, he was quite the vision to see. It was almost like looking into the past, at a Sundancer from 100 years before. He danced strongly, praying with his hair blowing in the wind, praying that the Creator answer his prayers for his loved ones. He also broke loose, easily, like the warrior he is.

Karla brought a special female energy into the arbor, with her commitment to pierce. This wasn't easy for me, as it was one of my first times piercing a woman. The first woman I pierced, was Princess Erena. But Karla was strong, and showed a lot of courage as she stood on the elk hide. She asked that both of her upper arms be pierced. I did what she asked, and after putting the harness on her, she danced back and pulled hard. It was very painful for her, I could tell, by the look on her face. But she never made one sound of pain, or complaint at all. She was as strong as anyone I've seen. After she broke loose, we danced for a while longer, then had a much needed break. That round had been long and hard, and the sun was really hot by this time.

We went back to dance, until sundown. The thirst was beginning to really affect everyone. I always tell everyone, whether it is a Sundance or a Sweat Lodge that the leader must always show compassion. And I was feeling for my Sundancers right then, as I had been there so many years before. Everyone knew they were in past the midpoint now, and the next day their commitment for that year would be done.

Rebecca had to leave the arbor by the end of the second day, because of her moon. She was really disappointed that she couldn't finish her commitment, but everyone understood.

Before I knew it, the last day arrived. It had rained a bit during the night, and I worried about the Sundancers, sleeping around the arbor. Sometime in the night, the flag was taken down to half mast. This would tell the dancers in the morning that we would be finished early. I had told them earlier that when we ended would be determined by the position of the flag on the morning of the last day.

When I arrived at the arbor, though it was still dark, all the dancers were up ready to greet the sun. They were all happy, and stepping a bit higher, knowing they had almost completed their first Sundance.

There was a surprise in store for me. While we were waiting around the fire, getting ready for our greeting the sun song to begin, Oriona approached me with tobacco. She wanted to Sundance for the last day, to finish Rebecca's commitment. I told her I would ask the other dancers, and they all agreed wholeheartedly. It choked me up, that my little girl had shown such maturity at her young age. This would be her second Sundance that she had danced at. She was strong, and wonderful. I was really proud of her.

Leslie and her friend, had driven all the way from Nebraska, and their contribution was 10 large, sweet watermelons. Larry had managed to get all of them put on ice, so the truck was ready with ice cold watermelons for each of the dancers.

Rod had asked his supporter, Bernice to make sure there were peaches and cantaloupe ready on ice, when he came out. All Sundancers, start to think of what they want first, when they come out of the Sundance. Some think of water, Gatorade, or something cold. Others think of that cup of coffee they've missed, or even a food they love. Many of them send out requests to those supporting them to be sure and have their favorite thing ready for them.

But there doesn't seem to be anything as good as that first taste of ice cold watermelon.

The day was completed about 1:00 p.m., and it was time for all the dancers to get their first drink of water. This would be a private, solemn ceremony. Each Sundancer, beginning with the ladies, would be under cover to receive their first drink of water. John and Larry brought in the ladle and bucket of water, in the arbor. The dancers took their time getting as much to drink as they wanted. When it was over, all the supporters lined up in the east direction to greet the dancers, and hug them for the first time since Thursday night. The first Mixblood Sundance was over.

That night, a huge storm came up. Because we had been stuck in the mud for a good part of the Sundance, I decided it would be best to pack up and leave before the rain began. So at about 3:00 a.m., we all began packing up our things and getting the trailer ready to go. Rose and Bernice pitched in and helped us get ready. It was quite a rush, because the storm was almost ready to pour rain on us all.

Rebecca had decided to venture out to Arizona, and be on her own for a while. And Stormy wanted to move to Nebraska, so she got a ride with Leslie. Stormy would stay with the Bush family.

Hard as it was to accept, it appeared that at 22, it was time for her to leave the nest. Mary had moved out in January, and Rockie was long gone, and in the Navy now.

Going home, it was only Dory, Stone, Oriona, Melody and I. It was amazing how quiet the house was that summer. I think Melody suffered from the "empty nest" syndrome. She had 6 children all at once, 9 years before, and now she was down to 3.

Lionel hadn't been able to make my Sundance, and he was still very sick. I was talking to him about the Sundance and all that happened when I got back. He knew he wasn't going to make the dance in South Dakota either. In fact, Monique wouldn't be able to make it either, because a lot of her time was spent trying to look after her dad. Lionel had since moved into a home, where people were taking care of him. I was worried about my brother.

At the end of July, I made a trip to California. I was going to combine a sales trip, with a visit with Lionel. First I went to St. Louis, to visit my Sundancers, and have a Sweat Lodge. While I was gone, Melody said Monique had called. Lionel was getting really bad, and she didn't know if he would live much longer.

They had called for David to come to California three times, to have a healing Sweat for Lionel. And all three times, something came up that David couldn't make it. Lionel was going down fast, and I knew he was really disappointed that David hadn't made it.

At the Sweat Lodge in St. Louis, I said I needed to go to the Sundance in South Dakota. I wanted to dance for Lionel, because he couldn't make it. Also my sister, Norma was quite ill, and she wasn't expected to last out the year. The only obstacle in my way, were the funds to get there. Like the Creator works, Joe came through with some money to get me there. And another woman that was in the Sweat Lodge gave me more money to make the trip. I was really grateful, and a bit worried about sending money home. But I just felt I had to get there. So I drove as fast as I could to Sundance, once more, to David's Sundance.

When I arrived at the Sundance grounds, it was late in the day on Tree Day. I only had my van to sleep in, so I parked where I usually do. This year our friends, the Bush family were in my usual place. Rebecca had taken the bus to Nebraska, to drive to the

Sundance with them.

Everyone was gone for the tree, so I just drank coffee with Jenny Bush. She treated me really well, and even made decaf coffee for me. Not long after I finished eating and drinking coffee, it was dusk, and everyone was coming back from getting the tree.

Though a lot of my friends were in the crowd, I couldn't see them very well in the dark. I went to the center when we were putting the tree up, to let David know I was there to help if he needed me. He greeted me warmly, and said it was good to see me. I told him I almost didn't make it.

Next morning, I let someone else wake everyone up. Jenny had got up early to fix coffee. My daughter was going in to dance her fourth year, and it was her Wo-Pila or "giveaway" this year.

Everyone was coming up to me saying, how sorry they were that Lionel wasn't there. He left a huge hole at the Sundance for me. As long as I'd Sundanced with David, Lionel had been there. So many memories of my brother were starting to flood my mind.

The Sundance began as usual. I just felt like I was going through the motions. I felt in my heart that this would be my last time at this Sundance. Not because of David, but it seemed to be time to move on. With the new direction of the Mixblood Sundance underway, my energy needed to be devoted to this path.

I was also witnessing a lot of disrespect to the elders, and I have never been able to tolerate this kind of behavior.

Most people don't notice the changes in themselves. But standing outside looking in, some of us can see them. I saw a lot of changes in the young people. Some of them I had known since they were small children.

I started to notice they were having less and less respect for the elders, including me. At times they even attempted to make fun of me, or make jokes at my expense.

Being very touchy on that or any related subject, in the beginning it hurt my feelings. After several times of this occurring, my feelings of being hurt,changed to anger. They had no right to treat elders in any other way except with respect. They hadn't spent even a small fraction of the time in the Sundance as the elders had. The young people I'm talking about, shouldn't have joked that way with the elders, as though they were equals.

I never said anything to them or the Sundance chief, because it is after all their Sundance. I was just happy and honored to have been allowed to take part in their most Spiritual Ceremony.

I believe this was the Great Spirit's way to let me know that it was time to move on. It was time for all the Mixbloods to move onto our own destiny, and to ask the Creator to bring us our own traditions. This he has done every step of the way. I give thanks for this on, almost, a daily basis.

Through extensive research, my wife has found out that there are several Metis or Mixblood organizations here in the United States. To the best of my knowledge, the U.A.M.S. has the distinction of being the only such organization to have its own Sundance with all it's new traditions.

The first three days went quickly, and nothing unusual happened. However, the last day bears mentioning, because I had prayed to the Creator to show me how I could help my brother, Lionel to get better. I also wanted the Creator to heal my sister, Norma. The answer I felt, was that if I wanted them to get better, I would have to go a step beyond what I did in the past. I was told I had to pierce myself. The thought of it scared me to death.

I took David some tobacco, and told him what I was told to do by the spirits, about piercing myself. But I was so afraid, not of doing it, but of failing to do it, I asked if he would stand by me. This way if I couldn't go on, he would finish the job for me. He said he'd be there.

When the Sundance Leaders started the piercing round, I prayed at the tree. Then I walked around it and stood on the Buffalo hide. Bo asked me if I was ready to pierce. I replied yes, but that I was going to pierce myself. He looked at me in surprise, then said okay. David took a spot about three or four feet in front of me. I asked Bo if he would help me by holding my flesh. I showed him where and he grabbed my skin. I started cutting with the scalpel. I felt a sharp pain go through my chest to the back of my head and down through my waist. And I said in a whisper, "This is for you my brother," speaking to Lionel. I nodded my head to Bo to insert the buffalo piercing bone. And the hole was still too small, so I had to cut it a little bigger. This time, when he started to put it in, I didn't remove the scalpel quickly enough, and as the bone pushed against it, it cut through my flesh.

I looked at David just then, and he said, "It's good, it's a good piercing." Somewhat relieved, I moved onto the other side. This time I was a little smarter. I started cutting my other side, while Bo stood there holding my flesh. This time I went deep and wide enough the first time. Bo had plenty of room to insert my piercing bone. Someone handed me a rope, and Bo put it over the piercing bone and tied it up for me.

He moved onto the next person. Both my daughters, Stormy and Becky were there, along with Arthur, Gil and some of my other nephews were standing behind me to support me. Before I knew it, it was time to break. My last time at the tree, I prayed hard for Norma and Lionel. I could feel the sting of tears in my eyes, and the thought of two people that I loved so dearly. I prayed this would help them. Then I ran backwards and broke free, nice and clean. I went back to the tree to pray again, and asked the Creator to hear my prayers and look at my sister and brother, with pity.

I turned around to see who would cut off the flesh for me to put on the tree. There was only this man, I didn't know, he was a "Heyokah" or a backwards person. So he took the two pieces of flesh off, and put them in my hand, before I finished asking him! I had to find a piece of red cloth, so I could put them on the tree.

This Sundance was over for me. But I had to go through to the end of the ceremony. All I could think of was leaving and heading for California to see Lionel once again. And this was how my last Sundance with the Lakota people happened.

Early the next morning, Rebecca and I left for Arizona. She wanted to hitch a ride back to Phoenix. We were also going to stop in Tucson to visit Norma at the hospital.

After a short visit with Norma in the hospital, Becky and I left for Ajo. I only stayed one night, took Becky to Phoenix, and headed to California.

In two days, I found myself at Paul's house in San Jose. While parked in Paul's driveway, it was five days before I got to see Lionel. Lionel was feeling better, and his whole situation seemed to have turned around. He had to move from the place he was in, and was busy packing. He planned to move back into his small trailer in San Juan Bautista for a while, until he could get a motor home. He wanted to travel around from place to place, selling crafts and going about his way.

As it turned out, Sonny was having an arts and craft show in San Juan Bautista the following weekend. So I prepared to set up there. For some reason, I couldn't seem to get motivated to make sales calls. Melody was anxious for me to send some money home, but I just couldn't seem to force myself to go and make sales.

All my old friends and I got to visit that weekend. Finally, Lionel came on Sunday. It was good to see my brother. But he almost looked like a walking skeleton. It was quite a difference from the year before, he had gone down a lot physically in one year. I just couldn't believe that my brother was so sick. Though he talked very positively, and said he was feeling better, he didn't look as good on the outside.

That Monday, we all went to our old haunt, "The Mission Cafe" in San Juan Bautista, for breakfast. There was Ray, Sonny, Lionel and I. We all sat down for a big, traditional Mexican breakfast. The owner, Jenny waited on us personally. She's a nice lady, and had served Lionel and me, at the same table, many times.

After breakfast, we went to his trailer, and Lionel gave me a drum. In all the years we'd known each other, I had never had a drum from him. He was surprised that he had never given me one, and told me to choose from two that he had finished. When we got outside, Sonny's wife, Elaine, took a picture of all of us. Lionel's dog, was in front of us, howling. It was quite the shot, and sadly, it was the last picture taken of my brother.

Ten days later, I was back home in Erie. The phone rang, and it was Sonny. He told me that Lionel had passed. Melody and I had been sitting outside, catching up on things. We both started to cry. Though I knew he was in a better place, the emptiness in my heart and the loss of my friend, was difficult to take. Sonny said his last words were, "Tighten the drum."

Lionel was the first member of the United American Metis/Mestizo Society to pass away. We retired his membership number, so no one else could have it. And his drum holds a place of honor in every Sweat Lodge and Sundance I attend.

In February, 2001, I was set up again at the Tucson show. Stormy and Becky were helping me at the booth, at Fred and Carol's Native show. We got a call, that my sister, Norma had passed away. There was hope that she would get better. As she wanted, she was at home when it happened. Norma was such a wonderful person. She was quiet, but was very intelligent. She'd been a good mother and wife, and the whole family would miss her terribly. At least I was near enough to be able to attend the funeral. So many people had come to pay respects.

We got a call that March from some people that lived about an hour's drive south east of Erie. A couple of years before, Melody and I had met them at a pow wow we were at near a town called, Tionesta. Anyway, the phone call led to my family being invited to a gathering they had, at Bill and Patsy Wall's house.

Well, we walked into the house, and met an amazing group of people. There were about 25 people in this one room, at Bill's house. Many of them had read my Sundance book, and were really excited about getting to know me. Melody and I were just as honored to meet all of them. They all seemed eager to learn about Native spirituality. So we talked and ate all afternoon. It was the beginning of a rich, and wonderful friendship.

Bill wanted me to build a Sweat Lodge on his land. He also had a beautiful property. It would turn out that we would have many spiritual gatherings and ceremonies at his place. And interesting enough, he's only a few miles from Oil City, PA., just as Brian had predicted.

That May, Melody had organized a tree planting. The United American Metis Society was going to plant 1,200 trees, close to Bill's house. I was really excited about it, because of all the Sundances I had been to, it was a chance to put back all the trees that were taken out for my spirituality.

On the Saturday we had the tree planting, there were about 50 people that had come to plant trees. The Forest Service had provided the trees, and the man that owned the land, gave us all lunch. Robert had arranged for water and pop. Rod, Anna and Joe drove in from St. Louis; Tonya and Marge, Mark, Lori and Tommy came from Ohio; a Girl Scout troop came from Meadville; several other members of U.A.M.S. arrived to participate in what I hoped would be an annual event. Even the Erie Times and Meadville Tribune had articles about it in the paper. It was time to walk our talk, and do something to help the environment. I realized that at every Sundance, there were about 100 trees that gave their life for us to dance. Afterwards we all camped out and had a Sweat Lodge at Sue's house. It turned into a wonderful gathering, and I was grateful so many had traveled long distances for the event.

The following June, we headed to Oklahoma on June 7th. We were going to attend a pow wow at Belle, MO., before heading to Keith and Karla's. John, the elder was the Master of Ceremonies, and many of the people that were coming to the Sundance were there. Redhawk made two flutes to be raffled off, as his donation for the Sundance. Melody made a sign, "$1.00 a ticket, or 5 for $5.00." You can't believe how many people bought 5 tickets. The power of suggestion, I guess.

Then the following Tuesday, my daughter, Sylvia and my grandson, Max, were flying in from Germany. My nephews, Joe and Bruce had made the arrangements and paid for her to come to my Sundance. It was supposed to be a surprise, but I don't think my heart could have taken it, if she just showed up at the Sundance. This way was better, as we got to spend a couple of days together before leaving for Oklahoma.

The Sundance had grown quite a bit this year. We went from 9 dancers the first year, and this year 20 people had pledged.

It was a much drier year this time. And we brought our big travel trailer with us, making it more comfortable. I had asked that everyone line up their trailers, facing away from the arbor. This way the cook shack would be blocked from view.

Bruce flew in from New York City the same day we arrived on June 16th, 2001. Jim and his wife, Sassy arrived two days later. Jim had pledged to Sundance. On June 18, Hawk, Pam, C.J., Sandy, Kevin, Redhawk and Lisa arrived. Not long after, John, the elder arrived, and this time he brought his wife, Lora. Barbara from Texas, drove up, she had pledged to Sundance. Then Chris (who was completely blind) and Kellean arrived, not long after Anna and Peggy all got there from St. Louis.

There were a number of people that wanted to Vision Quest this year. This time, I asked some of my Sundancers to go and get those people that were ready to come back. All my years of Sundancing was starting to wear on me. At times I felt like a hundred years old.

Bill and Patsy, from Pennsylvania, brought their son, Billy, and their friends, Floyd and Patty, all arrived in their huge travel trailer. Not long after, Joe arrived with Sylvia and Max.

Larry had built an incredible iron barreled barbeque, for the deluxe cook shack. This year we had a shade built, the size of a two-car garage to cover our food and serving tables. Everything was so much more organized this year. It helped to have so many more hands to help.

Becky drove in from Phoenix with her friend, Selena. And her twin, Mary flew in from Erie. Rod and his new girlfriend, Cindy arrived, followed by Richard, Shirley and Glen from St. Louis. Soon after, David and Gail arrived with their friend, Maria. And another Jim from Missouri had arrived with his big travel trailer. Everyone was putting up tents, and shades near their campsite. Again, this year we had six chemical toilets, with a hand cleanser.

Melody and I went to the airport in Oklahoma City, to meet with Crescencio "Mr. C" and his son, Alfredo. They had just flown in from California.

Sharon had flown from Ontario, down to Texas to meet with Nancy. Then they both drove up from Texas and arrived the afternoon of June 20th, and this time they drove up in Nancy's Mercedes. Their car was full of camping gear. Their tent was almost a three-room cabin. But they'd made it again, and had pledged to do all the cooking, and donate the food needed for the rest of the Sundance.

Pam, Sandy and Kellean were busy sewing some skirts for those that had pledged to dance, but didn't have a skirt. They did a great job, considering it was last minute. Everything was coming together, nicely.

Spaghetti was last meal for the pledgers, that Thursday

264

afternoon. And before we ate, we had a big prayer circle. Then two group pictures were taken, one of all the supporters, and the other of all the Sundancers. I was absolutely amazed at how many people were there. How it had grown in just a year.

That evening, all the Sundancers got ready to line up to go in, as the sun started to go down. I asked John to call everyone to the arbor. With everybody there, I gave them all a few last minute instructions, and encouragement. Then we all moved around to the west side of the arbor, and stood in two lines.

It made me so very proud to see all those that had pledged to Sundance this year: Bruce, Rod, Keith and Hawk, Karla, and Rebecca back for the second year. Oriona would dance on the last day. The new pledgers were Alfredo, Redhawk, Chris, Bill, Joe, Billy, Jim, (Hawk's son) Carl, Kevin, Cindy, Dorina, and Barbara. Mr. C, Floyd and John were my helpers. Mike, Jeremy and Larry's son, Jeff were the fire keepers.

Once again, the deep beautiful sound of Keith's Drum started welcoming us into the arbor. David had been designated as the head drummer this time. He'd been practicing all the songs a few days before. This "Going In" ceremony lasted about half an hour to an hour. This is our native heritage showing through, that's when we are on Indian time.

Once in, all the old guys started showing the new ones how to get situated. The call for the bedrolls started going out, and one at a time, each Sundancer went to John, who had them passed from the relatives, to get their sleeping bags. With that done, everyone settled down for the night. It was a clear night, with so many stars in the sky. I told everyone to get as much rest as possible, as it was going to be a long three days. Tomorrow's forecast was supposed to be a scorcher.

On Friday morning, everyone was assembled to bring in the sun. The drummers were gathered, and ready to begin singing our new "Greeting The Sun" song. Sometime in the year, Melody and I sat down, wrote the words and music for all the songs we needed. We had prayed about it, and asked for guidance. I was really grateful, that such beautiful songs came out of it. So everyone was learning the songs, as we went.

We had a break after the sun came up, then began our first full day in the sun. The dancers were dancing hard that day. Some of the Sundancers weren't pacing themselves as they should have. By the mid-afternoon, four of the dancers were already starting to weaken.

Chris really amazed me. He didn't want to be treated any differently, though he was completely blind. The only thing we did for him was to attach a rope from his spot to the tree, so he could rush the tree like everyone else. He was usually the first one to the tree. He turned out to be one of my strongest dancers.

That afternoon, we had the "Honoring Round." There were five chairs out this year, including one for Karla's mother who had passed, my sister, Norma had passed away in February, Lionel's chair, and at the last minute a young girl named, Lakota was honored. She was only 17 years old and the week before, had been beaten and killed on the Standing Rock reservation. We had only met her in Ohio for a few days, but felt close to her.

By late that afternoon, we began sharing the Sacred Pipe. All the Sundancers were sharing their pipes with the supporters, drummers, and fire keepers. The day had been so hot, and dry even the birds were flying around with a canteen! So with compassion, I ended the day before dark, so the dancers could rest up for the next day. It was going to be busy on Saturday. We would begin with the "Healing Round," followed by the "Piercing Round."

Around the camp, everyone was busy making prayer ties for their loved ones, visiting and getting to know each other. Naturally, not everyone got along, and some rumblings of politics were beginning to form between different campsites. Though I didn't know it at the time, it would get out of hand to the point, that many people would not be invited back to our Sundance. There simply cannot be gossip, or negative attitudes at the Sundance. It reflects on the Sundance, and all those that attend. We would come to learn that every Sundance that year was riddled with some sort of politics. Regardless, I decided to put a stop to it this year, and let others know it wouldn't be tolerated again.

So many beautiful things happened this year, that far outweighed any negativity. Mr. C from California was such a welcome addition to our Sundance family. He cooked, washed dishes, helped around the arbor, Billy helped him build a shower. It wasn't just the help, but it was his overall, positive attitude. When he was around the arbor, and the dancers were dancing, Mr. C would be high-stepping to the songs right along with them. Many of the dancers said he inspired them, with his support. Word was out that everyone fell in love with Mr. C, and we were grateful for him and his son, Alfredo making it to our Sundance.

The next day began with the promise of a healing. We were praying that all those that went into the arbor for a healing, would have their prayers answered. We were also praying for healing of the planet.

The "Healing Round" began with those that wanted a healing to line up, and one at a time, a Sundancer would escort the person into the arbor. They would be taken to the Sacred Tree to hold the tree and pray. Then another Sundancer would take them back. It was kind of like a relay, so each Sundancer would be a part of the healing. It was a slow, solemn round, but it seemed that all those that took part, felt the ceremony had worked in their lives in some way.

After a long break, I called everyone to get ready for the "Piercing Round." So many of the dancers were feeling weak by this time, but all the pledgers were determined to make it through this important round.

The drummers began the "Piercing Song." This song had a haunting quality to it, and many of the Sundancers, including myself, felt really moved by the song.

This year, Billy, Redhawk, Keith, Karla, Hawk, Bill, Barbara, Alfredo, and Rod committed to pierce. I also wanted to pierce myself again. While all the Sundancers were getting ready to Pierce, the scalpels, cloth, tobacco and bleach water were brought into the arbor. Each Sundancer nervously prepared for their private time to be pierced.

The "Piercing Song" continued throughout the round, and some of the singers had to be replaced, as they grew tired to the point some of the singers were losing their voice. Each one of the piercings went well, though at times it got a little chaotic. I was beginning to wonder how using only one rope was going to work, as this Sundance grew. Perhaps the following year, I would allow more than one rope, either that, or we would have to have more than one Piercing Round.

After everyone had been pierced, it was time for me to pierce myself. This year was a bit more difficult than last year, because there wasn't anyone there to help me. Sadly, the cuts I made cut right through, and I didn't get to insert the piercing bone on either side. All the other Sundancers said I had suffered enough, and it was the Creator showing compassion for me. But I was disappointed anyway. Joe stepped in and cut the flesh off my chest, like a surgeon. He had medical experience, and really helped during the whole piercing round.

We finished the round, shortly after I was done, and everyone rested for about two hours. A few of the Sundancers had fallen from exhaustion and the heat, it had been a very intense day all around.

When they went to sleep that night, they were all feeling good knowing that tomorrow was the last day.

Next morning, as the sky started clearing to the east, first thing each Sundancer did was to look at the flagpole. They wanted to see about when we would be getting out. Miraculously, the flag was just a little above half-mast. That meant early afternoon. That made them all happy.

So everyone was up, early getting dressed and ready for their last day. The men were dry shaving, after visiting the chemical toilets. The kidney's don't stop working though they weren't getting any water. The men put their finest skirt on for the last day. The women were changing, and combing their hair in the women's teepee. All the Sundancers wanted to look their very best they could, when they left the arbor. This was the day they had been searching for.

The drummers were in place, and the singing began. The skyline had some cloud cover to begin with, but as we began the "Greeting the Sun" song, the clouds started to clear. The sunlight had a path to shine through and bless us on this last day. We were all amazed at how fast it cleared up.

We danced for about twenty minutes, until the sun was well

up and shining on all of us. I waved at the drum to stop, which they did gratefully. Though they did change, they were beginning to get tired and voices were getting hoarse. We had the morning break.

We had two rounds of the Four Directions song, and all the dancers had an extra lift in their steps, or burst of energy. They all knew it would be over soon. They all looked like the first day, energized and refreshed.

After the final, Sharing of the Pipe with everyone, I wanted to dance a few more rounds. But I looked at the Sundancers, and some of them were looking very close to the edge. With compassion in mind, I decided to finish the Sundance. I asked them to rest, and prepare for their first drink of water.

Larry, Floyd, John and Mr. C, brought in the water buckets to give each one their drink. While the Sundancers were having their drink, the supporters prepared to greet them. They finally got through having their fill, and I assembled the dancers to return their pipes to them.

It was an emotional time, as each dancer made their way through the supporters. Everyone was hugging, and congratulating each Sundancer. It had been a very difficult time for many of them. But they all made it through, and some were even talking about next year.

Larry had a truck full of watermelons ready for every dancer, as they came out. Everyone was so happy to get the ice cold watermelons. The supporters and the Sundancers all sat on the grass, and had a watermelon feed. Many of the dancers were exhilarated that they had completed this incredibly difficult ceremony. After one of the dancers had his fill of watermelon, he jokingly said, "Uncle, that wasn't so hard, let's do another three days!" I loved their humor and resilience.

Soon after many of the participants began packing up, and heading home. To all those that were there, I thank each and every one of you for your sacrifice and support, for the people. You honor me.

So ended the 2nd Annual Mixblood Sundance.

Documenting my spiritual journey has been a good experience, and many times difficult to relive each Sundance.

Though the Sundance is over, the memories, the smells, and above all the new acquaintances that are found will live on in my heart until the next time we find ourselves together at a Sundance. I'm glad to have helped them find their road to the Sundance.

Native spirituality is not a matter of taking, and then taking some more. Always when we take, we give, and every time we give, we take. Balance is always practiced by the native people. When you see bumper stickers and T-shirts that say, "Walk in Balance in this life," we don't mean walking on a tightrope. We mean walking in balance with nature and with each other. It means respect for everything: plants, all animals, our Mother Earth, ourselves, and above all, respect for the Spirits.

If you take the life of a tree, plant two more, because then you are giving one of them a chance of survival: if one of them should die, there is still one to replace the one that you took.

People come from all over the world to attend the Sundance, from the mountains of Peru, from Europe and Tibet. There have been Aztecs, Navajos, Danes, Tohono O'Odhams, Apaches, Canadians, Germans, Afro-Americans, Japanese, and even a Buddhist monk. There are no racial or religious barriers for people who come to share the Sundance with us as long as they come in a good way, and with respect for our ways. There are representatives from all four races at the different Sundances. It is something we share with our brothers and sisters. It doesn't matter what color their skin is. We should pray, dance, and give thanks to the Creator together. That's what makes the Sundance so beautiful, so pure, and so powerful.

The Sundance was God sent to me. The Creator gave me something that would please me and fulfill my spiritual cravings. Every day, I thank the Creator for bringing me the Sundance and the Ceremonial Pipe. I found what had always been there for me. All I had to do was look and ask. After searching all over and in other beliefs, I had overlooked what was natively mine. It seems so simple now.

I had finally found a spiritual awareness within myself and was content with what I had found. I also felt a great weight lifted from my spirit. Although the spirit itself has no substance or physical restraints, I believe that when our spirits are without direction or focus, there is a great, almost physical stress put on our lives until we find our individual spirituality.

That spiritual stress then invades our physical body, creating an uneasy, restlessness. We find ourselves always looking for relief. We find ourselves searching until we get something we are content with. Some people choose Buddhism, Judaism, or Christianity, and some feel comfortable with Hinduism. There is something for everyone. It's just a matter of feeling good about what you find.

I've committed myself to the Sacred Pipe. I have committed myself to Sundancing every year as long as I live.

Many of us tend to forget our spirituality until we're in need of help, but the Sundance is never forgotten in my home. At every meal we give thanks. Sometimes we hold hands and form a prayer circle. Sometimes we don't. At every meal I give thanks to the Creator for having given the Sundance to me. Every time I wake up, I give thanks that I am here for my children one more day I don't ever know what that day is going to bring, but I hope that it will always bring tranquility to the world and peace to my family.

I always pray that people stop and realize what we are doing to our Mother Earth. Many don't seem to care about anything, except what is important to them. We should stop and realize that this is the only world we've got. This planet we are standing on is like our heart. This planet that we abuse daily, it's our heart. Without it we don't have a life. We don't survive. We don't exist.

Again and for the last time I want to ask you that same question I have asked. Why did God or the Creator decide to create us humans?

Here is my answer to that question.

I believe that God, the Creator, needs us to worship Him. Without us, He doesn't exist. No God is a God if He has no one to acknowledge Him. I believe that since He needs us to recognize Him as a God, it's His obligation to take care of us. In this way, He pays us back for our worship by answering our prayers. We can demand His help, and he has an obligation to give it to us. Our obligation is to worship and show respect.

I wonder sometimes why it took me so long to find the Sundance. It seems there were so many times in my life when I would have been a better person had I been Sundancing. As one Sundance Chief told me, it's very possible that I was just not ready, and the Spirits wanted me to wait until I was.

Now that you have finished reading this, you have knowledge that places you on a higher spiritual plateau. Make a commitment to yourself, always walk in balance and do not judge others. Be grateful for the things you receive and remember to give in return.

This journey has been a long and hard one for me, but in a good way. You have witnessed my hopes, fears, desires, heartbreaks, feelings, and the baring of my soul. All this was necessary, as it led me to. . .

. . . My road to the Sundance.

Afterword

My first experience with the Sundance happened many years ago. It awakened me spiritually and caused many changes in my life. It also brought about the events that left me feeling compelled to write this book and to pass on my message.

At the end of March of 1994, Melody and I had gone to New Mexico on a selling trip.

Our trip took us up through Santa Fe, then up to Taos to visit our friend, Lyn and Michael. Heading back to Albuquerque, the trip seemed to go by quickly although the road is slow and curvy. Melody was preoccupied and quiet most of the trip. I thought that the trip had been too short and felt uneasy, as though something had been left behind or left unsaid.

It felt like something that needed to be resolved in Taos, had not even been addressed. What was so funny was that I didn't even know what I needed answers to. I just knew I felt an emptiness that caused me to feel all these emotions. Perhaps the Spirits were preparing me for all the things from my past - for soon I would be reliving the past, however painful it might be. I know during the days before, while I was being led in this direction, I made life miserable for my wife and those around me.

Pulling into Albuquerque, we were treated to a beautiful picture that can only be seen in the West, a spectacular sunset. We thought of driving on to Arizona, but decided against it, since we were both tired. We found a motel, got something to eat, and went to bed early.

The next morning I was up early. Melody was having trouble detaching herself from the blankets. After I had my shower and while she had hers, I just kicked back and watched the news.

When she was done, she sat on the bed across from me. Suddenly an intense pain knifed through my head. "Oh my God," I thought, "I'm having a stroke."

I never experienced anything like it and it really scared me.

Melody saw me sitting there holding my head with both hands and knew I was in pain. She asked me if I was okay. I couldn't answer. I just kept holding my head and moaning from the pain. I tried to keep from making any sound but the pain was just too intense. Another moan escaped my lips.

By now Melody was really worried. She said, "Honey, are you all right?" Then she asked me again, but this time with a hint of panic in her voice. Then, "You want me to call a doctor?"

I shook my head and held my hand up to her to stop. In my head I was hearing voices. Though the pain was slowly subsiding, it was sharp enough that I was still conscious. Then I hear a voice say, "Don't worry, you're not sick. You're not having a stroke. You are fine."

Imagine that! My own mind was telling me not to worry, that I wasn't having a stroke. I felt I was losing my mind. My thought conversation continued. "Don't worry, you're fine. We have a message for you, and we wanted to get your attention."

"Who are 'we'?" I wondered.

Clearly, I received the answer. "We are the Spirits."

I asked, "What Spirits?"

"Just listen to what we have to tell you. You must write a book about your spiritual life. You must share all you have experienced with others. You must tell everything since the day we brought you the eagle whistles, that morning so long ago."

Through all these exchanges of thoughts in my head, all I was aware of, was the presence of my wife and her concern for me. I had no thoughts of where I was or anything else. It happened so fast that I didn't have time to reflect on other things.

"How do I do that?" I asked in my thoughts.

"You already have in your mind what you have lived through and suffered. You will know what to say. Say only the truth. But we will help you when you need it."

By now the pain in my head was gone, but I still felt drained and dazed. Apparently I didn't look very good, because my wife was still looking at me strangely, and she asked me again if I was all right. I told her that I felt better, and that I had been visited by the Spirits.

I sat thinking of what had occurred and shook my head in disbelief. I was telling myself that it hadn't really happened, that it was only thoughts running wildly through my head. But what about the pain? Had I actually had a stroke? I was still in a daze and not thinking straight.

Finally, Melody couldn't take my silence any longer: "What in the world happened to you, Honey? You looked awful! Please tell me what the Spirits told you."

"They said they had a message for me, and the pain was just to get my attention. They said to write a book about my spiritual life since the beginning, when they brought me the sound of the eagle whistle, when I heard them in Sacramento."

And so this book began. For a few weeks I ignored the call. I didn't want to write this book, and I didn't know why I had been told to share my experiences. So much of what I've seen and done, is personal. I didn't want to share my visions with everyone. Only the Spirits and I should know about them. Yet there was a voice inside me telling me to share what I know and what I've learned. I felt as though the Spirits would intervene and rearrange my thought patterns to include what they wanted me to do.

It was frustrating, as though I was in a constant thought battle against myself. One second I would think of something to write in the book, then I would reject it for one reason or another. Then again I would hear words in my mind that I had to write down. My mind was on the verge of bursting with ideas and refusals.

Suddenly one day I just couldn't keep it under restraint any longer. The Spirits simply would not be denied. The battle was over, I was overcome with a strong determination to start writing.

From what I have learned, the Spirits that the Creator designated to help us include a Human-like kind; The Animal Spirits; the Black, or Bad Spirits. I'll briefly try to explain how I believe they work.

The Human-like Spirits are the old people who have lived in the past. Though they are gone from this life, they continue to integrate with those of us on the earth to guide us on different paths in this life, but only if we are willing to accept these responsibilities. They can only guide us by bringing us thoughts, ideas, encouragement, and the ambition to do what they ask. Sometimes they make their presence known, most times they don't. Sometimes they say who they are. They come to us in different ways, but always when they do, it's very dramatic, so there's no doubt in your mind about what's going on.

Many people confuse random thoughts with visions. If every thought crossing our minds was a vision, we would be constantly confused. Our minds would tend to wander all over the universe, and our path and decisions would be constantly changing with our thoughts. There are ways of telling the difference.

The Animal Spirits are mostly to help us with both physical and material things; then there are the Black or Bad Spirits. There are people who feel more comfortable receiving their guidance from a Black, or Bad Spirit. But the Black Spirit's most important function is to form that very necessary element for our world, called "balance."

When I conceded to the Spirits, they took over my life and my family's life. I would write and write, all of it in longhand. Throughout the writing of this book and the editing of it, I always felt as though the Spirits never left my side. Anytime I got sidetracked or was getting lazy, they'd step in and inject me with enthusiasm to keep going, to keep writing.

Now we have this third edition done, and it will be the last. I feel I've come full circle, and have started a new beginning in my life with my own Sundance for all the Mixbloods in the world. For those that feel a pull to the Sundance but don't want to impose on those tribes that prefer they not be there. Now we are starting our own traditions. Many tribes are embracing the Sundance, though it isn't their own inherited way to worship. The beauty of a Sundance, is people don't have to give up their spirituality. There are many people from different faiths, that Sundance with us. And for others, such as myself, the Sundance is all there is.

One night after the book was finished, the Spirits came to me again in a dream. They told me the reason I had been picked to write this book was that I had shown my willingness to suffer for the people I was praying for. Also, although there were others with more knowledge of the Sundance, I was the Spirits' choice to put *my* experiences on paper.

The Spirits are concerned with the lack of interest shown by the younger people in all areas of spirituality. They are worried that the long-standing native tradition of the Sundance will be lost by the newer generations. No one really knows how old the Sundance is or how long it has been around. We do know that for us there are no other ways to worship.

At every Sweat Lodge ceremony someone always remembers to give thanks to our elders: those who had the courage and this spirituality so deeply rooted that they went into hiding when the government tried to take it from our people in the late 1800s. I equate the suppression of our spiritual beliefs by the government and established churches with the suppression of Jews and their beliefs, by the Nazis during World War II, and black people brought to America as slaves. I can't understand why people tried to force us to worship something other than what we wanted. All this without even trying to understand us and our beliefs.

The Sundance is a gathering of people assembled to pray and show their love for others, and to love, honor, and show respect for the world. Like the Jews, we were persecuted for not believing in Jesus Christ the same way. Yet all along we had the same God. Thanks to that God, the Sundance has survived. Perhaps this book will do what the Spirits intended it to do - help those searching for a spiritual path of their own. Or perhaps it will arouse people's curiosity about it and make then want to know more.

This is how I was compelled by the Spirits to do some of their work for them. To them I give my most profound thanks and gratitude for having selected me for this. They also know that if I'm called again to serve them in other ways, I will. For I have proven that to them many times over at the Sacred Tree, in our Sacred Sundance.

All my relations

If you cannot find this book in your local bookstore or library:

Write: Wo-Pila Publishing
                 P.O. Box 8966
                 Erie, PA. 16505-0966 U.S.A.

Website: www.MannyTwofeathers.com

Also look for Manny Twofeathers' other book:
                 Stone People Medicine:
                     A Native American Oracle
                 New World Library Publishing,
                 Novato, CA. ISBN: 1-57731137X
                 Boxed edition, with cards and book